MW01672201

THE UNITED METHODIST
MUSIC AND WORSHIP PLANNER
2008–2009

David L. Bone
Mary J. Scifres

Abingdon Press
Nashville

THE UNITED METHODIST MUSIC AND WORSHIP PLANNER 2008–2009

This book is printed on acid-free, recycled paper.

ISBN 978-0-687-64546-6

08 09 10 11 12 13 14 15 16 17—10 9 8 7 6 5 4 3 2 1

MANUFACTURED IN THE UNITED STATES OF AMERICA

CONTENTS

USING THIS PLANNER

This Planner has been created to give you as many ideas as possible about a given worship service. It is designed to be used along with a worship plan notebook that you create, and copies of *The United Methodist Hymnal, The United Methodist Book of Worship,* and *The Faith We Sing.*

Features of the Planner include:

- NEW!! Each week, **Primary Hymns and Songs for the Day** are suggested first. These suggestions include various helps for singing the hymns. These hymns and songs have the closest relationship to the scriptures and are widely known.
- The suggestions for each week are chosen to suggest a wide variety of styles, using *The United Methodist Hymnal, The United Methodist Book of Worship,* and *The Faith We Sing* to their fullest.
- Each item is referenced to scripture or occasion.
- At least one **communion hymn** is recommended for the first Sunday of each month and liturgical season. When appropriate, communion hymns related to the scriptures are noted on other days as well.
- **Opening (O)** and **Closing (C) hymns** are suggested for each worship service. Traditional folks songs and spirituals mayt be listed under **Hymn Suggestions** or under **Contemporary Suggestions**.
- **Visual Suggestions** are offered for each service. These suggestions are discussed in the following article. They are found in each week's "Other Suggestions" list. They have been compiled by Ashley M. Calhoun of Knoxville, Tennessee. Ashley is known for his inventive use of "found" items in creating visual worship settings. Worship committees and altar guilds can use these ideas to create unique worship centers and altar pieces.
- The planner also includes **Contemporary Suggestions** for use in contemporary or blended worship services. Music suggested here ranges in style from contemporary praise to Taize to spiritual to folk songs. Several resources are referenced in this section. Information about these resources can be found on page 7. Please note that contemporary songs may also be listed under Hymn Suggestions, Vocal Solos, or Other Suggestions.

Be sure to consult all the suggestions regardless of the type of service you are planning. Many items that are used in contemporary services are listed under "Hymn Suggestions" and resources for traditional services can be found in the "Contemporary" suggestions list. Don't let the designation deter you from using any item that will enhance your worship service. Planners should consult both lists when choosing congregational music, keeping in mind that under "Contemporary Suggestions" they will find not only praise choruses, but also global and ethnic music, folk music, and meditative music from traditions such as Taizé.

When planning any worship service, it is always best to start with the scripture and let it guide your thoughts and plans. If your church is not using the Revised Common Lectionary, but you know what the scripture will be for a service, look up that scripture in the Index of Scriptures on page 130.

As you read and study the scripture passages, read all of the suggested hymn texts. The hymns may remind you of anthems, solos, or keyboard selections. It is wise to mark your hymnal with the dates individual hymns are sung to avoid singing some too frequently. The **Hymn Resources** (see page 7) can enhance congregational singing, but should be used sparingly. Use a three-ring binder to organize your plans. For each service of worship, include a copy of one of the Worship Planning Sheets found on pages 00 (or design your own!) along with blank paper for listing further ideas. Do not simply "fill in the blanks" for each service, but use the Planning Sheet to guide your work.

If the Planner is new to you, you will want to be aware of several other items. The **Vocal Solo Suggestions** are taken from a group of ten collections that range from contemporary settings of hymn texts to well-known classics (see page 7). Augment these suggestions from your own library.

The **Anthem Suggestions** include new works as well as generally known works that are already in many church choral libraries. Your study of the scripture and hymn texts will lead you to anthems in your church library that are appropriate.

The **Other Suggestions** for each service are varied in their intent and function, but will often add to the non-musical aspects of planning worship. Add to this list as you study the scripture and hymn texts.

Use the suggestions in the Planner along with your own page of ideas to begin making decisions about worship. Will the choir sing a "Call to Worship"? Can a hymn verse serve as a prayer response? Can a particular anthem or vocal solo give direction to the sermon? What prayers will be used?

Once your decisions are made, complete the Worship Planning Sheet. Make a separate list of tasks related to that service. Planning worship is an awesome responsibility, but one that can be accomplished with an organized effort along with spiritual guidance.

VISUALS IN WORSHIP

Ashley M. Calhoun

The suggestions for visuals in this planner are meant to help worship leaders use objects and images to increase the impact of the gospel on a people who are increasingly oriented to visual forms of communication. These suggestions can be incorporated into many visual elements: hanging and processional banners, worship settings (whether on the altar, in the chancel or narthex), worship folder covers, and bulletin boards. Classical and contemporary works of art, sculpture, needlework, and photography can also be a meaningful addition to the worship service.

With more churches incorporating screens and video walls into their worship space, there is a tremendous potential for the use of still or moving imagery. Also, interpretive movement and drama can be very strong in their visual impact.

The visual suggestions in the Planner have several characteristics.

- The suggestions are not meant to give detailed plans, but to spark your imagination and creativity.
- Some are drawn literally from the lessons; others are thematic.
- The suggestions are organized by reference to the lectionary passages:
  O Old Testament reading
  P Psalm reading or Canticle
  E Epistle or New Testament reading
  G Gospel reading
- Chapter and verse numbers are sometimes given to indicate actual phrases in the scripture passage that can serve as visual elements.
- Themes such as "forgiveness," "love," "rejoicing," and so on are offered to encourage creative use of video and photographic images of people engaged in demonstrating those themes.

So much about worship is visual and intended to strengthen the proclamation of the gospel. The worship space is filled with visual elements that send a message, positive or negative. The Christian Year itself is a treasure trove of color, texture, symbolism, and visual imagery. The special Sundays and special days in the cultural and denominational calendars also give the opportunity for visual expression. Evaluate the visual aspects of your worship services and find ways to enhance the worship experience with a more thoughtful use of visual elements.

PLANNING CORPORATE WORSHIP WITH A TEAM

Planning worship provides an important opportunity for church staff members to work together as a team. Such planning also provides an opportunity for worship committees to find an important aspect of their ministry. Unfortunately, our fast-paced society and production focus in current culture pushes far too many pastors into a solo effort in worship planning. We call this all-too-common worship planning model "The Lonesome Approach."

The Lonesome Approach—A Non-Team Model for Worship Planning

- Preaching pastor picks the scripture readings, prayers, hymns and sermon title.
- Church secretary or pastor types and prints bulletins.
- Musician(s) pick up note in mailbox with hymn numbers for coming Sunday. If time permits, choir rehearses hymns during evening rehearsal. Anthem(s) and choral responses for Sunday are rehearsed as well.
- Preaching pastor writes sermon.
- Lay liturgist arrives early to review worship plans.
- Worship commences.

Is this how worship most often comes together in your church? If so, you may want to consider other models for planning worship. Although some find this "lonesome approach" convenient, worship planning with this approach is neither integrated into nor representative of the worshiping community. With this book you hold in your hands, we hope that pastors, musicians, and worship leaders find encouragement and assistance for planning worship in cooperation with one another. Perhaps the "Lonesome Approach" will one day be the exception rather than the rule.

We suggest that pastors, musicians, and worship leaders consider a **team-based approach to planning**. First, gather a team together. In doing so, review the talents of your church, looking for artists, visionaries, leaders, organizers, and workers. Choose team members, balancing gifts and talents, as well as time and commitment levels. Members of the worship planning team can expect to meet at least biannually. Some worship teams find weekly, monthly, or seasonal planning meetings helpful, but even two meetings a year can improve communication and coordination efforts immensely.

However often one plans, pastors need to know the time requirements for planning music. Choir directors can alert the pastor of the time needed to choose, obtain, and rehearse an anthem prior to a worship performance. Organists can communicate the time needed to choose, obtain, and rehearse organ compositions prior to use in worship. Likewise, organists and choir directors need to advise the pastor of the time needed to prepare congregational music for use in worship. (Pastors often discover that both playing and singing improve greatly on hymns rehearsed a few weeks in advance!) Finally, the musicians can communicate with the pastor of their visions for music ministry in worship.

Pastors, likewise, need to inform musicians of how they might interact not only in worship planning, but also in worship leadership. Some pastors establish cues to alert musicians when light background music is needed during worship. A pastor can educate musicians about their roles as worship leaders. Additionally, the pastor can communicate with the musicians what her or his visions are for music ministry in worship.

These initial communications are essential when worship planners begin to work together and also as personnel changes affect the worship planning team. Many models for the actual planning might be used, but one model is offered here. In order to use this model, the team needs several copies of this Planner (particularly for use of scripture readings and hymn lists), a Bible, hymnals, and *The United Methodist Book of Worship.* Musicians may find it helpful to have copies of the music collections suggested in this Planner as well as a single copy file of the anthem collection of your church. Copies of the worship planning sheet from pages 136-38 can be distributed to each team member for each Sunday being discussed.

A Team-based Model for Worship Planning

1. Prior to meeting, the pastor(s) need to have prepared preliminary scripture and sermon outlines; musicians need to have prepared repertoire lists as well as repertoire wish lists.

2. Team meets for a designated time period. (A retreat setting is appropriate, especially for initial planning.)

3. Meeting opens with prayer and discussion of worship and what it means to each team member. There is no need to come up with one particular philosophy or purpose of worship; the diversity in team members' opinions can enhance the planning and implementing processes.

4. Scriptures are read or reviewed, with emphasis on the pastor's primary focus.

5. Sermon topics or emphases are introduced and outlined by the pastor(s).

6. Seasonal needs are discussed and outlined.

7. Hymns are chosen by team, keeping in mind thematic and scriptural emphases; musical abilities; sermon topics; congregational hymn preferences; and desire to introduce new hymns.

8. Special ideas or plans for specific worship services are introduced and discussed (i.e., Palm Sunday cantata, Christmas Eve candlelight service, scripture drama, children's Sunday).

9. Spoken words (prayers, responsive readings, blessings) are chosen (by team or part of team, depending on number of participants).

10. Vocal, choral, and keyboard music is chosen (by team or part of team, depending on number of participants).

11. Services are reviewed for integration, unity and diversity.

12. Concerns regarding specific services are discussed.

13. Meeting closes with a brief hymn sing and prayer.

In any one of these steps, all members of the planning team may have valuable input. A pastor may have an idea for a choral anthem to enhance a sermon idea; a musician may have an insight into a sermon topic as it relates to the congregation. At any of these steps, all members of the team will find helpful suggestions in this Planner. The text of each scripture reading is provided, season and color are noted, visual images are listed for artists, hymn and music suggestions are offered, liturgical suggestions are provided, and other ideas are mentioned which may spark interest in an innovative type of worship service occasionally.

Worship planning need not be a point of departure for a worship staff. Rather it can be a point of unity and team-building. The team that works together models corporate worship for the congregation. If we expect people to walk in the church doors on Sunday mornings from their many walks of life to have a corporate experience, we need to avoid individual approaches for planning worship and turn to teams of planners. In so doing, we will find that the Holy Spirit has found a new freedom in which to work within the Body of Christ.

RESOURCE KEY

2000+ Hickman, Hoyt L., ed. *The Faith We Sing.* Nashville: Abingdon Press, 2000. Accompaniment, singer, guitar, and planning editions available. Cokesbury Order #090547 (Pew). Hymn numbers 2000 and higher listed under "Hymn Suggestions" are from this hymnal (referenced as S2000 in other listings).

BOW Langford, Andy, ed. *The United Methodist Book of Worship.* Nashville: The United Methodist Publishing House, 1992. Leader and accompaniment editions available. Cokesbury Order #035724.

UM Young, Carlton R., ed. *The United Methodist Hymnal.* Nashville: The United Methodist Publishing House, 1989. Cokesbury Order #431328.

HYMN RESOURCES

S-1 Smith, Gary Alan, ed. *The United Methodist Hymnal: Music Supplement.* Nashville: Abingdon Press, 1991. Cokesbury Order #431476.

S-2 Bennett, Robert C., ed. *The United Methodist Hymnal: Music Supplement II.* Nashville: Abingdon Press, 1993. Cokesbury Order #430135.

H-3 Hopson, Hal H. *The Creative Church Musician Series.* Carol Stream, IL: Hope Publishing

Handbell—Vol. 1. *The Creative Use of Handbells in Worship.* 1997. Cokesbury Order #921992.

Choir—Vol. 2. *The Creative Use of Choirs in Worship.* 1999. Cokesbury Order #732807.

Descant—*The Creative Use of Descants in Worship* 1999. Cokesbury Order #732864.

Organ—*The Creative Use of the Organ in Worship* (1997). Cokesbury Order #323904.

VOCAL SUGGESTION RESOURCES

V-1 Kimbrough, Steven, ed. *Sweet Singer.* Chapel Hill, NC: Hinshaw Music, 1987. Catalogue #CV-1 (Medium Voice). Cokesbury Order #811712.

V-2 Handel, George Frideric. *Messiah.* Various editions available.

V-3 Inman, Bryce. *I Can Only Imagine: 25 Modern Praise Favorites.* Word Music, 2002. Catalogue #080689-432286. Cokesbury Order #511461.

V-4 Scott, K. Lee. *Sing a Song of Joy.* Augsburg Fortress, 1989. Catalogue #0800647882 (Medium High Voice) or 0800652827 (Medium Low Voice). Cokesbury Order #9780800652821.

V-5 Courtney, Craig. *Music for the Master.* Beckenhorst. Songbook #VC1; Keyboard Accompaniment CD #VC1-CD. Cokesbury Order #508872.

V-6 Walters, Richard, arr. *Hymn Classics: Concert Arrangements of Traditional Hymns for Voice and Piano.* Hal Leonard Publishing, 1993. Catalogue #740033. (High Voice) or #740032 (Low Voice). Cokesbury Order #811290 and #811233.

V-7 Johnson, Hall, arr. *Thirty (30) Spirituals.* New York: G. Schirmer, Inc., 1949.

V-8 Wilson, John F., Don Doig, and Jack Schrader, ed. *Everything for the Church Soloist.* Hope Publishing Company, 1980. Catalogue #804. Cokesbury Order #810103.

V-9 Pote, Allen. *A Song of Joy,* Carol Stream, IL: Hope Publishing, 2003. Catalogue #8135.

V-10 (90) Inman, Bruce, and Ken Barker. *WOW the 90s Songbook.* Nashville: Word Music, 2000. Catalogue #080689-382284.

V-10 (03) Inman, Bryce, and Ken Barker. *WOW Hits 2003 Songbook.* Nashville: Word Music, 2002. Catalogue #080689-449284. Cokesbury Order #080689-449284.

CONTEMPORARY RESOURCES

R Webber, Robert, et al., ed. *Renew! Songs & Hymns for Blended Worship.* Hope Publishing Co., 1995. Accompaniment edition: #1998. Singer's Edition: #1997. Cokesbury Order #735812 and #835878.

SP Various. *Songs for Praise and Worship PVG Edition.* Word Music, 1992. Catalogue #080689-006395. Cokesbury Order #921013.

M Barker, Ken, ed. *More Songs for Praise and Worship.* Word Music, 2000. Choir/Worship Team Edition: Catalogue #0-80689-31317-2. Cokesbury Order #509802. Keyboard Edition: Catalogue #0-80689-39087-6. Cokesbury Order #509776.

MM Baker, Ken, ed. *More Songs for Praise and Worship 2.* Word Music, 2002. Choir/Worship Team Edition. Catalogue #512053. Keyboard Edition: Catalogue #512075. Piano/Guitar/Vocal Edition: Catalogue #512087.

WG *WOW Worship Green Songbook.* Integrity Music 2001. Catalogue #000768195567.

WO *WOW Worship Orange Songbook.* Integrity Music, 2000. Catalogue #000768172360.Cokesbury Order #323447.

WY *WOW Worship Yellow Songbook.* Brentwood-Benson Music Publishing. Catalogue #4575708397. Cokesbury Order #645757083977.

See also V-3 and V-10 suggestions under "Vocal Solos."

Exodus 12:1-14

1 The LORD said to Moses and Aaron in the land of Egypt:
2 This month shall mark for you the beginning of months; it
shall be the first month of the year for you.
3 Tell the whole congregation of Israel that on the tenth
of this month they are to take a lamb for each family, a lamb
for each household. 4 If a household is too small for a whole
lamb, it shall join its closest neighbor in obtaining one; the
lamb shall be divided in proportion to the number of peo-
ple who eat of it. 5 Your lamb shall be without blemish, a
year-old male; you may take it from the sheep or from the
goats. 6 You shall keep it until the fourteenth day of this
month; then the whole assembled congregation of Israel
shall slaughter it at twilight. 7 They shall take some of the
blood and put it on the two doorposts and the lintel of the
houses in which they eat it.
8 They shall eat the lamb that same night; they shall eat it
roasted over the fire with unleavened bread and bitter
herbs. 9 Do not eat any of it raw or boiled in water, but
roasted over the fire, with its head, legs, and inner organs.
10 You shall let none of it remain until the morning; any-
thing that remains until the morning you shall burn.
11 This is how you shall eat it: your loins girded, your san-
dals on your feet, and your staff in your hand; and you shall
eat it hurriedly. It is the passover of the LORD. 12 For I will
pass through the land of Egypt that night, and I will strike
down every firstborn in the land of Egypt, both human
beings and animals; on all the gods of Egypt I will execute
judgments: I am the LORD. 13 The blood shall be a sign for
you on the houses where you live: when I see the blood, I
will pass over you, and no plague shall destroy you when I
strike the land of Egypt.
14 This day shall be a day of remembrance for you. You
shall celebrate it as a festival to the LORD; throughout your
generations you shall observe it as a perpetual ordinance.

Psalm 149

1 Praise the LORD! Sing to the LORD a new song, his praise
in the assembly of the faithful. 2 Let Israel be glad in its
Maker; let the children of Zion rejoice in their King.
3 Let them praise his name with dancing, making melody to
him with tambourine and lyre. 4 For the LORD takes pleasure
in his people; he adorns the humble with victory. 5 Let the
faithful exult in glory; let them sing for joy on their couches.
6 Let the high praises of God be in their throats and two-
edged swords in their hands, 7 to execute vengeance on the
nations and punishment on the peoples, 8 to bind their
kings with fetters and their nobles with chains of iron, 9 to
execute on them the judgment decreed. This is glory for all
his faithful ones. Praise the LORD!

Romans 13:8-14

8 Owe no one anything, except to love one another; for
the one who loves another has fulfilled the law. 9 The com-
mandments, "You shall not commit adultery; You shall not
murder; You shall not steal; You shall not covet"; and any
other commandment, are summed up in this word, "Love
your neighbor as yourself." 10 Love does no wrong to a
neighbor; therefore, love is the fulfilling of the law.
11 Besides this, you know what time it is, how it is now the
moment for you to wake from sleep. For salvation is nearer
to us now than when we became believers; 12 the night is far
gone, the day is near. Let us then lay aside the works of
darkness and put on the armor of light; 13 let us live honor-
ably as in the day, not in reveling and drunkenness, not in
debauchery and licentiousness, not in quarreling and jeal-
ousy. 14 Instead, put on the Lord Jesus Christ, and make no
provision for the flesh, to gratify its desires.

Matthew 18:15-20

15 "If another member of the church sins against you, go
and point out the fault when the two of you are alone. If the
member listens to you, you have regained that one.
16 But if you are not listened to, take one or two others along
with you, so that every word may be confirmed by the evi-
dence of two or three witnesses. 17 If the member refuses to
listen to them, tell it to the church; and if the offender
refuses to listen even to the church, let such a one be to you
as a Gentile and a tax collector. 18 Truly I tell you, whatever
you bind on earth will be bound in heaven, and whatever
you loose on earth will be loosed in heaven. 19 Again, truly I
tell you, if two of you agree on earth about anything you ask,
it will be done for you by my Father in heaven. 20 For where
two or three are gathered in my name, I am there among
them."

Notes:

Primary Hymns and Songs for the Day

206 "I Want to Walk as a Child of the Light" (O) (Rom.)
S-2 #91. Descant
720 "Wake, Awake, for Night Is Flying" (Rom.)
H-3 Choir-174, 203; Organ-172
632 "Draw Us in the Spirit's Tether" (Rom., Matt., Communion)
H-3 Choir-62
S-1 #337. Performance note
2178 "Here Am I" (Matt.)
549 "Where Charity and Love Prevail" (Rom., Matt.) (C)
S-2 #162. Harmonization
2226 "Bind Us Together" (Rom., Matt.) (C)
R292, SP140

Hymn Suggestions

62 "All Creatures of Our God and King" (Ps.) (O)
448 "Go Down, Moses" (Exod.)
2060 "God the Sculptor of the Mountains" (Exod.)
2234 "Lead On, O Cloud of Presence" (Exod.)
2246 "Deep in the Shadows of the Past" (Exod.)
2045 "Sing a New Song to the Lord" (Ps.)
77 "How Great Thou Art" (Ps.)
149 "Cantemos al Señor" ("Let's Sing Unto the Lord") (Ps.)
513 "Soldiers of Christ, Arise" (Rom.)
551 "Awake, O Sleeper" (Rom.)
2172 "We Are Called" (Rom.)
2213 "Healer of Our Every Ill" (Rom.)
2254 "In Remembrance of Me" (Rom., Communion)
2260 "Let Us Be Bread" (Rom., Communion)
408 "The Gift of Love" (Rom., Matt.)
617 "I Come with Joy" (Rom., Matt., Communion)
390 "Forgive Our Sins as We Forgive" (Matt.)
557 "Blest Be the Tie That Binds" (Matt.)

Contemporary Suggestions

UM123 "El-Shaddai" (Exod.)
S-2 #54
S2270 "I Will Enter His Gates" (Exod., Ps.)
SP168
S2031 "We Bring the Sacrifice of Praise" (Exod., Ps.)
R3, SP1
M46 "I Will Celebrate" (Ps.)
R77, SP147, WO83
MM59 "Let Everything That Has Breath"
WY85
MM63 "I Could Sing of Your Love Forever"
WY44; V-3 p. 22 (vocal solo)
S2028 "Clap Your Hands" (Ps.)
UM432 "Jesu, Jesu" (Rom.)
R289, S-1 #63 (vocal part)
S2224 "Make Us One" (Rom.)
SP137
S2192 "Freedom Is Coming" (Rom.)
S2223 "They'll Know We Are Christians by Our Love" (Rom., Matt.)
SP240 "As We Gather" (Matt.)
R6

Vocal Solos

"Sing a Song of Joy" (Ps.)
V-4 p. 2
"All Creatures of Our God and King" (Ps.)
V-6 p. 55
"There's a Quiet Understanding" (Matt.)
V-8 p. 2

Anthems

"Raise Your Voices" (Exod., Ps.)
Arr. Roger Emerson; Brookfield Press 08745181
SATB with keyboard

"Be Our Light" (Rom.)
Michael Wolnaikowski; Walton Music HL08501578
SATB with organ

Other Suggestions

Visuals:
O Sin/salvation (black/gold), darkness/light, lamp, candles, Passover meal, lamb, blood, wine/bread
P Dancing figures, tambourine, lyre
E Paschal Lamb, portrait of Christ
E/G Reconciliation, bridges, alarm clock
G Worship, reconciliation, joined hands, four hands folded in prayer

Greeting: BOW378 (Ps.)
Act of Congregational Centering: BOW470 (Matt.)
Prayer of Confession: BOW484 or BOW488 (Matt.)
Litany: BOW496. The Ten Commandments (Rom.)
Call to Prayer: BOW202. "Where Two or Three Are Gathered" (Matt.)
Prayer: UM412. Prayer of John Chrysostom (Matt.)
Prayer: BOW507. For Creation (Ps.)
Prayer: BOW535. At the Beginning of a New School Year
Response: S2179, R226. "Live in Charity" ("Ubi Caritas") (Rom.)
For additional prayers and litanies, see *The Abingdon Worship Annual 2008.*

It's Unique!

For every church . . .
a songbook that will delight elders, young adults, teens, and children

Zion Still Sings

For Every Generation

Zion Still Sings **pulls together a vibrant, generation-spanning collection of over 220 songs and hymns.**

Just as *Songs of Zion* became a beloved songbook standard in churches all around the country, *Zion Still Sings* arrives 25 years later to stand alongside its predecessor.

It is the first songbook to contain very contemporary Black church music as well as standard music selections. Songs and hymns are presented the way they are sung in many churches, making it easier to learn these musical styles.

Pew Edition.
A collection of favorite songs and hymns from many sources. Its 6" x 9" size fits perfectly in pew racks along with standard denominational hymnals. Lexotone embossed cover.
CA8-9780687335275. Reg., ~~$12.00~~, **Sale $10.80**

Accompaniment Edition.
Features vocal and keyboard arrangements of the stylized embellishments that are part of the Black gospel tradition. Loose-leaf pages in a three-ring binder.
CA8-9780687335374. Reg., ~~$55.00~~, **Sale $49.50**

HIGHLIGHTS INCLUDE:

- African American spirituals
- Gospel
- Traditional hymns
- Contemporary
- 21st-century hymns
- Rap and Hip Hop

Music Resource Sale
January 25–April 30, 2008
10% Discount on *Zion Still Sings*

Published by
Abingdon Press

Cokesbury
Resources for the Christian Journey

store, web, phone
CMS@Cokesbury.com
1-877-877-8674 | FAX 615-749-6806

MPP86640001 PACP00423396-01

Exodus 14:19-31

19 The angel of God who was going before the Israelite army
moved and went behind them; and the pillar of cloud moved
from in front of them and took its place behind them. 20 It
came between the army of Egypt and the army of Israel. And
so the cloud was there with the darkness, and it lit up the
night; one did not come near the other all night.
21 Then Moses stretched out his hand over the sea. The LORD
drove the sea back by a strong east wind all night, and turned
the sea into dry land; and the waters were divided. 22 The
Israelites went into the sea on dry ground, the waters forming a
wall for them on their right and on their left. 23 The Egyptians
pursued, and went into the sea after them, all of Pharaoh's
horses, chariots, and chariot drivers. 24 At the morning watch the
LORD in the pillar of fire and cloud looked down upon the
Egyptian army, and threw the Egyptian army into panic. 25 He
clogged their chariot wheels so that they turned with difficulty.
The Egyptians said, "Let us flee from the Israelites, for the LORD
is fighting for them against Egypt."
26 Then the LORD said to Moses, "Stretch out your hand over
the sea, so that the water may come back upon the Egyptians,
upon their chariots and chariot drivers." 27 So Moses stretched
out his hand over the sea, and at dawn the sea returned to its
normal depth. As the Egyptians fled before it, the LORD tossed
the Egyptians into the sea. 28 The waters returned and covered
the chariots and the chariot drivers, the entire army of
Pharaoh that had followed them into the sea; not one of them
remained. 29 But the Israelites walked on dry ground through
the sea, the waters forming a wall for them on their right and
on their left.
30 Thus the LORD saved Israel that day from the Egyptians;
and Israel saw the Egyptians dead on the seashore. 31 Israel saw
the great work that the LORD did against the Egyptians. So the
people feared the LORD and believed in the LORD and in his
servant Moses.

Exodus 15:1*b*-11, 20-21

1b "I will sing to the LORD, for he has triumphed gloriously;
horse and rider he has thrown into the sea. 2 The LORD is my
strength and my might, and he has become my salvation; this is
my God, and I will praise him, my father's God, and I will exalt
him. 3 The LORD is a warrior; the LORD is his name. 4 "Pharaoh's
chariots and his army he cast into the sea; his picked officers
were sunk in the Red Sea. 5 The floods covered them; they went
down into the depths like a stone. 6 Your right hand, O LORD,
glorious in power—your right hand, O LORD, shattered the
enemy. 7 In the greatness of your majesty you overthrew your
adversaries; you sent out your fury, it consumed them like stub-
ble. 8 At the blast of your nostrils the waters piled up, the floods
stood up in a heap; the deeps congealed in the heart of the sea.
9 The enemy said, 'I will pursue, I will overtake, I will divide the
spoil, my desire shall have its fill of them. I will draw my sword,
my hand shall destroy them.' 10 You blew with your wind, the sea
covered them; they sank like lead in the mighty waters. 11 Who is
like you, O LORD, among the gods? Who is like you, majestic in
holiness, awesome in splendor, doing wonders?"
20 Then the prophet Miriam, Aaron's sister, took a tam-
bourine in her hand; and all the women went out after her
with tambourines and with dancing. 21 And Miriam sang to
them: "Sing to the LORD, for he has triumphed gloriously;
horse and rider he has thrown into the sea."

Romans 14:1-12

1 Welcome those who are weak in faith, but not for the pur-
pose of quarreling over opinions. 2 Some believe in eating any-
thing, while the weak eat only vegetables. 3 Those who eat must
not despise those who abstain, and those who abstain must not
pass judgment on those who eat; for God has welcomed them.
4 Who are you to pass judgment on servants of another? It is
before their own lord that they stand or fall. And they will be
upheld, for the Lord is able to make them stand.
5 Some judge one day to be better than another, while oth-
ers judge all days to be alike. Let all be fully convinced in their
own minds. 6 Those who observe the day, observe it in honor of
the Lord. Also those who eat, eat in honor of the Lord, since
they give thanks to God; while those who abstain, abstain in
honor of the Lord and give thanks to God.
7 We do not live to ourselves, and we do not die to ourselves.
8 If we live, we live to the Lord, and if we die, we die to the Lord; so
then, whether we live or whether we die, we are the Lord's.
9 For to this end Christ died and lived again, so that he might
be Lord of both the dead and the living.
10 Why do you pass judgment on your brother or sister? Or
you, why do you despise your brother or sister? For we will all
stand before the judgment seat of God. 11 For it is written, "As I
live, says the Lord, every knee shall bow to me, and every
tongue shall give praise to God." 12 So then, each of us will be
accountable to God.

Matthew 18:21-35

21 Then Peter came and said to him, "Lord, if another mem-
ber of the church sins against me, how often should I forgive?
As many as seven times?" 22 Jesus said to him, "Not seven times,
but, I tell you, seventy-seven times.
23 "For this reason the kingdom of heaven may be compared to
a king who wished to settle accounts with his slaves. 24 When he
began the reckoning, one who owed him ten thousand talents was
brought to him; 25 and, as he could not pay, his lord ordered him
to be sold, together with his wife and children and all his posses-
sions, and payment to be made. 26 So the slave fell on his knees
before him, saying, 'Have patience with me, and I will pay you
everything.' 27 And out of pity for him, the lord of that slave
released him and forgave him the debt. 28 But that same slave, as
he went out, came upon one of his fellow slaves who owed him a
hundred denarii; and seizing him by the throat, he said, 'Pay what
you owe.' 29 Then his fellow slave fell down and pleaded with him,
'Have patience with me, and I will pay you.' 30 But he refused; then
he went and threw him into prison until he would pay the debt.
31 When his fellow slaves saw what had happened, they were great-
ly distressed, and they went and reported to their lord all that had
taken place. 32 Then his lord summoned him and said to him,
'You wicked slave! I forgave you all that debt because you pleaded
with me. 33 Should you not have had mercy on your fellow slave, as
I had mercy on you?' 34 And in anger his lord handed him over to
be tortured until he would pay his entire debt. 35 So my heavenly
Father will also do to every one of you, if you do not forgive your
brother or sister from your heart."

Primary Hymns and Songs for the Day

2234 "Lead On, O Cloud of Presence" (Exod.) (O)
  H-3 Handbell-74; Choir-123; Descant-64; Organ-71
  S-1 #195-97. Various treatments
136 "O Mary, Don't You Weep" (Exod.)
149 "Cantemos al Señor" ("Let's Sing Unto the Lord") (Exod., Canticle)
  H-3 Choir-128; Organ-129
  S-2 #154. Performance note
356 "Pues Si Vivimos" ("When We Are Living") (Rom.)
  S-1 #320. Orff instrument arrangement
  H-3 Choir-218; Organ-155
390 "Forgive Our Sins as We Forgive" (Matt.)
  H-3 Choir-68; Descant-28; Organ-27
  S-1 #85. Choral harmonization
2169 "God, How Can We Forgive" (Rom., Matt.)
  H-3 Handbell-62, 95; Choir-59; Organ-77
  S-1 #211. Harmonization
389 "Freely, Freely" (Matt.) (C)
  S-1 #135. Vocal descant idea

Hymn Suggestions

315 "Come, Ye Faithful, Raise the Strain" (Exod.) (O)
105 "God of Many Names" (Exod.)
448 "Go Down, Moses" (Exod.)
508 "Faith, While Trees Are Still in Blossom" (Exod.)
2060 "God the Sculptor of the Mountains" (Exod.)
2107 "Wade in the Water" (Exod., Baptism)
2120 "Spirit, Spirit of Gentleness" (Exod.)
2238 "In the Midst of New Dimensions" (Exod.)
2246 "Deep in the Shadows of the Past" (Exod.)
168 "At the Name of Jesus" (Rom.)
169 "In Thee Is Gladness" (Rom.)
121 "There's a Wideness in God's Mercy" (Rom., Matt.)
170 "O How I Love Jesus" (Rom., Matt.)
187 "Rise, Shine, You People" (Matt.)
402 "Lord, I Want to Be a Christian" (Matt.)
560 "Help Us Accept Each Other" (Matt.)
2171 "Make Me a Channel of Your Peace" (Matt.)
2269 "Come, Share the Lord" (Matt., Communion)
463 "Lord, Speak to Me" (Rom.) (C)

Contemporary Suggestions

S2023 "How Majestic Is Your Name" (Exod.)
  R98, SP14
M1 "Ancient of Days" (Exod., Rom.)
UM176 "Majesty" (Exod., Rom.)
  SP73, WY33, R63
S2032 "My Life Is in You, Lord" (Exod., Rom.)
  SP204
SP58 "The Lord Reigns" (Exod.)
  M14
SP18 "I Exalt You" (Exod., Rom.)
  R44
MM99 "Shout to the North" (Exod., Ps.)
  WG114
S2070 "He Is Exalted" (Ps., Rom.)
  R238, SP66, WY198, WG71
S2071 "Jesus, Name Above All Names" (Rom.)
  R26, SP76
S2164 "Sanctuary" (Rom.)
  R185, M52
UM177 "He Is Lord" (Rom.)
  R29, SP122
MM56 "Come, Now Is the Time to Worship" (Rom.)
  WY178; V-3 p. 114 (vocal solo)
MM111 "The Heavens Shall Declare" (Rom.)

Vocal Solos

"Oh, Freedom" (Exod.)
V-7 p. 10
"That Someday Is Now" (Rom.)
V-8 p. 259
"My Father's Heart" (Rom.)
V-3 p. 134

Anthems

"Psalm of Praise" (Exod.)
James E. Clemens; Kjos 9022
SATB with percussion

"He Never Failed Me Yet" (Exod.)
Robert Ray, arr. Keith Christopher
Hal Leonard 08745113
TTBB with piano

Other Suggestions

Visuals:
O Symbols of hope: cloud, pillar of fire, rainbow, star
P Musical notes, sea, tambourine, dancing, Exod. 15:21*b*
E Reconciliation, unity, clasped hands, Christ, scales of justice
G Reconciliation, forgiveness, embrace, 70 x 7, no. 7, scales of justice

Call to Worship: UM149, st. 1. "Cantemos al Señor" ("Let's Sing Unto the Lord") (Exod.)
Prayer of Confession: BOW481 (Matt.)
Canticle: UM135. "Canticle of Moses and Miriam" (Exod.)
Canticle: UM167. "Canticle of Christ's Obedience" (Rom.)
Prayer: UM268. Lent (Exod.)
Prayer: BOW514. For the Mind of Christ (Rom., Matt.)
Response: BOW189 or BOW191. "May This Mind Be in Us" (Rom., Matt.)
Prayer: BOW517 or BOW547 (Exod.)
Prayer: BOW522. For Purity (Rom.)
Response: S2207. "Lord, Listen to Your Children" (Rom.)
Scripture Response: UM402, st. 2. "Lord I Want to Be a Christian" (Matt.)
Prayer of Thanksgiving: BOW556 (Exod.)
Blessing: UM666. "Shalom to You" (Exod., Matt.)

Exodus 16:2-15

[2] The whole congregation of the Israelites complained against Moses and Aaron in the wilderness. [3] The Israelites said to them, "If only we had died by the hand of the LORD in the land of Egypt, when we sat by the fleshpots and ate our fill of bread; for you have brought us out into this wilderness to kill this whole assembly with hunger."

[4] Then the LORD said to Moses, "I am going to rain bread from heaven for you, and each day the people shall go out and gather enough for that day. In that way I will test them, whether they will follow my instruction or not. [5] On the sixth day, when they prepare what they bring in, it will be twice as much as they gather on other days." [6] So Moses and Aaron said to all the Israelites, "In the evening you shall know that it was the LORD who brought you out of the land of Egypt, [7] and in the morning you shall see the glory of the LORD, because he has heard your complaining against the LORD. For what are we, that you complain against us?" [8] And Moses said, "When the LORD gives you meat to eat in the evening and your fill of bread in the morning, because the LORD has heard the complaining that you utter against him—what are we? Your complaining is not against us but against the LORD."

[9] Then Moses said to Aaron, "Say to the whole congregation of the Israelites, 'Draw near to the LORD, for he has heard your complaining.' " [10] And as Aaron spoke to the whole congregation of the Israelites, they looked toward the wilderness, and the glory of the LORD appeared in the cloud. [11] The LORD spoke to Moses and said, [12] "I have heard the complaining of the Israelites; say to them, 'At twilight you shall eat meat, and in the morning you shall have your fill of bread; then you shall know that I am the LORD your God.' "

[13] In the evening quails came up and covered the camp; and in the morning there was a layer of dew around the camp. [14] When the layer of dew lifted, there on the surface of the wilderness was a fine flaky substance, as fine as frost on the ground. [15] When the Israelites saw it, they said to one another, "What is it?" For they did not know what it was. Moses said to them, "It is the bread that the LORD has given you to eat."

Psalm 105:1-6, 37-45 (or Psalm 78)

[1] O give thanks to the LORD, call on his name, make known his deeds among the peoples. [2] Sing to him, sing praises to him; tell of all his wonderful works. [3] Glory in his holy name; let the hearts of those who seek the Lord rejoice. [4] Seek the Lord and his strength; seek his presence continually. [5] Remember the wonderful works he has done, his miracles, and the judgments he uttered, [6] O offspring of his servant Abraham, children of Jacob, his chosen ones.

[37] Then he brought Israel out with silver and gold, and there was no one among their tribes who stumbled. [38] Egypt was glad when they departed, for dread of them had fallen upon it. [39] He spread a cloud for a covering, and fire to give light by night. [40] They asked, and he brought quails, and gave them food from heaven in abundance. [41] He opened the rock, and water gushed out; it flowed through the desert like a river.

[42] For he remembered his holy promise, and Abraham, his servant. [43] So he brought his people out with joy, his chosen ones with singing. [44] He gave them the lands of the nations, and they took possession of the wealth of the peoples, [45] that they might keep his statutes and observe his laws. Praise the LORD!

Philippians 1:21-30

[21] For to me, living is Christ and dying is gain. [22] If I am to live in the flesh, that means fruitful labor for me; and I do not know which I prefer. [23] I am hard pressed between the two: my desire is to depart and be with Christ, for that is far better; [24] but to remain in the flesh is more necessary for you. [25] Since I am convinced of this, I know that I will remain and continue with all of you for your progress and joy in faith, [26] so that I may share abundantly in your boasting in Christ Jesus when I come to you again.

[27] Only, live your life in a manner worthy of the gospel of Christ, so that, whether I come and see you or am absent and hear about you, I will know that you are standing firm in one spirit, striving side by side with one mind for the faith of the gospel, [28] and are in no way intimidated by your opponents. For them this is evidence of their destruction, but of your salvation. And this is God's doing. [29] For he has graciously granted you the privilege not only of believing in Christ, but of suffering for him as well— [30] since you are having the same struggle that you saw I had and now hear that I still have.

Matthew 20:1-16

[1] "For the kingdom of heaven is like a landowner who went out early in the morning to hire laborers for his vineyard. [2] After agreeing with the laborers for the usual daily wage, he sent them into his vineyard. [3] When he went out about nine o'clock, he saw others standing idle in the marketplace; [4] and he said to them, 'You also go into the vineyard, and I will pay you whatever is right.' So they went. [5] When he went out again about noon and about three o'clock, he did the same. [6] And about five o'clock he went out and found others standing around; and he said to them, 'Why are you standing here idle all day?' [7] They said to him, 'Because no one has hired us.' He said to them, 'You also go into the vineyard.' [8] When evening came, the owner of the vineyard said to his manager, 'Call the laborers and give them their pay, beginning with the last and then going to the first.' [9] When those hired about five o'clock came, each of them received the usual daily wage. [10] Now when the first came, they thought they would receive more; but each of them also received the usual daily wage. [11] And when they received it, they grumbled against the landowner, [12] saying, 'These last worked only one hour, and you have made them equal to us who have borne the burden of the day and the scorching heat.' [13] But he replied to one of them, 'Friend, I am doing you no wrong; did you not agree with me for the usual daily wage? [14] Take what belongs to you and go; I choose to give to this last the same as I give to you. [15] Am I not allowed to do what I choose with what belongs to me? Or are you envious because I am generous?' [16] So the last will be first, and the first will be last."

Primary Hymns and Songs for the Day

553 "And Are We Yet Alive" (Phil.) (O)
H-3 Handbell-49; Choir-14; Descant-27; Organ-25
2238 "In the Midst of New Dimensions" (Exod.)
2036 "Give Thanks" (Ps., Matt.)
2149 "Living for Jesus" (Phil.)
433 "All Who Love and Serve Your City" (Matt., Ps.)
H-3 Choir-26, 65; Organ-19
S-1 #62. Descant
519 "Lift Every Voice and Sing" (Exod., Ps.) (C)
H-3 Choir-128

Hymn Suggestions

127 "Guide Me, O Thou Great Jehovah" (Exod., Ps.) (O)
132 "All My Hope Is Firmly Grounded" (Exod.)
586 "Let My People Seek Their Freedom" (Exod.)
631 "O Food to Pilgrims Given" (Exod., Communion)
731 "Glorious Things of Thee Are Spoken" (Exod., Matt.)
2126 "All Who Hunger" (Exod., Matt.)
2234 "Lead On, O Cloud of Presence" (Exod.)
2264 "Come to the Table" (Exod., Communion)
2279 "The Trees of the Field" (Ps.)
R302, SP128
124 "Seek the Lord" (Ps.)
169 "In Thee Is Gladness" (Phil.)
356 "Pues Si Vivimos" ("When We Are Living") (Phil.)
2153 "I'm Gonna Live So God Can Use Me" (Phil.)
2179 "Live in Charity" ("Ubi Caritas") (Phil.)
121 "There's a Wideness in God's Mercy" (Matt.)
339 "Come, Sinners, to the Gospel Feast" (Matt.)
340 "Come, Ye Sinners, Poor and Needy" (Matt.)
426 "Behold a Broken World" (Matt.)
435 "O God of Every Nation" (Matt.)
517 "By Gracious Powers" (Matt.)
581 "Lord, Whose Love Through Humble Service" (Matt.)
2177 "Wounded World that Cries for Healing" (Matt.)
2268 "As We Gather at Your Table" (Matt., Communion)
648 "God the Spirit, Guide and Guardian" (Exod.) (C)
671 "Lord, Dismiss Us with Thy Blessing" (Exod.) (C)

Contemporary Suggestions

M4 "Let It Rise" (Exod.)
S2132 "You Who Are Thirsty" (Exod., Communion)
WO63 "Hungry" ("Falling on My Knees") (Exod.)
WY52
S2144 "Why We Sing" (Ps.)
S2032 "My Life Is in You, Lord" (Phil.)
SP204
S2164 "Sanctuary" (Phil.)
R185, M52
S2224 "Make Us One" (Phil.)
SP137
S2131 "Humble Thyself in the Sight of the Lord" (Matt.)
R188, SP223
S2176 "Make Me a Servant" (Matt.)
SP193

Vocal Solos

"Patiently Have I Waited for the Lord" (Exod., Matt.)
V-4 p. 24
"God Will Make a Way" (Exod., Ps.)
WO43, SP40
"If My People Will Pray" (Exod., Ps.)
V-8 p. 66
"Leanin' on Dat Lamb" (Exod.)
V-7 p. 42

Anthems

"Triune God, Mysterious Being" (Exod.)
Alfred V. Fedak; Selah Pub. Co. 425-601
SATB with keyboard

"My Heart Is Longing" (Phil.)
Arr. Bradley Ellingboe; Kjos 9033
SATB with harp or piano and oboe or clarinet

Other Suggestions

Visuals:
- **O** Bread, quails, hungry being fed
- **P** Singing, praising, cloud, fire, bread, quails, rock/water
- **E** People at work, service to God with people (bowl/pitcher/towel)
- **G** Grapes, leaves, tools for work, clocks set at 6:00 A.M., 9:00 A.M., NOON, 3:00 P.M., 6:00 P.M.

Call to Worship: UM127. "Guide Me, O Thou Great Jehovah." A selected stanza may be used each Sunday from today until Nov., 3, when the Hebrew scripture tells of Israel's crossing the Jordan.
Greeting: BOW456 (Exod.)
Opening Prayer: BOW465 (Exod., Matt.)
Call to Prayer: S2132. "You Who Are Thirsty" (Exod.)
Prayer of Confession: BOW485 (Exod.)
Prayer: UM409. For Grace to Labor (Matt.)
Prayer: BOW514. For the Mind of Christ (Phil.)
Scripture response: UM731, st. 3. "Glorious Things of Thee Are Spoken" (Exod.)
Prayer of Thanksgiving: BOW552 or BOW557 (Exod.)
Response: S2195. "In the Lord I'll Be Ever Thankful" (Ps.)

Exodus 17:1-7

1 From the wilderness of Sin the whole congregation of
the Israelites journeyed by stages, as the LORD commanded.
They camped at Rephidim, but there was no water for the
people to drink. 2 The people quarreled with Moses, and
said, "Give us water to drink." Moses said to them, "Why do
you quarrel with me? Why do you test the LORD?" 3 But the
people thirsted there for water; and the people complained
against Moses and said, "Why did you bring us out of Egypt,
to kill us and our children and livestock with thirst?" 4 So
Moses cried out to the LORD, "What shall I do with this peo-
ple? They are almost ready to stone me." 5 The LORD said to
Moses, "Go on ahead of the people, and take some of the
elders of Israel with you; take in your hand the staff with
which you struck the Nile, and go. 6 I will be standing there
in front of you on the rock at Horeb. Strike the rock, and
water will come out of it, so that the people may drink."
Moses did so, in the sight of the elders of Israel. 7 He called
the place Massah and Meribah, because the Israelites quar-
reled and tested the LORD, saying, "Is the LORD among us or
not?"

Psalm 78:1-4, 12-16

1 Give ear, O my people, to my teaching; incline your ears
to the words of my mouth. 2 I will open my mouth in a para-
ble; I will utter dark sayings from of old, 3 things that we
have heard and known, that our ancestors have told us. 4 We
will not hide them from their children; we will tell to the
coming generation the glorious deeds of the LORD, and his
might, and the wonders that he has done.

12 In the sight of their ancestors he worked marvels in the
land of Egypt, in the fields of Zoan. 13 He divided the sea
and let them pass through it, and made the waters stand
like a heap. 14 In the daytime he led them with a cloud, and
all night long with a fiery light. 15 He split rocks open in the
wilderness, and gave them drink abundantly as from the
deep. 16 He made streams come out of the rock, and caused
waters to flow down like rivers.

Philippians 2:1-13

1 If then there is any encouragement in Christ, any conso-
lation from love, any sharing in the Spirit, any compassion
and sympathy, 2 make my joy complete: be of the same
mind, having the same love, being in full accord and of one
mind. 3 Do nothing from selfish ambition or conceit, but in
humility regard others as better than yourselves. 4 Let each
of you look not to your own interests, but to the interests of
others. 5 Let the same mind be in you that was in Christ
Jesus, 6 who, though he was in the form of God, did not
regard equality with God as something to be exploited, 7 but
emptied himself, taking the form of a slave, being born in
human likeness. And being found in human form, 8 he
humbled himself and became obedient to the point of
death—even death on a cross. 9 Therefore God also highly
exalted him and gave him the name that is above every
name, 10 so that at the name of Jesus every knee should
bend, in heaven and on earth and under the earth, 11 and
every tongue should confess that Jesus Christ is Lord, to the
glory of God the Father.

12 Therefore, my beloved, just as you have always obeyed
me, not only in my presence, but much more now in my
absence, work out your own salvation with fear and trem-
bling; 13 for it is God who is at work in you, enabling you
both to will and to work for his good pleasure.

Matthew 21:23-32

23 When he entered the temple, the chief priests and the
elders of the people came to him as he was teaching, and
said, "By what authority are you doing these things, and who
gave you this authority?" 24 Jesus said to them, "I will also ask
you one question; if you tell me the answer, then I will also
tell you by what authority I do these things. 25 Did the bap-
tism of John come from heaven, or was it of human origin?"
And they argued with one another, "If we say, 'From heav-
en,' he will say to us, 'Why then did you not believe him?'
26 But if we say, 'Of human origin,' we are afraid of the
crowd; for all regard John as a prophet." 27 So they answered
Jesus, "We do not know." And he said to them, "Neither
will I tell you by what authority I am doing these things.

28 "What do you think? A man had two sons; he went to
the first and said, 'Son, go and work in the vineyard today.'
29 He answered, 'I will not'; but later he changed his mind
and went. 30 The father went to the second and said the
same; and he answered, 'I go, sir'; but he did not go.
31 Which of the two did the will of his father?" They said,
"The first." Jesus said to them, "Truly I tell you, the tax col-
lectors and the prostitutes are going into the kingdom of
God ahead of you. 32 For John came to you in the way of
righteousness and you did not believe him, but the tax col-
lectors and the prostitutes believed him; and even after you
saw it, you did not change your minds and believe him."

Notes:

Primary Hymns and Songs for the Day

166 "All Praise to Thee, for Thou, O King Divine" (O) (Phil.)
  H-3 Handbell-58; Choir-65; Organ-152
  S-1 #314-18. Various treatments
2100 "Thou Didst Leave Thy Throne" (Phil.)
  H-3 Choir-200
M1 "Ancient of Days" (Exod., Ps., Phil.)
467 "Trust and Obey" (Phil., Matt.) (C)
  H-3 Choir-202
  S-1 #336. Harmonization

Hymn Suggestions

155 "All Hail the Power of Jesus' Name" (Phil., Matt.) (O)
127 "Guide Me, O Thou Great Jehovah" (Exod.)
132 "All My Hope Is Firmly Grounded" (Exod.)
506 "Wellspring of Wisdom" (Exod.)
586 "Let My People Seek Their Freedom" (Exod.)
117 "O God, Our Help in Ages Past" (Exod.)
340 "Come, Ye Sinners, Poor and Needy" (Exod., Matt.)
731 "Glorious Things of Thee Are Spoken" (Exod., Matt.)
168 "At the Name of Jesus" (Phil.)
193 "Jesus! the Name High Over All" (Phil.)
292 "What Wondrous Love Is This" (Phil.)
554 "All Praise to Our Redeeming Lord" (Phil.)
561 "Jesus, United by Thy Grace" (Phil.)
562 "Jesus, Lord, We Look to Thee" (Phil.)
692 "Creator of the Stars of Night" (Phil.)
2082 "Woke Up This Morning" (Phil.)
261 "Lord of the Dance" (Matt.)
343 "Come Back Quickly to the Lord" (Matt.)
536 "Precious Name" (Phil.) (C)
2186 "Song of Hope" ("Canto de Esperanza") (Phil.) (C)

Contemporary Suggestions

S2161 "To Know You More" (Phil.)
S2070 "He Is Exalted" (Phil.)
  R238, SP66, WY198, WG71
UM176 "Majesty" (Phil.)
  R63, SP73, WY33
UM177 "He Is Lord" (Phil.)
  R29, SP122
S2023 "How Majestic Is Your Name" (Phil.)
  R98, SP14
S2071 "Jesus, Name Above All Names" (Phil.)
  R26, SP76
SP18 "I Exalt You" (Phil.)
  R44
S2131 "Humble Thyself in the Sight of the Lord" (Phil.)
  R188, SP223
S2224 "Make Us One" (Phil.)
  SP137
SP234 "At the Name of Jesus" (Phil.)
  R133
M3 "Jesus, Your Name" (Phil.)
M30 "Knowing You" ("All I Once Held Dear") (Phil., Matt.)
M33 "Jesus, You Are My Life" (Phil.)
M38 "In the Secret" ("I Want to Know You") (Phil.)
  WO103; V-3 p. 36 (vocal solo)
M53 "Let It Be Said of Us" (Phil., Matt.)
MM91 "Take My Life" (Phil., Matt.)
  R150, H49
MM111 "The Heavens Shall Declare" (Phil.)
UM405 "Seek Ye First" (Matt.)
  SP182, WG110
S2167 "More Like You" (Phil., Matt.)

Vocal Solos

"This Is De Healin' Water" (Exod., Baptism)
V-7 p. 52
"My Father's Heart" (Phil.)
V-3 p. 134
"Christ Living Within You" (Phil.)
V-8 p. 177
"Into My Heart" (Phil.)
V-8 p. 121

Anthems

"Wondrous Love" (Phil.)
Arr. Paul J. Christiansen; Augsburg 11-1140
SATB *a cappella*

"Sombody's Runnin' From God" (Matt.)
Henry Hinnant; Hinshaw HMC2053
SSAATB *a cappella*

Other Suggestions

Visuals:
  O/P/G Rock, flowing water, sand, staff, images of baptism
  E Reminders of Crucifixion, Resurrection, Birth of Christ
  G Vineyard, grapes, vine, leaves, "Reconsider Your Call"
Call to Worship: WY178, MM56. "Come, Now Is the Time to Worship" (Phil.)
Greeting: BOW456 (Exod.)
Opening Prayer: BOW465 (Exod., Matt.)
Prayer of Confession: BOW485 (Exod.)
Canticle: UM167. "Canticle of Christ's Obedience" (Phil.) (see S-1, p. 381)
Scripture Response: UM731, st. 2. "Glorious Things of Thee Are Spoken" (Exod.)
Prayer: BOW514. For the Mind of Christ (Phil.)
Response: BOW189 or BOW191. "May This Mind Be in Us" (Phil.)
Prayer: BOW527. For the World and Its Peoples (Exod.)
Prayer: BOW529. A Prayer of Saint Patrick (Phil.)
Prayer: BOW539, BOW540, or BOW541 (Matt.)
Prayer of Thanksgiving: BOW552 or BOW557 (Exod.)
Blessing: BOW564 (Exod.)

Exodus 20:1-4, 7-9, 12-20
1 Then God spoke all these words:
2 I am the LORD your God, who brought you out of the
land of Egypt, out of the house of slavery; 3 you shall have no
other gods before me.
4 You shall not make for yourself an idol, whether in the
form of anything that is in heaven above, or that is on the
earth beneath, or that is in the water under the earth.
7 You shall not make wrongful use of the name of the
LORD your God, for the LORD will not acquit anyone who mis-
uses his name.
8 Remember the sabbath day, and keep it holy. 9 Six days
you shall labor and do all your work.
12 Honor your father and your mother, so that your days
may be long in the land that the LORD your God is giving
you.
13 You shall not murder.
14 You shall not commit adultery.
15 You shall not steal.
16 You shall not bear false witness against your neighbor.
17 You shall not covet your neighbor's house; you shall not
covet your neighbor's wife, or male or female slave, or ox, or
donkey, or anything that belongs to your neighbor.
18 When all the people witnessed the thunder and light-
ning, the sound of the trumpet, and the mountain smoking,
they were afraid and trembled and stood at a distance, 19 and
said to Moses, "You speak to us, and we will listen; but do not
let God speak to us, or we will die." 20 Moses said to the peo-
ple, "Do not be afraid; for God has come only to test you and
to put the fear of him upon you so that you do not sin."

Psalm 19
1 The heavens are telling the glory of God; and the firma-
ment proclaims his handiwork. 2 Day to day pours forth
speech, and night to night declares knowledge. 3 There is no
speech, nor are there words; their voice is not heard; 4 yet
their voice goes out through all the earth, and their words to
the end of the world. In the heavens he has set a tent for the
sun, 5 which comes out like a bridegroom from his wedding
canopy, and like a strong man runs its course with joy. 6 Its ris-
ing is from the end of the heavens, and its circuit to the end
of them; and nothing is hid from its heat. 7 The law of the
LORD is perfect, reviving the soul; the decrees of the LORD are
sure, making wise the simple; 8 the precepts of the LORD are
right, rejoicing the heart; the commandment of the LORD is
clear, enlightening the eyes; 9 the fear of the LORD is pure,
enduring forever; the ordinances of the LORD are true and
righteous altogether. 10 More to be desired are they than
gold, even much fine gold; sweeter also than honey, and
drippings of the honeycomb. 11 Moreover by them is your ser-
vant warned; in keeping them there is great reward. 12 But
who can detect their errors? Clear me from hidden faults.
13 Keep back your servant also from the insolent; do not let
them have dominion over me. Then I shall be blameless, and
innocent of great transgression. 14 Let the words of my mouth
and the meditation of my heart be acceptable to you, O
LORD, my rock and my redeemer.

Philippians 3:4*b*-14
4b If anyone else has reason to be confident in the flesh, I
have more: 5 circumcised on the eighth day, a member of the
people of Israel, of the tribe of Benjamin, a Hebrew born of
Hebrews; as to the law, a Pharisee; 6 as to zeal, a persecutor of
the church; as to righteousness under the law, blameless.
7 Yet whatever gains I had, these I have come to regard as
loss because of Christ. 8 More than that, I regard everything
as loss because of the surpassing value of knowing Christ
Jesus my Lord. For his sake I have suffered the loss of all
things, and I regard them as rubbish, in order that I may gain
Christ 9 and be found in him, not having a righteousness of
my own that comes from the law, but one that comes
through faith in Christ, the righteousness from God based on
faith. 10 I want to know Christ and the power of his resurrec-
tion and the sharing of his sufferings by becoming like him
in his death, 11 if somehow I may attain the resurrection from
the dead.
12 Not that I have already obtained this or have already
reached the goal; but I press on to make it my own, because
Christ Jesus has made me his own. 13 Beloved, I do not con-
sider that I have made it my own; but this one thing I do: for-
getting what lies behind and straining forward to what lies
ahead, 14 I press on toward the goal for the prize of the heav-
enly call of God in Christ Jesus.

Matthew 21:33-46
33 "Listen to another parable. There was a landowner who
planted a vineyard, put a fence around it, dug a wine press in
it, and built a watchtower. Then he leased it to tenants and
went to another country. 34 When the harvest time had come,
he sent his slaves to the tenants to collect his produce. 35 But
the tenants seized his slaves and beat one, killed another, and
stoned another. 36 Again he sent other slaves, more than the
first; and they treated them in the same way. 37 Finally he sent
his son to them, saying, 'They will respect my son.' 38 But
when the tenants saw the son, they said to themselves, 'This is
the heir; come, let us kill him and get his inheritance.' 39 So
they seized him, threw him out of the vineyard, and killed
him. 40 Now when the owner of the vineyard comes, what will
he do to those tenants?" 41 They said to him, "He will put
those wretches to a miserable death, and lease the vineyard
to other tenants who will give him the produce at the harvest
time."
42 Jesus said to them, "Have you never read in the scrip-
tures: 'The stone that the builders rejected has become the
cornerstone; this was the Lord's doing, and it is amazing in
our eyes'? 43 Therefore I tell you, the kingdom of God will be
taken away from you and given to a people that produces the
fruits of the kingdom. 44 The one who falls on this stone will
be broken to pieces; and it will crush anyone on whom it
falls."
45 When the chief priests and the Pharisees heard his para-
bles, they realized that he was speaking about them. 46 They
wanted to arrest him, but they feared the crowds, because
they regarded him as a prophet.

Primary Hymns and Songs for the Day

559 "Christ Is Made the Sure Foundation" (Matt.) (O)
  H-3 Choir-49; Descant-103; Organ-180
  S-1 #346. Descant
77 "How Great Thou Art" (Ps.)
  H-3 Choir-103; Organ-105
  S-1 #163. Harmonization
MM80 "God of Wonders" (Ps.)
  WY14; V-3 p. 184 (vocal solo)
368 "My Hope Is Built" (Phil., Matt.)
  H-3 Choir-191
  S-2 #171-72. Trumpet/vocal descants
620 "One Bread, One Body" (World Communion)
  H-3 Choir-156
546 "The Church's One Foundation" (Phil., Matt.) (C)
  H-3 Handbell-94; Choir-180; Descant-16; Organ-9
  S-1 #25-26. Descant/harmonization

Hymn Suggestions

404 "Every Time I Feel the Spirit" (Exod.) (O)
390 "Forgive Our Sins As We Forgive" (Exod.)
398 "Jesus Calls Us" (Exod., Phil.)
425 "O Crucified Redeemer" (Exod., Ps., Matt.)
529 "How Firm a Foundation" (Exod., Matt.)
2120 "Spirit, Spirit of Gentleness" (Exod.)
2230 "Lord, We Come to Ask Your Blessing" (Exod.)
149 "Cantemos al Señor" ("Let's Sing Unto the Lord") (Ps.)
685 "Now, on Land and Sea Descending" (Ps., Evening)
2012 "Let Us with a Joyful Mind" (Ps.)
175 "Jesus, the Very Thought of Thee" (Phil.)
701 "When We All Get to Heaven" (Phil.)
709 "Come, Let Us Join Our Friends Above" (Phil.)
298 "When I Survey the Wondrous Cross" (Phil.)
299 "When I Survey the Wondrous Cross" (Phil.)
363 "And Can It Be that I Should Gain" (Phil.)
433 "All Who Love and Serve Your City" (Matt.)
2213 "Healer of Our Every Ill" (Phil.)
2220 "We Are God's People" (Matt., World Communion)
2117 "Spirit of God" (World Communion)
2126 "All Who Hunger" (Communion)
2170 "God Made from One Blood" (World Communion)
2221 "In Unity We Lift Our Song" (World Communion)
413 "A Charge to Keep I Have" (Phil.) (C)

Contemporary Suggestions

S2018 "Honor and Praise" (Exod.)
S2040 "Awesome God" (Ps.)
  R245, SP11, WO9, WY3
MM58 "All Heaven Declares" (Ps.)
  R163
MM111 "The Heavens Shall Declare" (Ps.)
UM394 "Something Beautiful" (Phil.)
S2208 "Guide My Feet" (Phil.)
S2163 "He Who Began a Good Work in You" (Phil.)
  SP180, R134
S2161 "To Know You More" (Phil.)
M30 "Knowing You" ("All I Once Held Dear") (Phil.)
M38 "In the Secret" ("I Want to Know You") (Phil.)
  WO103; V-3 p. 36 (vocal solo)
MM76 "The Wonderful Cross" (Phil.)
  WY190
WY202 "Be Thou My Vision" (Phil.)
S2264 "Come to the Table" (Phil., Communion)
S2162 "Grace Alone" (Phil., Matt.)
  MM100
WY145 "In Christ Alone" (Matt.)
S2043 "Alleluia" (Matt.)
S2066 "Praise the Name of Jesus" (Matt., Ps.)
  R7, SP87
MM93 "Rock of Ages" (Matt., Ps.)
  WO125
S2224 "Make Us One" (World Communion)
  SP137

Vocal Solos

"Ev'ry Time I Feel De Spirit" (Exod.)
V-7 p. 78
"The Heavens Declare His Glory" (Ps.)
V-8 p. 248
"I Surrender All" (Phil.)
V-10 (90) p. 173
"The Body of the Lord" (World Communion)
V-8 p. 344

Anthems

"The Church of Christ Shall Stand" (Phil., Matt.)
Stan Pethel; Abingdon Press 9780687644704
SATB with piano (opt. brass and percussion)

"Face to Face" (Communion)
Mark Burrows; Abingdon Press 0687075629
SATB with keyboard

Other Suggestions

Visuals:
- **O** Clay tablets, Ten Commandments, lightning, trumpet, mountain
- **P** Tent, wedding canopy, planets/stars/space, gold, rock, honey/comb
- **E** "Yet," rubbish, portrait of Christ, resurrection, crown of laurel leaves, trophy
- **G** Vineyard, wine press, building cornerstone, fruit
- **World Communion:** Flags, costumes, artifacts of nations, unity, breads of the world, globe

Call to Worship: UM211, st. 3. "O Come, O Come, Emmanuel" (Exod.)
Greeting: BOW450 (Ps.) or BOW456 (Matt.)
Act of Congregational Centering: BOW470 (Phil.)
Prayer of Confession: BOW488 or BOW492 (World Communion)
Litany: UM556 or BOW495 (World Communion)
Litany: BOW496. The Ten Commandments (Exod.)
Prayer: UM564. For the Unity of Christ's Body (World Communion)
Prayers: BOW432 (World Communion)
Prayer: BOW524. For Strength (Phil.)
Prayer: BOW505. For the Church (World Communion)
Blessing: BOW562 (World Communion)

Exodus 32:1-14

1 When the people saw that Moses delayed to come down
from the mountain, the people gathered around Aaron, and
said to him, "Come, make gods for us, who shall go before us;
as for this Moses, the man who brought us up out of the land
of Egypt, we do not know what has become of him." 2 Aaron
said to them, "Take off the gold rings that are on the ears of
your wives, your sons, and your daughters, and bring them to
me." 3 So all the people took off the gold rings from their
ears, and brought them to Aaron.
4 He took the gold from them, formed it in a mold, and
cast an image of a calf; and they said, "These are your gods, O
Israel, who brought you up out of the land of Egypt!"
5 When Aaron saw this, he built an altar before it; and Aaron
made proclamation and said, "Tomorrow shall be a festival to
the LORD." 6 They rose early the next day, and offered burnt
offerings and brought sacrifices of well-being; and the people
sat down to eat and drink, and rose up to revel.
7 The LORD said to Moses, "Go down at once! Your people,
whom you brought up out of the land of Egypt, have acted
perversely; 8 they have been quick to turn aside from the way
that I commanded them; they have cast for themselves an
image of a calf, and have worshiped it and sacrificed to it, and
said, 'These are your gods, O Israel, who brought you up out
of the land of Egypt!' " 9 The LORD said to Moses, "I have seen
this people, how stiff-necked they are. 10 Now let me alone, so
that my wrath may burn hot against them and I may consume
them; and of you I will make a great nation."
11 But Moses implored the LORD his God, and said, "O
LORD, why does your wrath burn hot against your people,
whom you brought out of the land of Egypt with great power
and with a mighty hand? 12 Why should the Egyptians say, 'It
was with evil intent that he brought them out to kill them in
the mountains, and to consume them from the face of the
earth'? Turn from your fierce wrath; change your mind and
do not bring disaster on your people. 13 Remember Abraham,
Isaac, and Israel, your servants, how you swore to them by
your own self, saying to them, 'I will multiply your descen-
dants like the stars of heaven, and all this land that I have
promised I will give to your descendants, and they shall inher-
it it forever.' " 14 And the LORD changed his mind about the
disaster that he planned to bring on his people.

Psalm 106:1-6, 19-23

1 Praise the LORD! O give thanks to the LORD, for he is
good; for his steadfast love endures forever. 2 Who can utter
the mighty doings of the LORD, or declare all his praise?
3 Happy are those who observe justice, who do righteousness
at all times. 4 Remember me, O LORD when you show favor to
your people; help me when you deliver them; 5 that I may see
the prosperity of your chosen ones, that I may rejoice in the
gladness of your nation, that I may glory in your heritage.
6 Both we and our ancestors have sinned; we have committed
iniquity, have done wickedly.
19 They made a calf at Horeb and worshiped a cast image.
20 They exchanged the glory of God for the image of an ox
that eats grass. 21 They forgot God, their Savior, who had done
great things in Egypt, 22 wondrous works in the land of Ham,
and awesome deeds by the Red Sea. 23 Therefore he said he
would destroy them—had not Moses, his chosen one, stood
in the breach before him, to turn away his wrath from
destroying them.

Philippians 4:1-9

1 Therefore, my brothers and sisters, whom I love and long
for, my joy and crown, stand firm in the Lord in this way, my
beloved.
2 I urge Euodia and I urge Syntyche to be of the same
mind in the Lord. 3 Yes, and I ask you also, my loyal compan-
ion, help these women, for they have struggled beside me in
the work of the gospel, together with Clement and the rest of
my co-workers, whose names are in the book of life.
4 Rejoice in the Lord always; again I will say, Rejoice.
5 Let your gentleness be known to everyone. The Lord is near.
6 Do not worry about anything, but in everything by prayer
and supplication with thanksgiving let your requests be made
known to God. 7 And the peace of God, which surpasses all
understanding, will guard your hearts and your minds in
Christ Jesus.
8 Finally, beloved, whatever is true, whatever is honorable,
whatever is just, whatever is pure, whatever is pleasing, what-
ever is commendable, if there is any excellence and if there is
anything worthy of praise, think about these things. 9 Keep
on doing the things that you have learned and received and
heard and seen in me, and the God of peace will be with you.

Matthew 22:1-14

1 Once more Jesus spoke to them in parables, saying:
2 "The kingdom of heaven may be compared to a king who
gave a wedding banquet for his son. 3 He sent his slaves to call
those who had been invited to the wedding banquet, but they
would not come. 4 Again he sent other slaves, saying, 'Tell
those who have been invited: Look, I have prepared my din-
ner, my oxen and my fat calves have been slaughtered, and
everything is ready; come to the wedding banquet.' 5 But they
made light of it and went away, one to his farm, another to
his business, 6 while the rest seized his slaves, mistreated them,
and killed them. 7 The king was enraged. He sent his troops,
destroyed those murderers, and burned their city. 8 Then he
said to his slaves, 'The wedding is ready, but those invited
were not worthy. 9 Go therefore into the main streets, and
invite everyone you find to the wedding banquet.' 10 Those
slaves went out into the streets and gathered all whom they
found, both good and bad; so the wedding hall was filled with
guests.
11 "But when the king came in to see the guests, he noticed
a man there who was not wearing a wedding robe, 12 and he
said to him, 'Friend, how did you get in here without a wed-
ding robe?' And he was speechless. 13 Then the king said to
the attendants, 'Bind him hand and foot, and throw him into
the outer darkness, where there will be weeping and gnash-
ing of teeth.' 14 For many are called, but few are chosen."

Primary Hymns and Songs for the Day

160 "Rejoice, Ye Pure in Heart" (Phil.) (O)
H-3 Handbell-17, 90; Choir-166; Descant-73; Organ-85
S-1 #228. Descant
MM68 "Forever" (Ps.)
WY57
339 "Come, Sinners, to the Gospel Feast" (Matt.)
H-3 Choir-68; Descant-52; Organ-55
S-1 #164-66. Various treatments
427 "Where Cross the Crowded Ways of Life" (Matt.) (C)
H-3 Choir-178, 180; Organ-44
S-1 #141-43. Various treatments

Hymn Suggestions

161 "Rejoice, Ye Pure in Heart" (Phil.) (O)
115 "How Like a Gentle Spirit" (Exod.)
151 "God Created Heaven and Earth" (Exod.)
352 "It's Me, It's Me, O Lord" (Exod.)
426 "Behold a Broken World" (Exod.)
428 "For the Healing of the Nations" (Exod.)
443 "O God Who Shaped Creation" (Exod., Matt.)
450 "Creator of the Earth and Skies" (Exod.)
2120 "Spirit, Spirit of Gentleness" (Exod.)
2177 "Wounded World that Cries for Healing" (Exod., Ps.)
2182 "When God Restored Our Common Life" (Exod., Ps.)
2183 "Unsettled World" (Exod., Ps.)
121 "There's a Wideness in God's Mercy" (Exod., Matt.)
398 "Jesus Calls Us" (Exod, Matt.)
395 "Take Time to Be Holy" (Phil.)
526 "What a Friend We Have in Jesus" (Phil.)
562 "Jesus, Lord, We Look to Thee" (Phil.)
715 "Rejoice, the Lord Is King" (Phil.)
2197 "Lord of All Hopefulness" (Phil., Matt.)
2128 "Come and Find the Quiet Center" (Phil.)
2202 "Come Away with Me" (Phil.)
2205 "The Fragrance of Christ" (Phil.)
2212 "My Life Flows On" (Phil.)
2218 "You Are Mine" (Phil.)
340 "Come, Ye Sinners, Poor and Needy" (Matt.)
396 "O Jesus, I Have Promised" (Matt.)
348 "Softly and Tenderly Jesus Is Calling" (Matt.)
612 "Deck Thyself, My Soul, with Gladness" (Matt., Communion)
2175 "Together We Serve" (Matt.)
2197 "Lord of All Hopefulness" (Matt.)
2263 "Broken for Me" (Matt., Communion)
2265 "Time Now to Gather" (Matt., Communion)
2268 "As We Gather at Your Table" (Matt., Communion)
670 "Go Forth for God" (Phil.) (C)

Contemporary Suggestions

S2056 "God Is So Good" (Ps.)
S2036 "Give Thanks" (Ps.)
R266, SP170
S2195 "In the Lord I'll Be Ever Thankful" (Ps.)
M45 "God Is Good All the Time" (Ps.)
WO35
WG63 "Hallelujah" ("Your Love Is Amazing") (Ps.)
S2270 "I Will Enter His Gates" (Phil.)
SP168
S2145 "I've Got Peace Like a River" (Phil.)
S2156 "Give Peace" ("Da Pacem Cordium") (Phil.)
S2193 "Lord, Listen to Your Children Praying" (Phil.)
S2273 "Jesus, We Are Here" ("Jesu Tawa Pano") (Phil.)
BOW187
MM87 "Let the Peace of God Reign" (Phil.)

Vocal Solos

"Your Love, Oh Lord" (Ps.)
WY118
"A Song of Trust" (Phil.)
V-4 p. 20

Anthems

"Trust in the Lord" (Exod., Matt.)
James Brighton; Choristers Guild CGA-1054
Unison with keyboard (opt. oboe)

"God Is So Good" (Ps.)
Arr. John D. Horman; Abingdon Press 0687044073
Two-part treble with keyboard

Other Suggestions

Visuals:
O/P Gold, jewelry, golden calf, hands folded/lifted in prayer
E Praying hands, "Rejoice in the Lord always," "Again I say, Rejoice"
G Wedding garments, other wedding items (invitations, rings, flowers)
Call to Worship: S2271, BOW199. "Come! Come! Everybody Worship" (Ps., Phil.)
Greeting: BOW454 (Exod., Matt.)
Opening Prayer: BOW464 (Exod.)
Prayer of Confession: BOW479 or BOW482 (Exod.)
Call to Prayer: S2157. "Come and Fill Our Hearts" (Phil.)
Prayer: UM329 or UM459 (Phil.)
Prayer: UM392. Prayer for a New Heart (Exod., Phil.)
Prayer: BOW512. For Guidance (Phil.)
Prayer: BOW516. For the Nation (Exod.)
Prayer: BOW519. For Others (Phil., Matt.)
Prayer: BOW530. A Prayer of Saint Thomas Aquinas (Phil.)
Prayer: BOW544. For Leaders (Exod.)
Prayer and Response: S2201. "Prayers of the People" (Phil.)
Prayer of Thanksgiving: BOW552 (Exod., Phil.)
Response: S2195. "In the Lord I'll Be Ever Thankful" (Ps.)
Blessing: Philippians 4:8-9
Response: UM668. "Let Us Now Depart in Your Peace" (Phil.)

Exodus 33:12-23

[12] Moses said to the LORD, "See, you have said to me, 'Bring up this people'; but you have not let me know whom you will send with me. Yet you have said, 'I know you by name, and you have also found favor in my sight.' [13] Now if I have found favor in your sight, show me your ways, so that I may know you and find favor in your sight. Consider too that this nation is your people." [14] He said, "My presence will go with you, and I will give you rest." [15] And he said to him, "If your presence will not go, do not carry us up from here. [16] For how shall it be known that I have found favor in your sight, I and your people, unless you go with us? In this way, we shall be distinct, I and your people, from every people on the face of the earth."

[17] The LORD said to Moses, "I will do the very thing that you have asked; for you have found favor in my sight, and I know you by name." [18] Moses said, "Show me your glory, I pray." [19] And he said, "I will make all my goodness pass before you, and will proclaim before you the name, 'The LORD'; and I will be gracious to whom I will be gracious, and will show mercy on whom I will show mercy. [20] But," he said, "you cannot see my face; for no one shall see me and live." [21] And the LORD continued, "See, there is a place by me where you shall stand on the rock; [22] and while my glory passes by I will put you in a cleft of the rock, and I will cover you with my hand until I have passed by; [23] then I will take away my hand, and you shall see my back; but my face shall not be seen."

Psalm 99

[1] The LORD is king; let the peoples tremble! He sits enthroned upon the cherubim; let the earth quake! [2] The LORD is great in Zion; he is exalted over all the peoples. [3] Let them praise your great and awesome name. Holy is he! [4] Mighty King, lover of justice, you have established equity; you have executed justice and righteousness in Jacob. [5] Extol the LORD our God; worship at his footstool. Holy is he! [6] Moses and Aaron were among his priests, Samuel also was among those who called on his name. They cried to the LORD, and he answered them. [7] He spoke to them in the pillar of cloud; they kept his decrees, and the statutes that he gave them. [8] O LORD our God, you answered them; you were a forgiving God to them, but an avenger of their wrongdoings. [9] Extol the LORD our God, and worship at his holy mountain; for the LORD our God is holy.

1 Thessalonians 1:1-10

[1] Paul, Silvanus, and Timothy,

To the church of the Thessalonians in God the Father and the Lord Jesus Christ:

Grace to you and peace.

[2] We always give thanks to God for all of you and mention you in our prayers, constantly [3] remembering before our God and Father your work of faith and labor of love and steadfastness of hope in our Lord Jesus Christ. [4] For we know, brothers and sisters beloved by God, that he has chosen you, [5] because our message of the gospel came to you not in word only, but also in power and in the Holy Spirit and with full conviction; just as you know what kind of persons we proved to be among you for your sake. [6] And you became imitators of us and of the Lord, for in spite of persecution you received the word with joy inspired by the Holy Spirit, [7] so that you became an example to all the believers in Macedonia and in Achaia. [8] For the word of the Lord has sounded forth from you not only in Macedonia and Achaia, but in every place your faith in God has become known, so that we have no need to speak about it. [9] For the people of those regions report about us what kind of welcome we had among you, and how you turned to God from idols, to serve a living and true God, [10] and to wait for his Son from heaven, whom he raised from the dead—Jesus, who rescues us from the wrath that is coming.

Matthew 22:15-22

[15] Then the Pharisees went and plotted to entrap him in what he said. [16] So they sent their disciples to him, along with the Herodians, saying, "Teacher, we know that you are sincere, and teach the way of God in accordance with truth, and show deference to no one; for you do not regard people with partiality. [17] Tell us, then, what you think. Is it lawful to pay taxes to the emperor, or not?" [18] But Jesus, aware of their malice, said, "Why are you putting me to the test, you hypocrites? [19] Show me the coin used for the tax." And they brought him a denarius. [20] Then he said to them, "Whose head is this, and whose title?" [21] They answered, "The emperor's." Then he said to them, "Give therefore to the emperor the things that are the emperor's, and to God the things that are God's." [22] When they heard this, they were amazed; and they left him and went away.

Notes:

Primary Hymns and Songs for the Day

73 "O Worship the King" (Ps.) (O)
H-3 Handbell-90, 105; Choir-221; Descant-49; Organ-51
S-2 #71-74. Introduction/harmonizations
2070 "He Is Exalted" (Ps., Matt.)
444 "O Young and Fearless Prophet" (Matt.)
S-2 #27. Descant
399 "Take My Life, and Let It Be" (Matt.) (C)

Hymn Suggestions

126 "Sing Praise to God Who Reigns Above" (O) (Exod.)
103 "Immortal, Invisible, God Only Wise" (Exod.)
105 "God of Many Names" (Exod.)
124 "Seek the Lord" (Exod.)
361 "Rock of Ages, Cleft for Me" (Exod.)
523 "Saranam, Saranam" ("Refuge") (Exod.)
700 "Abide with Me" (Exod.)
66 "Praise, My Soul, the King of Heaven" (Ps.)
107 "La Palabra Del Señor Es Recta" ("Righteous and Just Is the Word of Our Lord") (Ps.)
715 "Rejoice, the Lord Is King" (Ps.)
716 "Rejoice, the Lord Is King" (Ps.)
717 "The Battle Hymn of the Republic" (Ps.)
2009 "O God Beyond All Praising" (Ps.)
2177 "Wounded World that Cries for Healing" (Ps.)
2183 "Unsettled World" (Ps.)
84 "Thank You, Lord" (1 Thess.)
537 "Filled with the Spirit's Power" (1 Thess.)
566 "Blest Be the Dear Uniting Love" (1 Thess.)
2220 "We Are God's People" (1 Thess.)
708 "Rejoice in God's Saints" (1 Thess.)
170 "O How I Love Jesus" (1 Thess., Matt.)
256 "We Would See Jesus" (Matt.)
261 "Lord of the Dance" (Matt.)
433 "All Who Love and Serve Your City" (Matt., Exod.)
558 "We Are the Church" (Laity Sunday)
529 "How Firm a Foundation" (Exod., 1 Thess.) (C)

Contemporary Suggestions

S2068 "I Love You, Lord" (Exod.)
R36, SP72
M38 "In the Secret" ("I Want to Know You") (Exod.)
WO103; V-3 p. 36 (vocal solo)
MM107 "Show Me Your Ways" (Exod.)
MM93 "Rock of Ages" (Exod., Ps.)
WO125
UM123 "El Shaddai" (Exod., Ps.)
S-2 #54 (verses for vocal solo)
S2040 "Awesome God" (Exod., Ps.)
R245, SP11, WO9, WY3; V-10 (90) p. 21 (vocal solo)
S2274 "Come, All You People" ("Uyai Mose") (Ps.)
SP18 "I Exalt You" (Ps.)
R44
SP68 "We Will Glorify" (Ps.)
SP78 "I Extol You" (Ps.)
S2150 "Lord, Be Glorified" (Ps., Matt.)
R172, SP196
S2065 "More Precious than Silver" (Matt.)
SP99
S2176 "Make Me a Servant" (Matt.)
SP193
M51 "Step By Step" (Matt., Exod.)
WY104
MM98 "Take This Life" (Matt., Stewardship)

Vocal Solos

"God, Our Ever Faithful Shepherd" (Exod., Ps.)
V-4 p. 15
"Praise to the Lord, the Almighty" (Ps.)
V-6 p. 18
"Did You Feel the Mountains Tremble?" (Ps.)
V-3 p. 140
MM69, WO25

Anthems

"God Is Our Refuge" (Exod.)
Allen Pote; Hope A 583
SATB with keyboard (opt. trumpets)

"Come All Christians, Be Committed" (Matt.)
Arr. Lloyd Larson; Brookfield Press 08745076
SATB with keyboard

Other Suggestions

Visuals:
O Rock, cleft rock, hand
P Earthquake, cloud, footstool
E Symbols of the Holy Spirit, Trinity
G Array of coins around an empty offering plate, cross

Call to Worship: S2274. "Come, All You People" ("Uyai Mose") (Ps.)
Greeting: BOW451 (Ps.)
Opening Prayer: BOW459 or BOW462 (Exod.)
Prayer of Confession: BOW480 (Exod.)
Canticle: UM125. "Canticle of Covenant Faithfulness" (Exod.)
Litany: BOW432. Litany for Laity Sunday.
Prayer: BOW518. For Others (1 Thess.)
Prayer: BOW524. For Strength (Exod., Ps.)
Prayer: BOW525. For Wisdom (Matt.)
Prayer: BOW539. For Disciples in the Marketplace (Matt.)
Prayer: BOW544. For Leaders (Exod., Matt.)
Prayer of Thanksgiving: BOW551 (Exod., Ps., Matt.)
Response: UM588. "All Things Come of Thee" (Matt., Stewardship)

Deuteronomy 34:1-12

[1] Then Moses went up from the plains of Moab to Mount Nebo, to the top of Pisgah, which is opposite Jericho, and the LORD showed him the whole land: Gilead as far as Dan, [2] all Naphtali, the land of Ephraim and Manasseh, all the land of Judah as far as the Western Sea, [3] the Negeb, and the Plain—that is, the valley of Jericho, the city of palm trees—as far as Zoar. [4] The LORD said to him, "This is the land of which I swore to Abraham, to Isaac, and to Jacob, saying, 'I will give it to your descendants'; I have let you see it with your eyes, but you shall not cross over there." [5] Then Moses, the servant of the LORD, died there in the land of Moab, at the LORD's command. [6] He was buried in a valley in the land of Moab, opposite Beth-peor, but no one knows his burial place to this day. [7] Moses was one hundred twenty years old when he died; his sight was unimpaired and his vigor had not abated. [8] The Israelites wept for Moses in the plains of Moab thirty days; then the period of mourning for Moses was ended.

[9] Joshua son of Nun was full of the spirit of wisdom, because Moses had laid his hands on him; and the Israelites obeyed him, doing as the LORD had commanded Moses.

[10] Never since has there arisen a prophet in Israel like Moses, whom the LORD knew face to face. [11] He was unequaled for all the signs and wonders that the LORD sent him to perform in the land of Egypt, against Pharaoh and all his servants and his entire land, [12] and for all the mighty deeds and all the terrifying displays of power that Moses performed in the sight of all Israel.

Psalm 90:1-6, 13-17

[1] Lord, you have been our dwelling place in all generations. [2] Before the mountains were brought forth, or ever you had formed the earth and the world, from everlasting to everlasting you are God. [3] You turn us back to dust, and say, "Turn back, you mortals." [4] For a thousand years in your sight are like yesterday when it is past, or like a watch in the night. [5] You sweep them away; they are like a dream, like grass that is renewed in the morning; [6] in the morning it flourishes and is renewed; in the evening it fades and withers.

[13] Turn, O LORD! How long? Have compassion on your servants! [14] Satisfy us in the morning with your steadfast love, so that we may rejoice and be glad all our days.
[15] Make us glad as many days as you have afflicted us, and as many years as we have seen evil. [16] Let your work be manifest to your servants, and your glorious power to their children.
[17] Let the favor of the Lord our God be upon us, and prosper for us the work of our hands—O prosper the work of our hands!

---

1 Thessalonians 2:1-8

[1] You yourselves know, brothers and sisters, that our coming to you was not in vain, [2] but though we had already suffered and been shamefully mistreated at Philippi, as you know, we had courage in our God to declare to you the gospel of God in spite of great opposition. [3] For our appeal does not spring from deceit or impure motives or trickery, [4] but just as we have been approved by God to be entrusted with the message of the gospel, even so we speak, not to please mortals, but to please God who tests our hearts. [5] As you know and as God is our witness, we never came with words of flattery or with a pretext for greed; [6] nor did we seek praise from mortals, whether from you or from others, [7] though we might have made demands as apostles of Christ. But we were gentle among you, like a nurse tenderly caring for her own children. [8] So deeply do we care for you that we are determined to share with you not only the gospel of God but also our own selves, because you have become very dear to us.

Matthew 22:34-46

[34] When the Pharisees heard that he had silenced the Sadducees, they gathered together, [35] and one of them, a lawyer, asked him a question to test him. [36] "Teacher, which commandment in the law is the greatest?" [37] He said to him, " 'You shall love the Lord your God with all your heart, and with all your soul, and with all your mind.' [38] This is the greatest and first commandment. [39] And a second is like it: 'You shall love your neighbor as yourself.' [40] On these two commandments hang all the law and the prophets."

[41] Now while the Pharisees were gathered together, Jesus asked them this question: [42] "What do you think of the Messiah? Whose son is he?" They said to him, "The son of David." [43] He said to them, "How is it then that David by the Spirit calls him Lord, saying, [44] 'The Lord said to my Lord, "Sit at my right hand, until I put your enemies under your feet" ' ? [45] If David thus calls him Lord, how can he be his son?" [46] No one was able to give him an answer, nor from that day did anyone dare to ask him any more questions.

Notes:

Primary Hymns and Songs for the Day

117 "O God, Our Help in Ages Past" (Ps.) (O)
H-3 Handbell-87; Choir-60, 143; Descant-93; Organ-132
S-1 #293-96. Various treatments
402 "Lord, I Want to Be a Christian" (Matt.)
H-3 Choir-130
410 "I Want a Principle Within" (Matt.)
2168 "Love the Lord Your God" (Matt.)
724 "On Jordan's Stormy Banks I Stand" (Deut.) (C)
H-3 Choir-155; Organ-117
S-1 #271. Orff instrument arrangement
#272. Transposition in D major

Hymn Suggestions

110 "A Mighty Fortress Is Our God" (Deut, Ps.) (O)
60 "I'll Praise My Maker While I've Breath" (Deut.)
108 "God Hath Spoken by the Prophets" (Deut.)
448 "Go Down, Moses" (Deut.)
(See especially stanzas 8-11.)
524 "Beams of Heaven as I Go" (Deut.)
703 "Swing Low, Sweet Chariot" (Deut.)
66 "Praise, My Soul, the King of Heaven" (Ps., 1 Thess.)
86 "Mountains Are All Aglow" (Ps., Deut.)
2206 "Without Seeing You" (Ps.)
118 "The Care the Eagle Gives Her Young" (1 Thess.)
463 "Lord, Speak to Me" (1 Thess.)
557 "Blest Be the Tie That Binds" (1 Thess.)
430 "O Master, Let Me Walk with Thee" (1 Thess., Matt.)
572 "Pass It On" (1 Thess., Matt.)
408 "The Gift of Love" (Matt.)
453 "More Love to Thee, O Christ" (Matt.)
500 "Spirit of God, Descend Upon My Heart" (Matt.)
549 "Where Charity and Love Prevail" (Matt.)
2213 "Healer of Our Every Ill" (Matt.)
2254 "In Remembrance of Me" (Matt., Communion)
590 "Christ Loves the Church" (Reformation Day)
672 "God Be with You Till We Meet Again" (1 Thess.)
673 "God Be with You Till We Meet Again" (1 Thess.)

Contemporary Suggestions

UM432 "Jesu, Jesu" (Matt.)
R289; S-1 #63. (vocal part)
S2037 "I Sing Praises to Your Name" (Matt.)
R79, SP27
S2071 "Jesus, Name Above All Names" (Matt.)
R26, SP76
S2161 "To Know You More" (Matt.)
S2167 "More Like You" (Matt.)
S2171 "Make Me a Channel of Your Peace" (Matt.)
S2188 "The Family Prayer Song" (Matt.)
M54
M40 "More Love, More Power" (Matt.)
WY131
M41 "You're Worthy of My Praise" (Matt.)
WG178
M49 "Refresh My Heart" (Matt.)
M53 "Let It Be Said of Us" (Matt.)
MM62 "Rise Up and Praise Him" (Matt.)
MM83 "Just Let Me Say" (Matt.)
MM98 "Take This Life" (Matt)
SP187 "With All of My Heart" (Matt.)
MM86; V-10(03) p. 148 (vocal solo)

Vocal Solos

"Over Yonder" (Exod.)
V-7 p. 38
"The Call" (Ps., Matt.)
V-4 p. 31
"The Gift of Love" (Matt.)
V-8 p. 120

Anthems

"Promised Land" (Deut.)
Natalie Sleeth; Heritage Music Press
Three-part mixed with keyboard (#HV405)
Two-part with keyboard (#S5775)

"Set Thy Love" (Matt.)
Fred Bock; Fred Bock Music BG2368
SATB with organ

Other Suggestions

Visuals:
O Portrait or bust of Moses, tears
P Tall grass, morning/evening, rejoicing, hands at work/praise
E Nurturing, caring for children
G Images of loving God, neighbor, self, worship, service to others, nurture, Matt. 22:37, 38

Greeting: BOW452 (1 Thess.) or BOW455 (Deut.)
Opening Prayer: BOW462 (Matt.)
Prayer of Confession: BOW476 or BOW489 (Matt.)
Prayer: UM268. Lent (Deut.)
Prayer: BOW518 (Matt.)
Response: S2179. "Live in Charity" ("Ubi Caritas") (Matt.)
Prayers: BOW501-506. For the Church (Reformation)
Canticle: UM646. "Canticle of Love" (Matt.) (see S-1, p. 387).
Scripture Response: UM92, st. 4. "For the Beauty of the Earth" (Matt.)
Blessing: BOW560 (Deut., Matt.)
Benediction: S2171. "Make Me a Channel of Your Peace" (Matt.)

Revelation 7:9-17

9 After this I looked, and there was a great multitude that
no one could count, from every nation, from all tribes and
peoples and languages, standing before the throne and
before the Lamb, robed in white, with palm branches in
their hands. 10 They cried out in a loud voice, saying
"Salvation belongs to our God who is seated on the throne,
and to the Lamb!" 11 And all the angels stood around the
throne and around the elders and the four living creatures,
and they fell on their faces before the throne and wor-
shiped God, 12 singing, "Amen! Blessing and glory and wis-
dom and thanksgiving and honor and power and might be
to our God forever and ever! Amen."
13 Then one of the elders addressed me, saying, "Who are
these, robed in white, and where have they come from?" 14 I
said to him, "Sir, you are the one that knows." Then he said
to me, "These are they who have come out of the great
ordeal; they have washed their robes and made them white
in the blood of the Lamb. 15 For this reason they are before
the throne of God, and worship him day and night within
his temple, and the one who is seated on the throne will
shelter them. 16 They will hunger no more, and thirst no
more; the sun will not strike them, nor any scorching heat;
17 for the Lamb at the center of the throne will be their
shepherd, and he will guide them to springs of the water of
life, and God will wipe away every tear from their eyes."

Psalm 34:1-10, 22

1 I will bless the LORD at all times; his praise shall continu-
ally be in my mouth. 2 My soul makes its boast in the LORD;
let the humble hear and be glad. 3 O magnify the LORD with
me, and let us exalt his name together. 4 I sought the LORD,
and he answered me, and delivered me from all my fears.
5 Look to him, and be radiant; so your faces shall never be
ashamed. 6 This poor soul cried, and was heard by the LORD,
and was saved from every trouble. 7 The angel of the LORD
encamps around those who fear him, and delivers them. 8 O
taste and see that the LORD is good; happy are those who
take refuge in him. 9 O fear the LORD, you his holy ones, for
those who fear him have no want. 10 The young lions suffer
want and hunger, but those who seek the LORD lack no
good thing.
22 The LORD redeems the life of his servants; none of
those who take refuge in him will be condemned.

1 John 3:1-3

1 See what love the Father has given us, that we should be
called children of God; and that is what we are. The reason
the world does not know us is that it did not know him.
2 Beloved, we are God's children now; what we will be has
not yet been revealed. What we do know is this; when he is
revealed, we will be like him, for we will see him as he is.
3 And all who have this hope in him purify themselves, just
as he is pure.

Matthew 5:1-12

1 When Jesus saw the crowds, he went up the mountain;
and after he sat down, his disciples came to him. 2 Then he
began to speak, and taught them, saying:
3 "Blessed are the poor in spirit, for theirs is the kingdom
of heaven.
4 "Blessed are those who mourn, for they will be com-
forted.
5 "Blessed are the meek, for they will inherit the earth.
6 "Blessed are those who hunger and thirst for righteous-
ness, for they will be filled.
7 "Blessed are the merciful, for they will receive mercy.
8 "Blessed are the pure in heart, for they will see God.
9 "Blessed are the peacemakers, for they will be called
children of God.
10 "Blessed are those who are persecuted for righteous-
ness' sake, for theirs is the kingdom of heaven.
11 "Blessed are you when people revile you and persecute
you and utter all kinds of evil against you falsely on my
account. 12 Rejoice and be glad, for your reward is great in
heaven, for in the same way they persecuted the prophets
who were before you."

Notes:

Primary Hymns and Songs for the Day

711 "For All the Saints" (All Saints) (O)
- H-3 Handbell-58; Choir-65; Organ-152
- S-1 #314-18. Various treatments

2155 "Blest Are They" (Matt.)
2108 "O How He Loves You and Me!" (1 John)
708 "Rejoice in God's Saints" (Rev., All Saints) (C)
- H-3 Handbell-90, 105; Choir-221; Descant-49; Organ-51
- S-2 #71-74. Introduction/harmonizations

Hymn Suggestions

2236 "Gather Us In" (Matt.) (O)
88 "Maker, in Whom We Live" (Rev.)
90 "Ye Watchers and Ye Holy Ones" (Rev.)
638 "This Is the Feast of Victory" (Rev., Communion)
655 "Fix Me, Jesus" (Rev.)
674 "See the Morning Sun Ascending" (Rev.)
709 "Come, Let Us Join Our Friends Above" (Rev., All Saints)
732 "Come, We That Love the Lord" (Rev.)
733 "Marching to Zion" (Rev.)
2126 "All Who Hunger" (Rev., Ps., Matt., Communion)
2261 "Life-giving Bread" (Ps., Communion)
2264 "Come to the Table" (Rev., Ps. Communion)
2267 "Taste and See" (Ps., Communion)
616 "Come, Sinners, to the Gospel Feast" (Ps.)
2248 "Baptized in Water" (1 John, Baptism)
547 "O Church of God, United" (Matt., All Saints)
568 "Christ for the World We Sing" (Matt., All Saints)
614 "For the Bread Which You Have Broken" (All Saints, Communion)
712 "I Sing a Song of the Saints of God" (Matt., All Saints)
2140 "Since Jesus Came Into My Heart" (Matt.)
2168 "Love the Lord Your God" (Matt., All Saints)
2190 "Bring Forth the Kingdom" (Matt.)
2221 "In Unity We Lift Our Song" (All Saints)
2262 "Let Us Offer to the Father" ("Te Ofrecemos Padre Nuestro") (Matt., Communion)
2283 "For All the Saints" (All Saints)
181 "Ye Servants of God" (Rev.) (C)

Contemporary Suggestions

M10 "Salvation Belongs to Our God" (Rev.)
M21 "Blessing, Honour and Glory" (Rev.)
R81
M27 "We Will Worship the Lamb of Glory" (Rev.)
M43 "We Declare Your Majesty" (Rev.)
SP60 "To Him Who Sits on the Throne" (Rev.)
R265, WG149
UM99 "My Tribute" ("To God Be the Glory") (Rev.)
R68; V-8 p. 5 (vocal solo)
S2058 "Shepherd Me, O God" (Rev., All Saints)
S2194 "O Freedom" (Rev.)
S2195 "In the Lord I'll Be Ever Thankful" (Rev.)
S2210 "Joy Comes with the Dawn" (Rev.)
S2272 "Holy Ground" (Rev.)
SP86, WO57
S2023 "How Majestic Is Your Name" (Ps.)
R98, SP14
MM60 "Better Is One Day" (Ps.)
WY170, WO13
SP50 "Think about His Love" (Ps., 1 John)
WG138
SP48 "Behold, What Manner of Love" (1 John)
S2039 "Holy, Holy" (1 John, Matt.)
R206, SP141
S2073 "Celebrate Love" (1 John)
S2085 "He Came Down" (1 John)
S2086 "Open Our Eyes, Lord" (Matt.)
SP199, R91
S2132 "You Who Are Thirsty" (Ps., Matt.)
S2036 "Give Thanks" (Matt.)
R266, SP170
MM57 "Open the Eyes of My Heart" (Matt.)
V-3 p. 162 (vocal solo)
MM75 "Trading My Sorrows" (Matt., All Saints)
WG155

Vocal Solos

"Ye Servants of God" (Rev.)
V-1 p. 41
"In Bright Mansions Above" (All Saints)
V-4 p. 39
"How Long Train Been Gone" (All Saints)
V-7 p. 17

Anthems

"When Shall I See?" (All Saints)
Bradley Ellingboe; Kjos 6326
Two-part mixed with piano

"Rejoice and Be Glad" (Matt.)
Glenn Pickett; Alfred 00-24234
SATB with piano

Other Suggestions

These scriptures and ideas may be used on November 2.

Visuals:
- **O** White robe, palm branches
- **P** "Taste and see," spices to taste, abundance, rejoicing, refuge
- **E** Images of saints of the congregation
- **G** Images of people living the Beatitudes, mountain

Greeting: BOW414 (All Saints) or BOW449 (Ps.)
Prayer: UM392. Prayer for a New Heart (Matt.)
Response: S2277. "Lord, Have Mercy" (Rev.)
Prayer: UM713 or BOW415 (All Saints Day)
Prayer: BOW512. For Guidance (Rev., 1 John)
Prayer: BOW522. For Purity (1 John)
Memorial Prayer: UM461, BOW500, or BOW548 (All Saints)
Response: BOW219 "Beloved, Now We Are the Saints of God" (1 John, All Saints)

Joshua 3:7-17

7 The LORD said to Joshua, "This day I will begin to exalt
you in the sight of all Israel, so that they may know that I
will be with you as I was with Moses. 8 You are the one who
shall command the priests who bear the ark of the
covenant, 'When you come to the edge of the waters of
the Jordan, you shall stand still in the Jordan.' "
9 Joshua then said to the Israelites, "Draw near and hear
the words of the LORD your God." 10 Joshua said, "By this
you shall know that among you is the living God who with-
out fail will drive out from before you the Canaanites,
Hittites, Hivites, Perizzites, Girgashites, Amorites, and
Jebusites: 11 the ark of the covenant of the Lord of all the
earth is going to pass before you into the Jordan. 12 So now
select twelve men from the tribes of Israel, one from each
tribe. 13 When the soles of the feet of the priests who bear
the ark of the LORD, the Lord of all the earth, rest in the
waters of the Jordan, the waters of the Jordan flowing
from above shall be cut off; they shall stand in a single
heap."
14 When the people set out from their tents to cross over
the Jordan, the priests bearing the ark of the covenant
were in front of the people. 15 Now the Jordan overflows all
its banks throughout the time of harvest. So when those
who bore the ark had come to the Jordan, and the feet of
the priests bearing the ark were dipped in the edge of the
water, 16 the waters flowing from above stood still, rising
up in a single heap far off at Adam, the city that is beside
Zarethan, while those flowing toward the sea of the
Arabah, the Dead Sea, were wholly cut off. Then the peo-
ple crossed over opposite Jericho. 17 While all Israel were
crossing over on dry ground, the priests who bore the ark
of the covenant of the LORD stood on dry ground in the
middle of the Jordan, until the entire nation finished
crossing over the Jordan.

Psalm 107:1-7, 33-37

1 O give thanks to the LORD, for he is good; for his stead-
fast love endures forever. 2 Let the redeemed of the LORD
say so, those he redeemed from trouble 3 and gathered in
from the lands, from the east and from the west, from the
north and from the south. 4 Some wandered in desert
wastes, finding no way to an inhabited town; 5 hungry and
thirsty, their soul fainted within them. 6 Then they cried to
the LORD in their trouble, and he delivered them from
their distress; 7 he led them by a straight way, until they
reached an inhabited town.
33 He turns rivers into a desert, springs of waters into
thirsty ground, 34 a fruitful land into a salty waste, because
of the wickedness of its inhabitants. 35 He turns a desert
into pools of water, a parched land into springs of water.
36 And there he lets the hungry live, and they establish a
town to live in; 37 they sow fields, plant vineyards, and get a
fruitful yield.

1 Thessalonians 2:9-13

9 You remember our labor and toil, brothers and sisters;
we worked night and day, so that we might not burden any
of you while we proclaimed to you the gospel of God. 10 You
are witnesses, and God also, how pure, upright, and blame-
less our conduct was toward you believers. 11 As you know, we
dealt with each one of you like a father with his children,
12 urging and encouraging you and pleading that you lead a
life worthy of God, who calls you into his own kingdom and
glory.
13 We also constantly give thanks to God for this, that
when you received the word of God that you heard from us,
you accepted it not as a human word but as what it
really is, God's word, which is also at work in you believers.

Matthew 23:1-12

1 Then Jesus said to the crowds and to his disciples,
2 "The scribes and the Pharisees sit on Moses' seat; 3 there-
fore, do whatever they teach you and follow it; but do not
do as they do, for they do not practice what they teach.
4 They tie up heavy burdens, hard to bear, and lay them on
the shoulders of others; but they themselves are unwilling to
lift a finger to move them. 5 They do all their deeds to be
seen by others; for they make their phylacteries broad and
their fringes long. 6 They love to have the place of honor at
banquets and the best seats in the synagogues, 7 and to be
greeted with respect in the marketplaces, and to have peo-
ple call them rabbi. 8 But you are not to be called rabbi, for
you have one teacher, and you are all students. 9 And call no
one your father on earth, for you have one Father—the one
in heaven. 10 Nor are you to be called instructors, you have
one instructor, the Messiah. 11 The greatest among you will
be your servant. 12 All who exalt themselves will be humbled,
and all who humble themselves will be exalted."

Notes:

Primary Hymns and Songs for the Day

127 "Guide Me, O Thou Great Jehovah" (Josh.) (O)
- H-3 Handbell-25, 51, 58; Choir-89; Descant-26; Organ-23
- S-1 #76-77. Descant/harmonization

404 "Every Time I Feel the Spirit" (Josh.)

416 "Come Out the Wilderness" (Josh.) (See especially stanzas 6, 7, 9, 10, 11.)

581 "Lord, Whose Love Through Humble Service" (Matt.)
- H-3 Choir-51, 67

430 "O Master, Let Me Walk with Thee" (Matt.) (C)
- H-3 Handbell-81; Choir-147; Descant-74; Organ-87
- S-2 #118. Descant

Hymn Suggestions

128 "He Leadeth Me: O Blessed Thought" (Josh.)
448 "Go Down, Moses" (Josh.)
474 "Precious Lord, Take My Hand" (Josh.)
508 "Faith, While Trees Are Still in Blossom" (Josh.)
519 "Lift Every Voice and Sing" (Josh., Ps.)
629 "You Satisfy the Hungry Heart" (Ps., Communion)
631 "O Food to Pilgrims Given" (Ps., Communion)
2009 "O God Beyond All Praising" (Ps.)
2264 "Come to the Table" (Ps.)
84 "Thank You, Lord" (Josh, Ps., 1 Thess.)
364 "Because He Lives" (Josh., Ps., 1 Thess.)
558 "We Are the Church" (1 Thess.)
601 "Thy Word Is a Lamp" (1 Thess.)
649 "How Shall They Hear the Word of God" (1 Thess.)
163 "Ask Ye What Great Thing I Know" (1 Thess., Matt.)
433 "All Who Love and Serve Your City" (1 Thess., Matt.)
2153 "I'm Gonna Live So God Can Use Me" (1 Thess., Matt.)
432 "Jesu, Jesu" (Matt.)
463 "Lord, Speak to Me" (Matt.)
571 "Go, Make of All Disciples" (Matt.)
632 "Draw Us in the Spirit's Tether" (Matt., Communion)
2168 "Love the Lord Your God" (Matt.)
2175 "Together We Serve" (Matt., Communion)
2268 "As We Gather at Your Table" (Matt., Communion)
724 "On Jordan's Stormy Banks I Stand" (Josh.) (C)
670 "Go Forth for God" (1 Thess.) (C)

Contemporary Suggestions

S2272 "Holy Ground" (Josh.)
- SP86, WO57

M36 "Awesome in This Place" (Josh.)
- WG14

S2132 "You Who Are Thirsty" (Ps.)
S2195 "In the Lord I'll Be Ever Thankful" (Ps., 1 Thess.)
MM68 "Forever" (Ps.)
- WY57

MM99 "Shout to the North" (Ps.)
- WG114

WG63 "Hallelujah" ("Your Love Is Amazing") (Ps.)

WO63 "Hungry" ("Falling On My Knees") (Ps.)
- WY52

WY118 "Your Love, Oh Lord" (Ps.)
S2164 "Sanctuary" (1 Thess.)
- R185, M52

S2031 "We Bring the Sacrifice of Praise" (1 Thess., Matt.)
- R3, SP1

S2222 "The Servant Song" (Matt.)
- R148, SP193

S2176 "Make Me a Servant" (Matt.)
- SP193

S2131 "Humble Thyself in the Sight of the Lord" (Matt.)
- R188, SP223

M40 "More Love, More Power" (Matt.)
- WY131

Vocal Solos

"Stan' Still Jordan" (Josh.)
V-7 p. 62
"Take My Life" (Matt.)
V-8 p. 262

Anthems

"On Jordan's Stormy Banks I Stand" (Josh.)
Arr. Dale Grotenhuis; Curtis C8307
SATB with keyboard

"Whoever Would Be Great Among You" (Matt.)
Ronald A. Nelson; Augsburg 9780800645809
SAB with keyboard or guitar

Other Suggestions

Today may also be celebrated as All Saints Sunday, using suggestions for Nov. 1, 2008.

Visuals:
- **O** Flowing water
- **P** Water, bubbling water, sand, grapes, wheat
- **E** Man encouraging child, open Bible
- **G** Christ as teacher, servanthood (bowl/pitcher/towel), boxes symbolizing burdens, phylacteries, chair

Call to Worship: S2271, BOW199. "Come! Come! Everybody Worship" (Ps., 1 Thess.)
Greeting: BOW453 (Ps.)
Opening Prayer: BOW460 (Matt.)
Prayer of Confession: BOW476 (Matt.)
Prayer: BOW511. For God's Reign (Matt.)
Prayer: BOW540. For Those Who Work (1 Thess.)
Prayer: UM353. Ash Wednesday (1 Thess.)
Prayer of Thanksgiving: BOW550 or BOW555 (1 Thess., Matt.)
Closing Prayer: BOW567 (Matt.)
Benediction: UM672 or UM673, st. 2. "God Be with You till We Meet Again" (Josh.)

Joshua 24:1-3*a*, 14-25

1 Then Joshua gathered all the tribes of Israel to Shechem, and summoned the elders, the heads, the judges, and the officers of Israel; and they presented themselves before God. 2 And Joshua said to all the people, "Thus says the LORD, the God of Israel: Long ago your ancestors—Terah and his sons Abraham and Nahor—lived beyond the Euphrates and served other gods. 3 Then I took your father Abraham from beyond the River and led him through all the land of Canaan and made his offspring many.

14 "Now therefore revere the LORD, and serve him in sincerity and in faithfulness; put away the gods that your ancestors served beyond the River and in Egypt, and serve the LORD. 15 Now if you are unwilling to serve the LORD, choose this day whom you will serve, whether the gods your ancestors served in the region beyond the River or the gods of the Amorites in whose land you are living; but as for me and my household, we will serve the LORD."

16 Then the people answered, "Far be it from us that we should forsake the LORD to serve other gods; 17 for it is the LORD our God who brought us and our ancestors up from the land of Egypt, out of the house of slavery, and who did those great signs in our sight. He protected us along all the way that we went, and among all the peoples through whom we passed; 18 and the LORD drove out before us all the peoples, the Amorites who lived in the land. Therefore we also will serve the LORD, for he is our God."

19 But Joshua said to the people, "You cannot serve the LORD, for he is a holy God. He is a jealous God; he will not forgive your transgressions or your sins. 20 If you forsake the LORD and serve foreign gods, then he will turn and do you harm, and consume you, after having done you good." 21 And the people said to Joshua, "No, we will serve the LORD!" 22 Then Joshua said to the people, "You are witnesses against yourselves that you have chosen the LORD, to serve him." And they said, "We are witnesses." 23 He said, "Then put away the foreign gods that are among you, and incline your hearts to the LORD, the God of Israel." 24 The people said to Joshua, "The LORD our God we will serve, and him we will obey." 25 So Joshua made a covenant with the people that day, and made statutes and ordinances for them at Shechem.

Psalm 78:1-7

1 Give ear, O my people, to my teaching; incline your ears to the words of my mouth. 2 I will open my mouth in a parable; I will utter dark sayings from of old, 3 things that we have heard and known, that our ancestors have told us. 4 We will not hide them from their children; we will tell to the coming generation the glorious deeds of the LORD, and his might, and the wonders that he has done. 5 He established a decree in Jacob, and appointed a law in Israel, which he commanded our ancestors to teach to their children; 6 that the next generation might know them, the children yet unborn, and rise up and tell them to their children, 7 so that they should set their hope in God, and not forget the works of God, but keep his commandments.

1 Thessalonians 4:13-18

13 But we do not want you to be uninformed, brothers and sisters, about those who have died, so that you may not grieve as others do who have no hope. 14 For since we believe that Jesus died and rose again, even so, through Jesus, God will bring with him those who have died. 15 For this we declare to you by the word of the Lord, that we who are alive, who are left until the coming of the Lord, will by no means precede those who have died. 16 For the Lord himself, with a cry of command, with the archangel's call and with the sound of God's trumpet, will descend from heaven, and the dead in Christ will rise first. 17 Then we who are alive, who are left, will be caught up in the clouds together with them to meet the Lord in the air; and so we will be with the Lord forever. 18 Therefore encourage one another with these words.

Matthew 25:1-13

1 "Then the kingdom of heaven will be like this. Ten bridesmaids took their lamps and went to meet the bridegroom. 2 Five of them were foolish, and five were wise. 3 When the foolish took their lamps, they took no oil with them; 4 but the wise took flasks of oil with their lamps. 5 As the bridegroom was delayed, all of them became drowsy and slept. 6 But at midnight there was a shout, 'Look! Here is the bridegroom! Come out to meet him.' 7 Then all those bridesmaids got up and trimmed their lamps. 8 The foolish said to the wise, 'Give us some of your oil, for our lamps are going out.' 9 But the wise replied, 'No! there will not be enough for you and for us; you had better go to the dealers and buy some for yourselves.' 10 And while they went to buy it, the bridegroom came, and those who were ready went with him into the wedding banquet; and the door was shut. 11 Later the other bridesmaids came also, saying, 'Lord, lord, open to us.' 12 But he replied, 'Truly I tell you, I do not know you.' 13 Keep awake therefore, for you know neither the day nor the hour."

Notes:____

Primary Hymns and Songs for the Day

662 "Stand Up and Bless the Lord" (Josh.) (O)
  H-3 Handbell-79; Choir-141; Descant-95; Organ-143
  S-1 #306-8. Various treatments
2188 "The Family Prayer Song" (Josh.)
2220 "We Are God's People" (Josh., Matt.)
718 "Lo, He Comes with Clouds Descending" (1 Thess.)
  H-3 Handbell-93; Choir-129; Descant-50; Organ-53
  S-1 #157. Descant
719 "My Lord, What a Morning" (1 Thess.)
  H-3 Choir-139
720 "Wake, Awake, for Night Is Flying" (Matt.) (C)
  H-3 Choir-174, 203; Organ-172

Hymn Suggestions

116 "The God of Abraham Praise" (Josh.) (O)
391 "O Happy Day, That Fixed My Choice" (Josh.)
411 "Dear Lord, Lead Me Day by Day" (Josh.)
472 "Near to the Heart of God" (Josh.)
551 "Awake, O Sleeper" (Josh., Matt.)
717 "The Battle Hymn of the Republic" (Josh., 1 Thess.)
2130 "The Summons" (Josh., Matt.)
2153 "I'm Gonna Live So God Can Use Me" (Josh., Matt.)
2166 "Christ Beside Me" (Josh., Matt.)
2175 "Together We Serve" (Josh., Matt.)
2242 "Walk with Me" (Josh., Matt.)
2245 "Within the Day-to-Day" (Josh., Matt.)
701 "When We All Get to Heaven" (1 Thess.)
704 "Steal Away to Jesus" (1 Thess.)
715 "Rejoice, the Lord Is King" (1 Thess.)
716 "Rejoice, the Lord Is King" (1 Thess.)
2147 "There Are Some Things I May Not Know" ("Yes, God Is Real") (1 Thess.)
440 "Let There Be Light" (Matt.)
540 "I Love Thy Kingdom, Lord" (Matt.)
722 "I Want to Be Ready" (Matt.)
2149 "Living for Jesus" (Matt.)
702 "Sing with All the Saints in Glory" (1 Thess.) (C)

Contemporary Suggestions

UM328 "Surely the Presence of the Lord" (Josh.)
  R167, SP243
S2161 "To Know You More" (Josh.)
S2165 "Cry of My Heart" (Josh.)
  M39, WG32
S2208 "Guide My Feet" (Josh.)
S2240 "One God and Father of Us All" (Josh.)
S2272 "Holy Ground" (Josh.)
  SP86, WO57
M41 "You're Worthy of My Praise" (Josh.)
  WG178
M51 "Step By Step" (Josh.)
  WY104
MM97 "I Give You My Heart" (Josh.)
  WY71
S2192 "Freedom Is Coming" (Josh., 1 Thess., Matt.)
S2040 "Awesome God" (Ps.)
  R245, SP11, WO9, WY3; V-10 (90) p. 21 (vocal solo)
SP158 "The Battle Belongs to the Lord" (1 Thess.)
  R244
SP151 "Blow the Trumpet in Zion" (1 Thess.)
WO68 "I Believe In Jesus" (1 Thess.)
S2194 "O Freedom" (1 Thess., Matt.)
M17 "This Kingdom" (1 Thess., Matt.)
M31 "I See the Lord" (1 Thess., Matt.)
  WO72
MM111 "The Heavens Shall Declare" (1 Thess., Matt.)
WO155 "We Will Dance" (1 Thess., Matt.)
WY25 "Imagine" (1 Thess., Matt.)
  V-3 p. 8 (vocal solo)

Vocal Solos

"Here I Am" (Josh.)
V-9 p. 19
"Every Move I Make" (Josh.)
WY76, WG41
"Gospel Train" (Josh., 1 Thess.)
V-7 p. 74

Anthems

"Guide My Feet" (Josh.)
Arr. Leck/Ellis; Hal Leonard 08745189
SATB with piano

"Keep Your Lamps!" (Matt.)
Arr. Andre Thomas; Hinshaw Music HMC-577
SATB with conga drums

Other Suggestions

Visuals:
  O "Choose this day whom you will serve," "As for me and my household," servanthood (bowl/pitcher/towel)
  P Christ as teacher, open Bible
  E Trumpet, clouds, resurrection, encouragement
  G Ten lamps, oil, wedding garments, bouquet, clock set at 12:00
Call to Worship: UM719, refrain. "My Lord, What a Morning" (1 Thess.)
Act of Congregational Centering: BOW472 (Josh.)
Greeting: BOW450 (1 Thess., Matt.)
Opening Prayer: BOW468 (Josh.)
Call to Prayer: UM704, refrain. "Steal Away to Jesus" (1 Thess.)
Prayer of Confession: BOW483 or BOW490 (Josh., Matt.)
Prayer: BOW510. For Discernment (Josh.)
Prayer: BOW511 or BOW513 (1 Thess., Matt.)
Prayer: BOW528. A Prayer of Susanna Wesley (Matt.)
Prayer of Thanksgiving: BOW551 (Josh.) or BOW556 (Ps.)
Blessing: BOW562 (Josh.)

Judges 4:3-7

1 The Israelites again did what was evil in the sight of the LORD, after Ehud died. 2 So the LORD sold them into the hand of King Jabin of Canaan, who reigned in Hazor; the commander of his army was Sisera, who lived in Harosheth-ha-goiim. 3 Then the Israelites cried out to the LORD for help; for he had nine hundred chariots of iron, and had oppressed the Israelites cruelly twenty years.

4 At that time Deborah, a prophetess, wife of Lappidoth, was judging Israel. 5 She used to sit under the palm of Deborah between Ramah and Bethel in the hill country of Ephraim; and the Israelites came up to her for judgment. 6 She sent and summoned Barak son of Abinoam from Kedesh in Naphtali, and said to him, "The LORD, the God of Israel, commands you, 'Go, take position at Mount Tabor, bringing ten thousand from the tribe of Naphtali and the tribe of Zebulun. 7 I will draw out Sisera, the general of Jabin's army, to meet you by the Wadi Kishon with his chariots and his troops; and I will give him into your hand.' "

Psalm 123

1 To you I lift up my eyes, O you who are enthroned in the heavens! 2 As the eyes of servants look to the hand of their master, as the eyes of a maid to the hand of her mistress, so our eyes look to the LORD our God, until he has mercy upon us. 3 Have mercy upon us, O LORD, have mercy upon us, for we have had more than enough of contempt. 4 Our soul has had more than its fill of the scorn of those who are at ease, of the contempt of the proud.

1 Thessalonians 5:1-11

1 Now concerning the times and the seasons, brothers and sisters, you do not need to have anything written to you. 2 For you yourselves know very well that the day of the Lord will come like a thief in the night. 3 When they say, "There is peace and security," then sudden destruction will come upon them, as labor pains come upon a pregnant woman, and there will be no escape! 4 But you, beloved, are not in darkness, for that day to surprise you like a thief; 5 for you are all children of light and children of the day; we are not of the night or of darkness. 6 So then let us not fall asleep as others do, but let us keep awake and be sober; 7 for those who sleep sleep at night, and those who are drunk get drunk at night. 8 But since we belong to the day, let us be sober, and put on the breastplate of faith and love, and for a helmet the hope of salvation. 9 For God has destined us not for wrath but for obtaining salvation through our Lord Jesus Christ, 10 who died for us, so that whether we are awake or asleep we may live with him. 11 Therefore encourage one another and build up each other, as indeed you are doing.

Matthew 25:14-30

14 "For it is as if a man, going on a journey, summoned his slaves and entrusted his property to them; 15 to one he gave five talents, to another two, to another one, to each according to his ability. Then he went away. 16 The one who had received the five talents went off at once and traded with them, and made five more talents. 17 In the same way, the one who had the two talents made two more talents. 18 But the one who had received the one talent went off and dug a hole in the ground and hid his master's money. 19 After a long time the master of those slaves came and settled accounts with them. 20 Then the one who had received the five talents came forward, bringing five more talents, saying, 'Master, you handed over to me five talents; see, I have made five more talents.' 21 His master said to him, 'Well done, good and trustworthy slave; you have been trustworthy in a few things, I will put you in charge of many things; enter into the joy of your master.' 22 And the one with the two talents also came forward, saying, 'Master, you handed over to me two talents; see, I have made two more talents.' 23 His master said to him, 'Well done, good and trustworthy slave; you have been trustworthy in a few things, I will put you in charge of many things; enter into the joy of your master.' 24 Then the one who had received the one talent also came forward, saying, 'Master, I knew that you were a harsh man, reaping where you did not sow, and gathering where you did not scatter seed; 25 so I was afraid, and I went and hid your talent in the ground. Here you have what is yours.' 26 But his master replied, 'You wicked and lazy slave! You knew, did you, that I reap where I did not sow, and gather where I did not scatter? 27 Then you ought to have invested my money with the bankers, and on my return I would have received what was my own with interest. 28 So take the talent from him, and give it to the one with the ten talents. 29 For to all those who have, more will be given, and they will have an abundance; but from those who have nothing, even what they have will be taken away. 30 As for this worthless slave, throw him into the outer darkness, where there will be weeping and gnashing of teeth.' "

Notes:

Primary Hymns and Songs for the Day

206 "I Want to Walk as a Child of the Light" (O) (1 Thess.)
S-2 #91. Descant
81 "¡Canta, Débora, Canta!" (Judg.)
S-1 #81. Tambourine part
2150 "Lord, Be Glorified" (Matt.)
399 "Take My Life, and Let It Be" (Matt.)
413 "A Charge to Keep I Have" (Matt.) (C)
H-3 Descant-19; Organ-14
S-1 #46. Choral harmonization

Hymn Suggestions

150 "God Who Stretched the Spangled Heavens" (Matt.) (O)
108 "God Hath Spoken By the Prophets" (Judg.)
107 "La Palabra Del Señor Es Recta" ("Righteous and Just Is the Word of Our Lord") (Judg.)
121 "There's a Wideness in God's Mercy" (Ps.)
482 "Lord, Have Mercy" (Ps.)
485 "Let Us Pray to the Lord" (Ps.)
247 "O Morning Star, How Fair and Bright" (1 Thess.)
289 "Ah, Holy Jesus" (1 Thess.)
301 "Jesus, Keep Me Near the Cross" (1 Thess.)
356 "Pues Si Vivimos" ("When We Are Living") (1 Thess.)
551 "Awake, O Sleeper" (1 Thess.)
2172 "We Are Called" (1 Thess.)
2175 "Together We Serve" (1 Thess., Matt.)
2214 "Lead Me, Guide Me" (1 Thess.)
2236 "Gather Us In" (1 Thess.)
2284 "Joy in the Morning" (1 Thess.)
87 "What Gift Can We Bring" (Matt.)
433 "All Who Love and Serve Your City" (Matt.)
508 "Faith, While Trees Are Still in Blossom" (Matt.)
650 "Give Me the Faith Which Can Remove" (Matt.)
2153 "I'm Gonna Live So God Can Use Me" (Matt.)
581 "Lord, Whose Love Through Humble Service" (Matt.) (C)

Contemporary Suggestions

UM483 "Kyrie Eleison" ("Lord, Have Mercy") (Ps.)
UM484 (different tunes)
S2192 "Freedom Is Coming" (1 Thess.)
S2194 "O Freedom" (1 Thess.)
S2204 "Light of the World" (1 Thess.)
S2235b "We Are Marching" ("Siyahamba") (1 Thess.)
R306
M19 "Shine on Us" (1 Thess.)
MM64 "Hear Our Praises" (1 Thess.)
SP144 "Song for the Nations" ("May We Be a Shining Light") (1 Thess.)
R303
WY139 "Here I Am to Worship" (1 Thess.)
S2032 "My Life Is in You, Lord" (Matt.)
SP204
M53 "Let It Be Said of Us" (Matt.)
MM115 "When It's All Been Said and Done" (Matt.)
WO97 "In That Day" (Matt.)

Vocal Solos

"I Will Lift Up Mine Eyes" (Ps.)
V-9 p. 27
"Let De Heb'n-Light Shine on Me" (1 Thess.)
V-7 p. 66
"Redeeming Grace" (1 Thess., Matt.)
V-4 p. 47
"Take My Life, and Let It Be" (Matt.)
V-8 p. 262

Anthems

"Take and Receive, O Lord" (Matt.)
Allen Pote; Hope C5131
SATB with piano (opt. C or B-flat instruments)

"What Gift Can We Bring" (Matt.)
Jane Marshall; Hope CY 3370
SATB with keyboard

Other Suggestions

Visuals:
O Manacles
P Hand
E Robber's mask, light/dark, awake/asleep, lantern
G Three piles of coins (large, medium, small), bank bag, time/talent survey, nos. 1, 2 and 5 (nos. 10, 4, and 1)

Today's parable from Matthew lends itself well to a stewardship emphasis.
Greeting: BOW450 (1 Thess., Matt.)
Opening Prayer: BOW460 (1 Thess., Matt.)
Prayer of Confession: BOW476, BOW478, or BOW480 (1 Thess., Matt.)
Response: S2275. "Kyrie" or S2277. "Lord, Have Mercy" (Ps.)
Baptism Response: S2249, BOW175. "God Claims You" (1 Thess.)
Prayer: UM403. For True Life (1 Thess., Matt.)
Prayer: UM481. Prayer of Saint Francis (Ps.)
Prayer: BOW508. Psalm of the Woodlands (Matt.)
Prayer: BOW540. For Those Who Work (Matt.)
Response: BOW179. "For the Gift of Creation" (Matt.)
Dismissal: BOW559 (1 Thess., Matt.)

Ezekiel 34:11-16, 20-24

11 For thus says the Lord GOD: I myself will search for my
sheep, and will seek them out. 12 As shepherds seek out their
flocks when they are among their scattered sheep, so I will
seek out my sheep. I will rescue them from all the places to
which they have been scattered on a day of clouds and thick
darkness. 13 I will bring them out from the peoples and gath-
er them from the countries, and will bring them into their
own land; and I will feed them on the mountains of Israel,
by the watercourses, and in all the inhabited parts of the
land. 14 I will feed them with good pasture, and the moun-
tain heights of Israel shall be their pasture; there they shall
lie down in good grazing land, and they shall feed on rich
pasture on the mountains of Israel. 15 I myself will be the
shepherd of my sheep, and I will make them lie down, says
the Lord GOD. 16 I will seek the lost, and I will bring back the
strayed, and I will bind up the injured, and I will strengthen
the weak, but the fat and the strong I will destroy. I will feed
them with justice.

20 Therefore, thus says the Lord GOD to them: I myself
will judge between the fat sheep and the lean sheep.
21 Because you pushed with flank and shoulder, and butted
at all the weak animals with your horns until you scattered
them far and wide, 22 I will save my flock, and they shall no
longer be ravaged; and I will judge between sheep and
sheep.

23 I will set up over them one shepherd, my servant David,
and he shall feed them: he shall feed them and be their
shepherd. 24 And I, the LORD, will be their God, and my ser-
vant David shall be prince among them; I, the LORD, have
spoken.

Psalm 100

1 Make a joyful noise to the LORD, all the earth.
2 Worship the LORD with gladness; come into his presence
with singing. 3 Know that the LORD is God. It is he that made
us, and we are his; we are his people, and the sheep of his
pasture. 4 Enter his gates with thanksgiving, and his courts
with praise. Give thanks to him, bless his name. 5 For the
LORD is good; his steadfast love endures forever, and his
faithfulness to all generations.

Ephesians 1:15-23

15 I have heard of your faith in the Lord Jesus and your
love toward all the saints, and for this reason 16 I do not
cease to give thanks for you as I remember you in my
prayers. 17 I pray that the God of our Lord Jesus Christ, the
Father of glory, may give you a spirit of wisdom and revela-
tion as you come to know him, 18 so that, with the eyes of
your heart enlightened, you may know what is the hope to
which he has called you, what are the riches of his glorious
inheritance among the saints, 19 and what is the immeasur-
able greatness of his power for us who believe, according to
the working of his great power. 20 God put this power to
work in Christ when he raised him from the dead and seat-
ed him at his right hand in the heavenly places, 21 far above
all rule and authority and power and dominion, and above
every name that is named, not only in this age but also in
the age to come. 22 And he has put all things under his feet
and has made him the head over all things for the church,
23 which is his body, the fullness of him who fills all in all.

Matthew 25:31-46

31 "When the Son of Man comes in his glory, and all the
angels with him, then he will sit on the throne of his glory.
32 All the nations will be gathered before him, and he will
separate people one from another as a shepherd separates
the sheep from the goats, 33 and he will put the sheep at his
right hand and the goats at the left. 34 Then the king will say
to those at his right hand, 'Come, you that are blessed by my
Father, inherit the kingdom prepared for you from the
foundation of the world; 35 for I was hungry and you gave
me food, I was thirsty and you gave me something to drink,
I was a stranger and you welcomed me, 36 I was naked and
you gave me clothing, I was sick and you took care of me, I
was in prison and you visited me.' 37 Then the righteous will
answer him, 'Lord, when was it that we saw you hungry and
gave you food, or thirsty and gave you something to drink?
38 And when was it that we saw you a stranger and welcomed
you, or naked and gave you clothing? 39 And when was it
that we saw you sick or in prison and visited you?' 40 And the
king will answer them, 'Truly I tell you, just as you did it to
one of the least of these who are members of my family, you
did it to me.' 41 Then he will say to those at his left hand,
'You that are accursed, depart from me into the eternal fire
prepared for the devil and his angels; 42 for I was hungry and
you gave me no food, I was thirsty and you gave me nothing
to drink, 43 I was a stranger and you did not welcome me,
naked and you did not give me clothing, sick and in prison
and you did not visit me.' 44 Then they also will answer,
'Lord, when was it that we saw you hungry or thirsty or a
stranger or naked or sick or in prison, and did not take care
of you?' 45 Then he will answer them, 'Truly I tell you, just as
you did not do it to one of the least of these, you did not do
it to me.' 46 And these will go away into eternal punishment,
but the righteous into eternal life."

Notes:

Primary Hymns and Songs for the Day

75 "All People That on Earth Do Dwell" (Ps.) (O)
H-3 Handbell-45; Choir-24; Descant-84, 85; Organ-107
S-1 #257-59. Various treatments
S-2 #140. Descant
2182 "When God Restored Our Common Life" (Ezek., Matt.)
MM77 "Above All" (Eph.)
WO2; V-3 p. 17 or V-10(03) p. 18 (vocal solo)
434 "Cuando El Pobre" ("When the Poor Ones") (Matt.)
591 "Rescue the Perishing" (Matt.)
581 "Lord, Whose Love Through Humble Service" (C) (Matt.)
H-3 Choir-51, 67

Hymn Suggestions

131 "We Gather Together" (Matt., Thanksgiving) (O)
66 "Praise, My Soul, the King of Heaven" (Ezek., Christ the King)
115 "How Like a Gentle Spirit" (Ezek.)
132 "All My Hope Is Firmly Grounded" (Ezek.)
381 "Savior, Like a Shepherd Lead Us" (Ezek., Ps.)
2123 "Loving Spirit" (Ezek.)
2177 "Wounded World that Cries for Healing" (Ezek.)
2178 "Here Am I" (Ezek., Matt.)
2180 "Why Stand So Far Away, My God?" (Ezek.)
61 "Come, Thou Almighty King" (Ps., Eph., Christ the King)
62 "All Creatures of Our God and King" (Ps., Christ the King)
94 "Praise God, from Whom All Blessings Flow" (Ps.)
694 "Come, Ye Thankful People, Come" (Ps., Matt., Thanksgiving)
73 "O Worship the King" (Eph., Christ the King)
79 "Holy God, We Praise Thy Name" (Eph., Christ the King) (See especially stanzas 1, 5-7.)
96 "Praise the Lord Who Reigns Above" (Eph., Christ the King)
103 "Immortal, Invisible, God Only Wise" (Eph.)
175 "Jesus, the Very Thought of Thee" (Eph.)
178 "Hope of the World" (Eph.)
368 "My Hope Is Built" (Eph.)
711 "For All the Saints" (Eph.)
2147 "There Are Some Things I May Not Know" ("Yes, God Is Real") (Eph.)
2220 "We Are God's People" (Eph.)
2269 "Come, Share the Lord" (Eph., Matt., Christ the King, Communion)
192 "There's a Spirit in the Air" (Matt.)
433 "All Who Love and Serve Your City" (Matt.)
2126 "All Who Hunger" (Matt., Communion)
2175 "Together We Serve" (Matt.)
2254 "In Remembrance of Me" (Matt., Communion)
2268 "As We Gather at Your Table" (Matt., Communion)

Contemporary Suggestions

S2036 "Give Thanks" (Ezek., Matt.)
R266, SP170
S2055 "You Are My Hiding Place" (Ezek.)
S2058 "Shepherd Me, O God"
MM92 "All Things Are Possible" (Ezek.)
WG8
S2017 "Come, Rejoice in God" ("Jubilate Servite") (Ps.)
S2035 "Praise, Praise, Praise the Lord" (Ps.)
S2270 "I Will Enter His Gates" (Ps.)
SP168
S2244 "People Need the Lord" (Matt.)
S2075 "King of Kings" (Christ the King)
R268, SP94

Vocal Solos

"God, Our Ever Faithful Shepherd" (Ezek., Matt.)
V-4 p. 15
"Reach Out to Your Neighbor" (Matt.)
V-8 p. 372
"Praise to the Lord, the Almighty" (Christ the King)
V-6 p. 18

Anthems

"Make a Joyful Noise" (Ps.)
Gary Alan Smith; Abingdon Press 9780687645817
SATB, *a cappella*

"The Morning Trumpet" (Matt.)
Arr. Joanne Brown LeDoux; Abingdon Press 099838
Two-part with keyboard (opt. trumpet)

Other Suggestions

Visuals:
O Sheep, good shepherd
P Instruments, worship, singing
E Portraits of Christ or local church saints, church history
G Christ descending, angels, food, drink, clothes, visitation, medicine bag, prison ministry, Bible, crown, rich fabric, Christ as King

Call to Worship: S2274 "Come, All You People" (Ps.)
Response: UM93. "Let All the World in Every Corner Sing" (Ps.)
Greeting: BOW420 (Christ the King)
Greeting: BOW450 or BOW452 (Ps.) or BOW454 (Ezek.)
Opening Prayer: BOW460 (Matt.)
Canticle: UM74 or UM91 (Ps.)
Call to Confession: S2138, st. 3. "Sunday's Palms Are Wednesday's Ashes" (Matt.)
Prayer of Confession: BOW476 or BOW481 (Matt.)
Prayer: UM323. Ascension (Eph.)
Prayer: UM721 or BOW421or BOW511 (Christ the King)
Prayer: BOW522, BOW529, or BOW546 (Matt.)
Prayer of Thanksgiving: BOW555 (Ps., Matt.)
Response: UM67. "We, Thy People, Praise Thee" (Ps.)
Blessing: BOW564 (Matt.)

Deuteronomy 8:7-18

7 For the LORD your God is bringing you into a good
land, a land with flowing streams, with springs and under-
ground waters welling up in valleys and hills, 8 a land of
wheat and barley, of vines and fig trees and pomegranates, a
land of olive trees and honey, 9 a land where you may eat
bread without scarcity, where you will lack nothing, a land
whose stones are iron and from whose hills you may mine
copper. 10 You shall eat your fill and bless the LORD your
God for the good land that he has given you.
11 Take care that you do not forget the LORD your God, by
failing to keep his commandments, his ordinances, and his
statutes, which I am commanding you today. 12 When you
have eaten your fill and have built fine houses and live in
them, 13 and when your herds and flocks have multiplied,
and your silver and gold is multiplied, and all that you have
is multiplied, 14 then do not exalt yourself, forgetting the
LORD your God, who brought you out of the land of Egypt,
out of the house of slavery, 15 who led you through the great
and terrible wilderness, an arid wasteland with poisonous
snakes and scorpions. He made water flow for you from flint
rock, 16 and fed you in the wilderness with manna that your
ancestors did not know, to humble you and to test you, and
in the end to do you good. 17 Do not say to yourself, "My
power and the might of my own hand have gotten me this
wealth." 18 But remember the LORD your God, for it is he
who gives you power to get wealth, so that he may confirm
his covenant that he swore to your ancestors, as he is doing
today.

Psalm 65

1 Praise is due to you, O God, in Zion; and to you shall
vows be performed, 2 O you who answer prayer! To you all
flesh shall come. 3 When deeds of iniquity overwhelm us,
you forgive our transgressions. 4 Happy are those whom you
choose and bring near to live in your courts. We shall be sat-
isfied with the goodness of your house, your holy temple.
5 By awesome deeds you answer us with deliverance, O God
of our salvation; you are the hope of all the ends of the
earth and of the farthest seas. 6 By your strength you estab-
lished the mountains; you are girded with might. 7 You
silence the roaring of the seas, the roaring of their waves,
the tumult of the peoples. 8 Those who live at earth's far-
thest bounds are awed by your signs; you make the gateways
of the morning and the evening shout for joy. 9 You visit the
earth and water it, you greatly enrich it; the river of God is
full of water; you provide the people with grain, for so you
have prepared it. 10 You water its furrows abundantly, set-
tling its ridges, softening it with showers, and blessing its
growth. 11 You crown the year with your bounty; your wagon
tracks overflow with richness. 12 The pastures of the wilder-
ness overflow, the hills gird themselves with joy, 13 the mead-
ows clothe themselves with flocks, the valleys deck them-
selves with grain, they shout and sing together for joy.

2 Corinthians 9:6-15

6 The point is this: the one who sows sparingly will also
reap sparingly, and the one who sows bountifully will also
reap bountifully. 7 Each of you must give as you have made
up your mind, not reluctantly or under compulsion, for
God loves a cheerful giver. 8 And God is able to provide you
with every blessing in abundance, so that by always having
enough of everything, you may share abundantly in every
good work. 9 As it is written, "He scatters abroad, he gives to
the poor; his righteousness endures forever." 10 He who sup-
plies seed to the sower and bread for food will supply and
multiply your seed for sowing and increase the harvest of
your righteousness. 11 You will be enriched in every way for
your great generosity, which will produce thanksgiving to
God through us; 12 for the rendering of this ministry not
only supplies the needs of the saints but also overflows with
many thanksgivings to God. 13 Through the testing of this
ministry you glorify God by your obedience to the confes-
sion of the gospel of Christ and by the generosity of your
sharing with them and with all others, 14 while they long for
you and pray for you because of the surpassing grace of God
that he has given you. 15 Thanks be to God for his indescrib-
able gift!

Luke 17:11-19

11 On the way to Jerusalem Jesus was going through the
region between Samaria and Galilee. 12 As he entered a vil-
lage, ten lepers approached him. Keeping their distance,
13 they called out, saying, "Jesus, Master, have mercy on us!"
14 When he saw them, he said to them, "Go and show your-
selves to the priests." And as they went, they were made
clean. 15 Then one of them, when he saw that he was healed,
turned back, praising God with a loud voice. 16 He prostrated
himself at Jesus' feet and thanked him. And he was a
Samaritan. 17 Then Jesus asked, "Were not ten made clean?
But the other nine, where are they? 18 Was none of them
found to return and give praise to God except this foreign-
er?" 19 Then he said to him, "Get up and go on your way;
your faith has made you well."

Notes:

Primary Hymns and Songs for the Day

694 "Come, Ye Thankful People, Come" (2 Cor., Thanksgiving) (O)
H-3 Handbell-54; Choir-58; Descant-94; Organ-137
S-1 #302-3. Harmonizations with descant
92 "For the Beauty of the Earth" (Ps.)
H-3 Choir-33, 65; Descant-30; Organ-29
S-1 #93-96. Various treatments
583 "Sois la Semilla" ("You Are the Seed") (2 Cor.)
2036 "Give Thanks" (2 Cor.)
R266, SP170
60 "I'll Praise My Maker While I've Breath" (Luke) (C)
H-3 Choir-109; Organ-105
S-2 #141. Harmonization

Hymn Suggestions

139 "Praise to the Lord, the Almighty" (Deut., Thanksgiving) (O)
86 "Mountains Are All Aglow" (Deut., Ps., 1 Cor.)
87 "What Gift Can We Bring" (Deut.)
92 "For the Beauty of the Earth" (Deut., Thanksgiving)
97 "For the Fruits of This Creation" (Deut.)
102 "Now Thank We All Our God" (Deut., Thanksgiving)
586 "Let My People Seek Their Freedom" (Deut.)
637 "Una Espiga" ("Sheaves of Summer") (Ps., Communion)
2061 "Praise Our God Above" ("Harvest Song") (Deut., Ps., Thanksgiving)
66 "Praise, My Soul, The King of Heaven" (Luke, Thanksgiving)
263 "When Jesus the Healer Passed Through Galilee" (Luke)
273 "Jesus' Hands Were Kind Hands" (Luke)
372 "How Can We Sinners Know" (Luke)
551 "Awake, O Sleeper" (Luke)
2104 "An Outcast Among Outcasts" (Luke)
565 "Father, We Thank You" (Thanksgiving, Communion)
563 "Father, We Thank You" (alternate tune)
617 "I Come with Joy" (Thanksgiving, Communion)
2044 "My Gratitude Now Accept, O God" ("Gracias, Señor") (Thanksgiving)
2262 "Let Us Offer to the Father" ("Te Ofrecemos Padre Nuestro") (Thanksgiving, Communion)
2265 "Time Now to Gather" (Thanksgiving, Communion)
2283 "For All the Saints" (Thanksgiving)
2279 "The Trees of the Field" (Ps.) (C)
R302, SP128

Contemporary Suggestions

S2271 "Come! Come! Everybody Worship" (2 Cor.)
BOW199
S2150 "Lord, Be Glorified" (2 Cor.)
R172, SP196
S2162 "Grace Alone" (2 Cor.)
MM100
M13 "Be Glorified" (2 Cor.)
M37 "He Is Able" (2 Cor.)
WO49
M35 "White as Snow" (Luke)
UM84 "Thank You, Lord" (Luke, Thanksgiving)
UM394 "Something Beautiful" (Luke)
S2079 "Jesus Be Praised" (Luke)
S2081 "Thank You, Jesus" ("Tino Tenda, Jesu") (Luke)
BOW203
S2195 "In the Lord I'll Be Ever Thankful" (2 Cor., Luke)

Vocal Solos

"O For a Thousand Tongues to Sing" (Luke)
V-1 p. 32
"Praise Forevermore" (Luke, Thanksgiving)
V-3 p. 68
"When I Praise" (Luke, Thanksgiving)
V-3 p. 170
"I Just Came to Praise the Lord" (Luke, Thanksgiving)
V-8 p. 294
"Now Thank We All Our God" (Thanksgiving)
V-6 p. 8

Anthems

"O For a Thousand Tongues to Sing" (Luke)
Carlton R. Young: Abingdon Press 9780687646111
SATB with piano (opt. bass and claves)

"It Is a Good Thing to Give Thanks" (Thanksgiving)
Eugene Butler; Agape EB9213
Three-part mixed with keyboard

Other Suggestions

Visuals:
O Flowing water, wheat, barley, figs, etc.
P Cornucopia with fruit, vegetables, water, sheep, sea, mountains, grain
E Seed, bread, people in ministry, 2 Cor. 9:15
G Nos. 1 and 9, healing, praise, Luke 17:19*b*
Act of Congregational Centering: BOW471 (Thanks)
Greeting: BOW417 (Thanksgiving Day)
Opening Prayer: BOW464 (Deut., Matt., Thanks)
Canticle: UM74. "Canticle of Thanksgiving" (see S-1, p. 374)
Prayer of Confession: BOW485 or BOW494 (Thanksgiving)
Response: S2275. "Kyrie" (Luke)
Prayer: BOW507. For Creation (Thanksgiving)
Prayer: BOW521. A Vision of Hope (2 Cor., Thanks)
Prayer: BOW532 (Luke)
Prayer of Thanksgiving: BOW418 or BOW557 (Deut.)
Response: BOW203, S2081. "Thank You, Jesus" (Luke)
Blessing: BOW565 (Deut., Thanksgiving)

Isaiah 64:1-9

[1]O that you would tear open the heavens and come down, so that the mountains would quake at your presence—[2]as when fire kindles brushwood and the fire causes water to boil—to make your name known to your adversaries, so that the nations might tremble at your presence! [3]When you did awesome deeds that we did not expect, you came down, the mountains quaked at your presence. [4]From ages past no one has heard, no ear has perceived, no eye has seen any God besides you, who works for those who wait for him. [5]You meet those who gladly do right, those who remember you in your ways. But you were angry, and we sinned; because you hid yourself we transgressed. [6]We have all become like one who is unclean, and all our righteous deeds are like a filthy cloth. We all fade like a leaf, and our iniquities, like the wind, take us away. [7]There is no one who calls on your name, or attempts to take hold of you; for you have hidden your face from us, and have deliviered us into the hand of our iniquity. [8]Yet, O LORD, you are our Father; we are the clay, and you are our potter; we are all the work of your hand. [9]Do not be exceedingly angry, O LORD, and do not remember iniquity forever. Now consider, we are all your people.

Psalm 80:1-7, 17-19

[1]Give ear, O Shepherd of Israel, you who lead Joseph like a flock! You who are enthroned upon the cherubim, shine forth [2]before Ephraim and Benjamin and Manasseh. Stir up your might, and come to save us! [3]Restore us, O God; let your face shine, that we may be saved. [4]O LORD God of hosts, how long will you be angry with your people's prayers? [5]You have fed them with the bread of tears, and given them tears to drink in full measure. [6]You make us the scorn of our neighbors; our enemies laugh among themselves. [7]Restore us, O God of hosts; let your face shine, that we may be saved.

[17]But let your hand be upon the one at your right hand, the one whom you made strong for yourself. [18]Then we will never turn back from you; give us life, and we will call on your name. [19]Restore us, O LORD God of hosts; let your face shine, that we may be saved.

---

1 Corinthians 1:3-9

[3]Grace to you and peace from God our Father and the Lord Jesus Christ.

[4]I give thanks to my God always for you because of the grace of God that has been given you in Christ Jesus, [5]for in every way you have been enriched in him, in speech and knowledge of every kind—[6]just as the testimony of Christ has been strengthened among you—[7]so that you are not lacking in any spiritual gift as you wait for the revealing of our Lord Jesus Christ. [8]He will also strengthen you to the end, so that you may be blameless on the day of our Lord Jesus Christ. [9]God is faithful; by him you were called into the fellowship of his Son, Jesus Christ our Lord.

Mark 13:24-37

[24] "But in those days, after that suffering, the sun will be darkened, and the moon will not give its light, [25]and the stars will be falling from heaven, and the powers in the heavens will be shaken. [26]Then they will see 'the Son of Man coming in clouds' with great power and glory. [27]Then he will send out the angels, and gather his elect from the four winds, from the ends of the earth to the ends of heaven.

[28] "From the fig tree learn its lesson: as soon as its branch becomes tender and puts forth its leaves, you know that summer is near. [29]So also, when you see these things taking place, you know that he is near, at the very gates. [30]Truly I tell you, this generation will not pass away until all these things have taken place. [31]Heaven and earth will pass away, but my words will not pass away.

[32] "But about that day or hour no one knows, neither the angels in heaven, nor the Son, but only the Father. [33]Beware, keep alert; for you do not know when the time will come. [34]It is like a man going on a journey, when he leaves home and puts his slaves in charge, each with his work, and commands the doorkeeper to be on the watch. [35]Therefore, keep awake—for you do not know when the master of the house will come, in the evening, or at midnight, or at cockcrow, or at dawn, [36]or else he may find you asleep when he comes suddenly. [37]And what I say to you I say to all: Keep awake."

Notes:

Primary Hymns and Songs for the Day

196 "Come, Thou Long-Expected Jesus" (O) (Mark, Ps.)
  H-3 Handbell-46; Choir-26, 134; Descant-53; Organ-56
  S-1 #168-71. Various treatments
382 "Have Thine Own Way, Lord" (Isa.)
  S-2 #2. Instrumental descant
2152 "Change My Heart, O God" (Isa.)
719 "My Lord, What a Morning" (Mark)
  H-3 Choir-139
706 "Soon and Very Soon" (Mark) (C)

Hymn Suggestions

115 "How Like a Gentle Spirit" (Isa.)
132 "All My Hope Is Firmly Grounded" (Isa.)
518 "O Thou, in Whose Presence" (Isa.)
140 "Great Is Thy Faithfulness" (Ps., 1 Cor.)
195 "Send Your Word" (Ps., 1 Cor.)
247 "O Morning Star, How Fair and Bright" (Ps., Mark, Advent)
373 "Nothing Between" (Ps., 1 Cor.)
627 "O the Depth of Love Divine" (Communion, 1 Cor.)
714 "I Know Whom I Have Believed" (1 Cor., Mark)
202 "People, Look East" (Mark)
718 "Lo, He Comes with Clouds Descending" (Mark)
720 "Wake, Awake, for Night Is Flying" (Mark)
730 "O Day of God, Draw Nigh" (Mark, Advent)
2210 "Joy Comes with the Dawn" (Mark)
626 "Let All Mortal Flesh Keep Silence" (Mark, Communion)
636 "Christian People, Raise Your Song" (Communion)
2100 "Thou Didst Leave Thy Throne" (Advent)

Contemporary Suggestions

S2086 "Open Our Eyes, Lord" (Isa.)
  SP199, R91
S2253 "Water, River, Spirit, Grace" (Isa., Baptism)
M26 "The Power of Your Love" (Isa.)
  WG133
MM57 "Open the Eyes of My Heart" (Isa.)
  V-3 p. 162 (vocal solo)
MM85 "The Potter's Hand" (Isa.)
MM112 "Jesus, Lover of My Soul" (Isa.)
  WO111
MM87 "Let the Peace of God Reign" (1 Cor.)
UM171 "There's Something About That Name" (Mark)
  R26, SP89
S2192 "Freedom Is Coming" (Mark)
S2194 "O Freedom" (Mark)
M1 "Ancient of Days" (Mark)
M25 "No Greater Love" (Mark)

Vocal Solos

"But Who May Abide" (Isa., Mark)
V-2
"Then Shall the Righteous Shine Forth" (Isa., Mark)
V-8 p. 274
"Did You Feel the Mountains Tremble?" (Isa., Mark)
V-3 p. 140
MM69, WO25
"Great Day!" (Mark)
V-7 p. 14
"Patiently Have I Waited" (Advent)
V-4 p. 24

Anthems

"Adonai" (Isa.)
Mark A. Miller; Abingdon Press 9780687644308
SATB with piano (opt. solo)

"People, Look East" (Mark)
Daniel Nelson; Concordia 98-3770
SATB with piano

Other Suggestions

Visuals:
- **O** Fire, volcanic imagery, dirty cloth, leaf, potter, potter's wheel, lump of clay, water
- **P** Angels, water (tears), dried leaves, rough cloth (burlap), shepherd
- **E** Portrait of Christ, pile of gifts, 1 Cor. 1:9
- **G** Eclipse of sun/moon, stars, angels, fig tree, alarm clock, crowing rooster

Greeting: BOW243 (Mark)
Advent Wreath Readings: BOW262 (Advent)
Response: S2090. "Light the Advent Candle" (Advent)
Canticle: UM205. Canticle of Light and Darkness (Ps.) (see S-1, p. 383)
Opening Prayer: BOW254 (Mark)
Prayer of Confession: BOW486 (Isa., Ps.)
Prayer: BOW500. For Blessing, Mercy, and Courage (Isa., Ps.)
Litany: BOW433. "Gracious God, Eternal God" (Student Day)
Great Thanksgiving for Advent: BOW54
Blessing: BOW560 (Ps.)
Benediction: BOW190. "Benediction" (Ps.)

Isaiah 40:1-11

1 Comfort, O comfort my people, says your God. 2 Speak tenderly to Jerusalem, and cry to her that she has served her term, that her penalty is paid, that she has received from the LORD's hand double for all her sins. 3 A voice cries out: "In the wilderness prepare the way of the LORD, make straight in the desert a highway for our God. 4 Every valley shall be lifted up, and every mountain and hill be made low; the uneven ground shall become level, and the rough places a plain. 5 Then the glory of the LORD shall be revealed, and all people shall see it together, for the mouth of the LORD has spoken." 6 A voice says, "Cry out!" And I said, "What shall I cry?" All people are grass, their constancy is like the flower of the field. 7 The grass withers, the flower fades, when the breath of the LORD blows upon it; surely the people are grass. 8 The grass withers, the flower fades; but the word of our God will stand forever. 9 Get you up to a high mountain, O Zion, herald of good tidings; lift up your voice with strength, O Jerusalem, herald of good tidings, lift it up, do not fear; say to the cities of Judah, "Here is your God!" 10 See, the Lord GOD comes with might, and his arm rules for him; his reward is with him, and his recompense before him. 11 He will feed his flock like a shepherd; he will gather the lambs in his arms, and carry them in his bosom, and gently lead the mother sheep.

Psalm 85:1-2, 8-13

1 LORD, you were favorable to your land; you restored the fortunes of Jacob. 2 You forgave the iniquity of your people; you pardoned all their sin.

8 Let me hear what God the LORD will speak, for he will speak peace to his people, to his faithful, to those who turn to him in their hearts. 9 Surely his salvation is at hand for those who fear him, that his glory may dwell in our land. 10 Steadfast love and faithfulness will meet; righteousness and peace will kiss each other. 11 Faithfulness will spring up from the ground, and righteousness will look down from the sky. 12 The LORD will give what is good, and our land will yield its increase. 13 Righteousness will go before him, and will make a path for his steps.

---

2 Peter 3:8-15*a*

8 But do not ignore this one fact, beloved, that with the Lord one day is like a thousand years, and a thousand years are like one day. 9 The Lord is not slow about his promise, as some think of slowness, but is patient with you, not wanting any to perish, but all to come to repentance. 10 But the day of the Lord will come like a thief, and then the heavens will pass away with a loud noise, and the elements will be dissolved with fire, and the earth and everything that is done on it will be disclosed.

11 Since all these things are to be dissolved in this way, what sort of persons ought you to be in leading lives of holiness and godliness, 12 waiting for and hastening the coming of the day of God, because of which the heavens will be set ablaze and dissolved, and the elements will melt with fire? 13 But, in accordance with his promise, we wait for new heavens and a new earth, where righteousness is at home.

14 Therefore, beloved, while you are waiting for these things, strive to be found by him at peace, without spot or blemish; 15 and regard the patience of our Lord as salvation.

Mark 1:1-8

1 The beginning of the good news of Jesus Christ, the Son of God.

2 As it is written in the prophet Isaiah, "See, I am sending my messenger ahead of you, who will prepare your way; 3 the voice of one crying out in the wilderness: 'Prepare the way of the Lord, make his paths straight,' " 4 John the baptizer appeared in the wilderness, proclaiming a baptism of repentance for the forgiveness of sins. 5 And people from the whole Judean countryside and all the people of Jerusalem were going out to him, and were baptized by him in the river Jordan, confessing their sins. 6 Now John was clothed with camel's hair, with a leather belt around his waist, and he ate locusts and wild honey. 7 He proclaimed, "The one who is more powerful than I is coming after me; I am not worthy to stoop down and untie the thong of his sandals. 8 I have baptized you with water; but he will baptize you with the Holy Spirit."

Notes:

Primary Hymns and Songs for the Day

211 "O Come, O Come, Emmanuel" (Ps., Mark) (O)
H-3 Handbell-14, 79; Choir-141; Organ-168
S-1 #342. Handbell accompaniment
207 "Prepare the Way of the Lord" (Isa., Mark)
R92
171 "There's Something About That Name" (2 Pet., Mark)
R26, SP89
2089 "Wild and Lone the Prophet's Voice" (Mark)
567 "Heralds of Christ" (Isa., Mark) (C)

Hymn Suggestions

108 "God Hath Spoken by the Prophets" (Isa., Mark) (O)
202 "People, Look East" (Isa., Advent)
203 "Hail to the Lord's Anointed" (Isa., Mark)
209 "Blessed Be the God of Israel" (Isa., Mark)
210 "Toda la Tierra" ("All Earth Is Waiting") (Isa.)
2142 "Blessed Quietness" (Isa., Advent)
213 "Lift Up Your Heads, Ye Mighty Gates" (Ps., 2 Pet.)
117 "O God Our Help in Ages Past" (2 Pet.)
233 "En el Frio Invernal" ("Cold December Flies Away") (2 Pet., Advent)
383 "This Is a Day of New Beginnings" (2 Pet., Communion)
384 "Love Divine, All Loves Excelling" (2 Pet.)
666 "Shalom to You" (2 Pet., Closing)
730 "O Day of God, Draw Nigh" (2 Pet., Advent)
220 "Angels from the Realms of Glory" (Mark)
473 "Lead Me, Lord" (Mark)
619 "Now the Silence" (Communion, Advent)
626 "Let All Mortal Flesh Keep Silence" (Communion, Advent)
2255 "In the Singing" (Communion, Advent)

Contemporary Suggestions

UM186 "Alleluia" (Isa., Mark)
R136, SP108; S-2 #3-4
S2006 "Lord God, Almighty" (Isa.)
R40
S2049 "God Is Here Today" ("Dios Está Aquí) (Isa.)
S2143 "O Lord, Your Tenderness" (Isa.)
M4 "Let It Rise" (Isa.)
MM62 "Rise Up and Praise Him" (Isa.)
WG104
MM103 "How Great Are You, Lord" (Isa., Ps.)
WO43 "God Will Make a Way" (Isa., Mark)
SP40
S2192 "Freedom Is Coming" (2 Pet.)
S2194 "O Freedom" (2 Pet.)
SP130 "While We Are Waiting, Come" (2 Pet., Advent)
S2071 "Jesus, Name Above All Names" (Mark)
R26, SP76
UM204 "Emmanuel, Emmanuel" (Advent)
R28

Vocal Solos

"Comfort Ye"
"Every Valley"
"O Thou That Tellest Good Tidings to Zion" (Isa.)
V-2
"He Shall Feed His Flock Like a Shepherd" (Isa.)
V-2
V-8 p. 334
"So Great Is His Mercy" (Isa.)
V-8 p. 251
"God, Our Ever Faithful Shepherd" (Isa.)
V-4 p. 15
"My Lord, What a Mornin' " (2 Pet.)
V-7 p. 68
"Consume Me" (Mark)
V-3 p. 148

Anthems

"Lift Up Your Heads" (Ps., 2 Pet.)
Mark Burrows; Abingdon Press 0687343755
SATB with piano

"A Prayer of Promise" (Ps., Mark)
Stan Pethel; Abingdon Press 9780687646616
SATB with piano

Other Suggestions

Visuals:
O God's outstretched hand, Bible, straight highway, wilderness, places of solitude, city streets, prairies, mountaintop, shepherd carrying a lamb, sheep
P Kiss, images of peace, reconciliation
E Fire, upheaval/ peace, calm
G Wilderness, water, rough fabric, leather, honeycomb, sandals, fire/dove (Holy Spirit)

Introit: UM207 or BOW211. "Prepare the Way" (Mark)
Greeting: BOW240 (Ps.) or BOW307 (2 Pet.)
Greeting: BOW241 or BOW248 (Isa., Mark)
Advent Wreath Readings: BOW262 (Advent)
Response: S2090. "Advent Song" (Advent)
Opening Prayer: BOW250 (Isa., Mark)
Opening Prayer: BOW464 (Ps., 2 Pet.)
Canticle: UM199. "Canticle of Mary" (Isa.) (see S-1, p. 382)
Canticle: UM205. "Canticle of Light and Darkness" (Isa.) (see S-1, p. 383)
Prayer of Confession: BOW478 (1 Pet.)
Prayer: UM201. Advent.
Prayer : BOW521. A Vision of Hope (Ps., 2 Pet.)
Great Thanksgiving for Advent: BOW54
Blessing: BOW246 (Isa.)

Isaiah 61:1-4, 8-11

1 The spirit of the Lord God is upon me, because the Lord has anointed me; he has sent me to bring good news to the oppressed, to bind up the brokenhearted, to proclaim liberty to the captives, and release to the prisoners; 2 to proclaim the year of the Lord's favor, and the day of vengeance of our God; to comfort all who mourn; 3 to provide for those who mourn in Zion—to give them a garland instead of ashes, the oil of gladness instead of mourning, the mantle of praise instead of a faint spirit. They will be called oaks of righteousness, the planting of the Lord, to display his glory. 4 They shall build up the ancient ruins, they shall raise up the former devastations; they shall repair the ruined cities, the devastations of many generations.

8 For I the Lord love justice, I hate robbery and wrongdoing; I will faithfully give them their recompense, and I will make an everlasting covenant with them. 9 Their descendants shall be known among the nations, and their offspring among the peoples; all who see them shall acknowledge that they are a people whom the Lord has blessed. 10 I will greatly rejoice in the Lord, my whole being shall exult in my God; for he has clothed me with the garments of salvation, he has covered me with the robe of righteousness, as a bridegroom decks himself with a garland, and as a bride adorns herself with her jewels. 11 For as the earth brings forth its shoots, and as a garden causes what is sown in it to spring up, so the Lord God will cause righteousness and praise to spring up before all the nations.

Psalm 126

1 When the Lord restored the fortunes of Zion, we were like those who dream. 2 Then our mouth was filled with laughter, and our tongue with shouts of joy; then it was said among the nations, "The Lord has done great things for them." 3 The Lord has done great things for us, and we rejoiced. 4 Restore our fortunes, O Lord, like the watercourses in the Negeb. 5 May those who sow in tears reap with shouts of joy. 6 Those who go out weeping, bearing the seed for sowing, shall come home with shouts of joy, carrying their sheaves.

1 Thessalonians 5:16-24

16 Rejoice always, 17 pray without ceasing, 18 give thanks in all circumstances; for this is the will of God in Christ Jesus for you. 19 Do not quench the Spirit. 20 Do not despise the words of prophets, 21 but test everything; hold fast to what is good; 22 abstain from every form of evil.

23 May the God of peace himself sanctify you entirely; and may your spirit and soul and body be kept sound and blameless at the coming of our Lord Jesus Christ. 24 The one who calls you is faithful, and he will do this.

John 1:6-8, 19-28

6 There was a man sent from God, whose name was John. 7 He came as a witness to testify to the light, so that all might believe through him. 8 He himself was not the light, but he came to testify to the light.

19 This is the testimony given by John when the Jews sent priests and Levites from Jerusalem to ask him, "Who are you?" 20 He confessed and did not deny it, but confessed, "I am not the Messiah." 21 And they asked him, "What then? Are you Elijah?" He said, "I am not." "Are you the prophet?" He answered, "No." 22 Then they said to him, "Who are you? Let us have an answer for those who sent us. What do you say about yourself?" 23 He said, "I am the voice of one crying out in the wilderness, 'Make straight the way of the Lord,' " as the prophet Isaiah said.

24 Now they had been sent from the Pharisees. 25 They asked him, "Why then are you baptizing if you are neither the Messiah, nor Elijah, nor the prophet?" 26 John answered them, "I baptize with water. Among you stands one whom you do not know, 27 the one who is coming after me; I am not worthy to untie the thong of his sandal." 28 This took place in Bethany across the Jordan where John was baptizing.

Notes:

Primary Hymns and Songs for the Day

57 "O For a Thousand Tongues to Sing" (Isa.) (O)
H-3 Handbell-79; Choir-142; Descant-17; Organ-12
S-1 #33-38. Various treatments
203 "Hail to the Lord's Anointed" (Isa.)
H-3 Handbell-16, 22, 68; Choir-101; Descant-37
S-1 #114. Descant
#115. Harmonization
670 "Go Forth for God" (1 Thess.) (C)
S-1 #138-9. Harmonization with descant
#140. Harmonization
H-3 Handbell-77; Choir-63; Organ-106
240 "Hark! the Herald Angels Sing" (John) (C)
H-3 Handbell-26, 67; Choir-91; Descant-75; Organ-89
S-1 #234-36. Harmonizations/descant

Hymn Suggestions

2236 "Gather Us In" (Isa., John) (O)
59 "Mil Voces Para Celebrar" (Isa.)
64 "Holy, Holy, Holy! Lord God Almighty" (Isa.)
65 "Santo! Santo! Santo!" (Isa.)
196 "Come, Thou Long-Expected Jesus" (Isa.)
200 "Tell Out, My Soul" (Isa.)
333 "I'm Goin'a Sing When the Spirit Says Sing" (Isa.)
573 "O Zion, Haste" (Isa.)
2019 "Holy" ("Santo") (Isa.)
2117 "Spirit of God" (Isa.)
2120 "Spirit of Gentleness" (Isa., Ps., John)
2172 "We Are Called" (Isa., John)
2177 "Wounded World that Cries for Healing" (Isa.)
2182 "When God Restored Our Common Life" (Ps.)
2210 "Joy Comes with the Dawn" (Ps.)
2279 "The Trees of the Field" (Ps.)
160 "Rejoice, Ye Pure in Heart" (Ps., 1 Thess.)
161 "Rejoice, Ye Pure in Heart" (Ps., 1 Thess.)
2205 "The Fragrance of Christ" (1 Thess.)
108 "God Hath Spoken by the Prophets" (John)
173 "Christ, Whose Glory Fills the Skies" (John)
182 "Word of God, Come Down on Earth" (John)
188 "Christ Is the World's Light" (John)
195 "Send Your Word" (John)
206 "I Want to Walk as a Child of the Light" (John)
214 "Savior of the Nations, Come" (John)
473 "Lead Me, Lord" (John)
567 "Heralds of Christ" (John)
2214 "Lead Me, Guide Me" (John)
2089 "Wild and Lone the Prophet's Voice" (John, Advent)
2092 "Like a Child" (Advent)
2241 "The Spirit Sends Us Forth to Serve" (Isa.) (C)

Contemporary Suggestions

S2109 "Hosanna! Hosanna!" (Isa.)
S2039 "Holy, Holy" (Isa.)
S2118 "Holy Spirit, Come to Us" (Isa., Advent)
S2143 "O Lord, Your Tenderness" (Isa.)
S2210 "Joy Comes with the Dawn" (Isa.)
MM75 "Trading My Sorrows" (Isa.)
WG155
S2074 "Shout to the Lord" (Ps.)
M16, WY126; V-3 p. 56 (vocal solo)
S2017 "Come, Rejoice in God" (1 Thess.)
S2164 "Sanctuary" (1 Thess.)
S2186 "Song of Hope" ("Canto de Esperanza") (1 Thess.)
S2193 "Lord, Listen to Your Children Praying" (1 Thess.)
S2195 "In the Lord I'll Be Ever Thankful" (1 Thess.)
S2273 "Jesus, We Are Here" (1 Thess.)
MM68 "Forever" (1 Thess.)
WY57
SP150 "Rejoice" (1 Thess.)
UM207 "Prepare the Way of the Lord" (John)
S2005 "Arise, Shine" (John)
S2071 "Jesus, Name Above All Names" (John)
S2204 "Light of the World" (John)
SP48 "Behold, What Manner of Love" (John)
SP176 "Arise, Shine, for Your Light Is Come" (John)
WY125 "Here I Am to Worship" (John)

Vocal Solos

"Come, Thou Long-Expected Jesus" (Isa.)
V-1 p. 5
"Rejoice Greatly, O Daughter of Zion" (Ps.)
V-2

Anthems

"Sing a Song of Advent" (Isa., John)
Hal H. Hopson; Choristers Guild CGA1040
Unison/two-part with keyboard (opt. flute and handbells)

"Thou Shalt Know Him" (Isa., John)
Mark Sirett; Augsburg 11-10645
SATB *a cappella*

Other Suggestions

Visuals:
O Garland, oil, mantle, oak tree, rich garments/jewelry
P Praise, tears of joy, sheaves of wheat
E Praying hands, 1 Thess. 5:16, 17
G Water/baptism, light, John 1:23 (Christ candle)
Introit: S2202. "Come Away with Me" (1 Thess.)
Introit: UM202, st. 3. "People, Look East" (Advent)
Greeting: BOW241 (John)
Greeting: BOW242 or BOW453 (Ps., 1 Thess.)
Canticle: UM205. "Canticle of Light and Darkness" (John)
Opening Prayer: BOW252 (Isa., John)
Call to Prayer: S2118. "Holy Spirit, Come to Us" (Isa.)
Prayer of Confession: UM201. Advent (Isa., John)
Prayer: UM489. For God's Gifts (John)
Prayer: BOW513. For Justice (Isa.)
Prayer of Thanksgiving/Intercession: BOW255 (John, Advent)

2 Samuel 7:1-11, 16

1 Now when the king was settled in his house, and the LORD had given him rest from all his enemies around him, 2 the king said to the prophet Nathan, "See now, I am living in a house of cedar, but the ark of God stays in a tent." 3 Nathan said to the king, "Go, do all that you have in mind; for the LORD is with you."

4 But that same night the word of the LORD came to Nathan: 5 Go and tell my servant David: Thus says the LORD: Are you the one to build me a house to live in? 6 I have not lived in a house since the day I brought up the people of Israel from Egypt to this day, but I have been moving about in a tent and a tabernacle. 7 Wherever I have moved about among all the people of Israel, did I ever speak a word with any of the tribal leaders of Israel, whom I commanded to shepherd my people Israel, saying, "Why have you not built me a house of cedar?" 8 Now therefore thus you shall say to my servant David: Thus says the LORD of hosts: I took you from the pasture, from following the sheep to be prince over my people Israel; 9 and I have been with you wherever you went, and have cut off all your enemies from before you; and I will make for you a great name, like the name of the great ones of the earth. 10 And I will appoint a place for my people Israel and will plant them, so that they may live in their own place, and be disturbed no more; and evildoers shall afflict them no more, as formerly, 11 from the time that I appointed judges over my people Israel; and I will give you rest from all your enemies. Moreover the LORD declares to you that the LORD will make you a house. 16 Your house and your kingdom shall be made sure forever before me; your throne shall be established forever.

Luke 1:46b-55

46b My soul magnifies the Lord, 47 and my spirit rejoices in God my Savior, 48 for he has looked with favor on the lowliness of his servant. Surely, from now on all generations will call me blessed; 49 for the Mighty One has done great things for me, and holy is his name. 50 His mercy is for those who fear him from generation to generation. 51 He has shown strength with his arm; he has scattered the proud in the thoughts of their hearts. 52 He has brought down the powerful from their thrones, and lifted up the lowly; 53 he has filled the hungry with good things, and sent the rich away empty. 54 He has helped his servant Israel, in remembrance of his mercy, 55 according to the promise he made to our ancestors, to Abraham and to his descendants forever."

Romans 16:25-27

25 Now to God who is able to strengthen you according to my gospel and the proclamation of Jesus Christ, according to the revelation of the mystery that was kept secret for long ages 26 but is now disclosed, and through the prophetic writings is made known to all the Gentiles, according to the command of the eternal God, to bring about the obedience of faith— 27 to the only wise God, through Jesus Christ, to whom be the glory forever! Amen.

Luke 1:26-38

26 In the sixth month the angel Gabriel was sent by God to a town in Galilee called Nazareth, 27 to a virgin engaged to a man whose name was Joseph, of the house of David. The virgin's name was Mary. 28 And he came to her and said, "Greetings, favored one! The Lord is with you." 29 But she was much perplexed by his words and pondered what sort of greeting this might be. 30 The angel said to her, "Do not be afraid, Mary, for you have found favor with God. 31 And now, you will conceive in your womb and bear a son, and you will name him Jesus. 32 He will be great, and will be called the Son of the Most High, and the Lord God will give to him the throne of his ancestor David. 33 He will reign over the house of Jacob forever, and of his kingdom there will be no end." 34 Mary said to the angel, "How can this be, since I am a virgin?" 35 The angel said to her, "The Holy Spirit will come upon you, and the power of the Most High will overshadow you; therefore the child to be born will be holy; he will be called Son of God. 36 And now, your relative Elizabeth in her old age has also conceived a son; and this is the sixth month for her who was said to be barren. 37 For nothing will be impossible with God." 38 Then Mary said, "Here am I, the servant of the Lord; let it be with me according to your word." Then the angel departed from her.

Notes:

Primary Hymns and Songs for the Day

250 "Once in Royal David's City" (Luke) (O)
H-3 Handbell-83; Choir-68, 156; Descant-57; Organ-63
S-1 #182-84. Various treatments

198 "My Soul Gives Glory to My God" (Luke)

2036 "Give Thanks" (Luke)
R266, SP170

218 "It Came Upon the Midnight Clear" (2 Sam., Luke) (C)
H-3 Handbell-72; Choir-113; Descant-22; Organ-19
S-2 #39. Descant

Hymn Suggestions

203 "Hail to the Lord's Anointed" (2 Sam.) (O)
209 "Blessed Be the God of Israel" (2 Sam.)
211 "O Come, O Come, Emmanuel" (2 Sam.)
241 "That Boy-Child of Mary" (2 Sam., Luke)
98 "To God Be the Glory" (Rom.)
103 "Immortal, Invisible, God Only Wise" (Rom.)
197 "Ye Who Claim the Faith of Jesus" (Luke)
200 "Tell Out, My Soul" (Luke)
202 "People, Look East" (Luke)
214 "Savior of the Nations, Come" (Luke)
215 "To a Maid Engaged to Joseph" (Luke)
216 "Lo, How a Rose E'er Blooming" (Luke)
221 "In the Bleak Midwinter" (Luke)
228 "He Is Born" ("Il Est Né") (Luke)
234 "O Come, All Ye Faithful" (Luke)
272 "Sing of Mary, Pure and Lowly" (Luke)
276 "The First One Ever" (Luke)
2093 "The Snow Lay on the Ground" (Luke)
2098 "The Virgin Mary Had a Baby Boy" (Luke)
2099 "Joseph Dearest, Joseph Mine" (Luke)
2120 "Spirit of Gentleness" (Luke)
2122 "She Comes Sailing on the Wind" (Luke)
2151 "I'm So Glad Jesus Lifted Me" (Luke)
2155 "Blest Are They" (Luke)

Contemporary Suggestions

M37 "He Is Able" (Rom.)
WO49
S2029 "Praise to the Lord" (Luke)
S2033 "Glory to God" ("Gloria a Dios") (Luke)
M17 "This Kingdom" (Luke)
MM88 "Holy Spirit, Rain Down" (Luke)
MM99 "Shout to the North" (Luke)
WG114
SP220 "You Are My All in All" (Luke)
WY39
WG54 "Good To Me" (Luke)

Vocal Solos

"Behold, a Virgin Shall Conceive" (Luke)
V-2
"The Virgin's Slumber Song" (Luke)
V-4 p. 28
"Glory Hallelujah to de New-Born King" (Luke)
V-7 p. 80

Anthems

"Lo, How a Rose E'er Blooming" (Luke)
Donald Bailey; Gentry Publications JG2251
SATB divisi, *a cappella*

"Magnificat and Nunc Dimitis" (Luke)
Helen Kemp; Choristers Guild CGA954
Unison with piano (opt. C instrument and handbells)

Other Suggestions

Visuals:
O Cedar, crown, tent, ark of the covenant (chest)
P Luke 1:46*b*, food, hungry being fed
E Open Bible, Christ, servant, obedience
G Luke 1:28ff., angel, Mary, Annunciation, servant imagery, Luke 1:38

Greeting: BOW246 (Luke)
Advent Wreath Readings: BOW262 (Advent)
Response: S2090. "Advent Song" (Advent)
Opening Prayer: BOW253 (Advent) or BOW473 (Winter)
Canticle: UM208. "Canticle of Zechariah" (2 Sam.) (see S-1, p. 384)
Canticle: UM112, Response 2. "Canticle of Wisdom" (Rom.)
Canticle: UM199. "Canticle of Mary" (Luke) (see S-1, p. 382)
As an alternative to reading the Canticle of Mary (the Magnificat reading), have the choir lead the congregation in singing UM198, "My Soul Gives Glory to My God."
Prayers: BOW256 and BOW257 (Luke)
Prayer: BOW527. For the World (2 Sam., Luke)
Blessing: BOW563

Isaiah 9:2-7

2 The people who walked in darkness have seen a great light; those who lived in a land of deep darkness—on them light has shined. 3 You have multiplied the nation, you have increased its joy; they rejoice before you as with joy at the harvest, as people exult when dividing plunder. 4 For the yoke of their burden, and the bar across their shoulders, the rod of their oppressor, you have broken as on the day of Midian. 5 For all the boots of the tramping warriors and all the garments rolled in blood shall be burned as fuel for the fire. 6 For a child has been born for us, a son given to us; authority rests upon his shoulders; and he is named Wonderful Counselor, Mighty God, Everlasting Father, Prince of Peace. 7 His authority shall grow continually, and there shall be endless peace for the throne of David and his kingdom. He will establish and uphold it with justice and with righteousness from this time onward and forevermore. The zeal of the LORD of hosts will do this.

Psalm 96

1 O sing to the LORD a new song; sing to the LORD, all the earth. 2 Sing to the LORD, bless his name; tell of his salvation from day to day. 3 Declare his glory among the nations, his marvelous works among all the peoples. 4 For great is the LORD, and greatly to be praised; he is to be revered above all gods. 5 For all the gods of the peoples are idols, but the LORD made the heavens. 6 Honor and majesty are before him; strength and beauty are in his sanctuary. 7 Ascribe to the LORD, O families of the peoples, ascribe to the LORD glory and strength. 8 Ascribe to the LORD the glory due his name; bring an offering, and come into his courts. 9 Worship the LORD in holy splendor; tremble before him, all the earth. 10 Say among the nations, "The LORD is king! The world is firmly established; it shall never be moved. He will judge the peoples with equity." 11 Let the heavens be glad, and let the earth rejoice; let the sea roar, and all that fills it; 12 let the field exult, and everything in it. Then shall all the trees of the forest sing for joy 13 before the LORD; for he is coming, for he is coming to judge the earth. He will judge the world with righteousness, and the peoples with his truth.

Titus 2:11-14

11 For the grace of God has appeared, bringing salvation to all, 12 training us to renounce impiety and worldly passions, and in the present age to live lives that are self-controlled, upright, and godly, 13 while we wait for the blessed hope and the manifestation of the glory of our great God and Savior, Jesus Christ. 14 He it is who gave himself for us that he might redeem us from all iniquity and purify for himself a people of his own who are zealous for good deeds.

Luke 2:1-20

1 In those days a decree went out from Emperor Augustus that all the world should be registered. 2 This was the first registration and was taken while Quirinius was governor of Syria. 3 All went to their own towns to be registered. 4 Joseph also went from the town of Nazareth in Galilee to Judea, to the city of David called Bethlehem, because he was descended from the house and family of David. 5 He went to be registered with Mary, to whom he was engaged and who was expecting a child. 6 While they were there, the time came for her to deliver her child. 7 And she gave birth to her firstborn son and wrapped him in bands of cloth, and laid him in a manger, because there was no place for them in the inn.

8 In that region there were shepherds living in the fields, keeping watch over their flock by night. 9 Then an angel of the Lord stood before them, and the glory of the Lord shone around them, and they were terrified. 10 But the angel said to them, "Do not be afraid; for see—I am bringing you good news of great joy for all the people: 11 to you is born this day in the city of David a Savior, who is the Messiah, the Lord. 12 This will be a sign for you: you will find a child wrapped in bands of cloth and lying in a manger." 13 And suddenly there was with the angel a multitude of the heavenly host, praising God and saying, 14 "Glory to God in the highest heaven, and on earth peace among those whom he favors!"

15 When the angels had left them and gone into heaven, the shepherds said to one another, "Let us go now to Bethlehem and see this thing that has taken place, which the Lord has made known to us." 16 So they went with haste and found Mary and Joseph, and the child lying in the manger. 17 When they saw this, they made known what had been told them about this child; 18 and all who heard it were amazed at what the shepherds told them. 19 But Mary treasured all these words and pondered them in her heart. 20 The shepherds returned, glorifying and praising God for all they had heard and seen, as it had been told them.

Notes:

Primary Hymns and Songs for the Day

234 "O Come, All Ye Faithful" (Isa., Luke) (O)
(See especially stanzas 1, 3, and 4.)
H-3 Handbell-78; Descant-12; Organ-2
S-1 #7-13. Various treatments
238 "Angels We Have Heard on High" (Luke) (festive close)
H-3 Handbell-47; Choir-31; Descant-43; Organ-45
239 "Silent Night, Holy Night" (Luke) (quiet close)

Hymn Suggestions

562 "Jesus, Lord, We Look to Thee" (Isa.)
567 "Heralds of Christ" (Isa.)
2172 "We Are Called" (Isa.)
2236 "Gather Us In" (Isa.)
2001 "We Sing to You, O God" (Ps.)
2011 "We Sing of Your Glory" (Ps., Luke)
2255 "In the Singing" (Titus, Communion)
2266 "Here Is Bread, Here Is Wine" (Titus, Communion)
217 "Away in a Manger" (Luke)
219 "What Child Is This" (Luke)
224 "Good Christian Friends, Rejoice" (Luke)
227 "The Friendly Beasts" (Luke)
229 "Infant Holy, Infant Lowly" (Luke)
230 "O Little Town of Bethlehem" (Luke)
235 "Rock-a-Bye, My Dear Little Boy" (Luke)
236 "While Shepherds Watched Their Flocks" (Luke)
242 "Love Came Down at Christmas" (Luke)
245 "The First Noel" (Luke)
248 "On This Day Earth Shall Ring" (Luke)
251 "Go, Tell It on the Mountain" (Luke)
2092 "Like a Child" (Luke)
2093 "The Snow Lay on the Ground" (Luke)
2096 "Rise Up, Shepherd, and Follow" (Luke)
2097 "One Holy Night in Bethlehem" (Luke)
2276 "Glory to God in the Highest" (Luke)

Contemporary Suggestions

UM174 "His Name Is Wonderful" (Isa.)
R30, SP90
S2075 "King of Kings" (Isa.)
R268, SP94
S2232 "Come Now, O Prince of Peace" ("O-So-So") (Isa.)
S2204 "Light of the World" (Isa.)
S2023 "How Majestic Is Your Name" (Isa.)
R98, SP14
S2071 "Jesus, Name Above All Names" (Isa.)
R26, SP76
S2037 "I Sing Praises to Your Name" (Ps.)
R79, SP27
S2074 "Shout to the Lord" (Ps.)
M16, WY126; V-3 p. 56 (vocal solo)
S2088 "Lord, I Lift Your Name on High" (Luke)
R4, M2
S2072 "Amen, Amen" (Luke)

Vocal Solos

"For Unto Us a Child Is Born" (Isa.)
V-2
"A Scottish Christmas Song" (Luke, Christmas)
V-4 p. 4
"Mary Had a Baby" (Luke)
V-7 p. 46
"O Holy Night" (Luke)
V-8 p. 93
"Sing Noel!" (Christmas)
V-9 p. 13

Anthems

"A Child Is Born in Bethlehem" (Luke)
Philip Stopford; Hal Leonard 08745637
SATB with organ

"Wexford Carol" (Luke)
Arr. Dale Warland; G. Schirmer 50486222
SATB *a cappella* with flute

Other Suggestions

Visuals:
O Joy, praise, Isa. 9:6*b*
P Musical notes, sea, field, trees, branches upraised, Ps. 96:12*b*
E Titus 2:11, Christ Child, manger
G Christ Child, manger, Mary, Joseph, shepherds/angels, peace, joy, Luke 2:14, 19

Introit: UM244, sts. 1 and 4 " 'Twas in the Moon of Wintertime" (Luke, Christmas)
Introit: UM72 or S2033. "Gloria" (Luke)
Greeting: BOW271 (Luke) or BOW273 (Titus)
Christ Candle Prayer: BOW277 (Isa., Luke)
Response: S2090. "Advent Song" (Advent)
Opening Prayer: BOW276 or UM231 (Luke, Christmas)
Response: UM256, st. 1. "We Would See Jesus" (Luke)
Canticle: UM82 or UM83 "Canticle of God's Glory" (Luke)
Canticle: UM91. "Canticle of Praise to God" (Ps.)
Canticle: UM205. "Canticle of Light and Darkness" (Isa.)
Prayer of Intercession : BOW279 (Luke)
Response: UM241, sts. 2 and 5. "That Boy-Child of Mary" (Luke)
Great Thanksgiving for Christmas Eve: BOW56

Isaiah 61:10–62:3

10 I will greatly rejoice in the LORD, my whole being shall
exult in my God; for he has clothed me with the garments
of salvation, he has covered me with the robe of righteous-
ness, as a bridegroom decks himself with a garland, and as a
bride adorns herself with her jewels. 11 For as the earth
brings forth its shoots, and as a garden causes what is sown
in it to spring up, so the Lord GOD will cause righteousness
and praise to spring up before all the nations.
1 For Zion's sake I will not keep silent, and for
Jerusalem's sake I will not rest, until her vindication shines
out like the dawn, and her salvation like a burning torch.
2 The nations shall see your vindication, and all the kings
your glory; and you shall be called by a new name that the
mouth of the LORD will give. 3 You shall be a crown of beauty
in the hand of the LORD, and a royal diadem in the hand of
your God.

Psalm 148

1 Praise the LORD! Praise the LORD from the heavens;
praise him in the heights! 2 Praise him, all his angels; praise
him, all his host! 3 Praise him, sun and moon; praise him, all
you shining stars! 4 Praise him, you highest heavens, and you
waters above the heavens! 5 Let them praise the name of the
LORD, for he commanded and they were created. 6 He estab-
lished them forever and ever; he fixed their bounds, which
cannot be passed. 7 Praise the LORD from the earth, you sea
monsters and all deeps, 8 fire and hail, snow and frost,
stormy wind fulfilling his command! 9 Mountains and all
hills, fruit trees and all cedars! 10 Wild animals and all cattle,
creeping things and flying birds! 11 Kings of the earth and all
peoples, princes and all rulers of the earth! 12 Young men
and women alike, old and young together! 13 Let them
praise the name of the LORD, for his name alone is exalted;
his glory is above earth and heaven. 14 He has raised up a
horn for his people, praise for all his faithful, for the people
of Israel who are close to him. Praise the LORD!

Galatians 4:4-7

4 But when the fullness of time had come, God sent his
Son, born of a woman, born under the law, 5 in order to
redeem those who were under the law, so that we might
receive adoption as children. 6 And because you are chil-
dren, God has sent the Spirit of his Son into our hearts, cry-
ing, "Abba! Father!" 7 So you are no longer a slave but a
child, and if a child then also an heir, through God.

Luke 2:22-40

22 When the time came for their purification according to
the law of Moses, they brought him up to Jerusalem to pre-
sent him to the Lord 23 (as it is written in the law of the
Lord, "Every firstborn male shall be designated as holy to
the Lord"), 24 and they offered a sacrifice according to what
is stated in the law of the Lord, "a pair of turtledoves or two
young pigeons."
25 Now there was a man in Jerusalem whose name was
Simeon; this man was righteous and devout, looking for-
ward to the consolation of Israel, and the Holy Spirit
rested on him. 26 It had been revealed to him by the Holy
Spirit that he would not see death before he had seen the
Lord's Messiah. 27 Guided by the Spirit, Simeon came into
the temple; and when the parents brought in the child
Jesus, to do for him what was customary under the law,
28 Simeon took him in his arms and praised God, saying,
29 "Master, now you are dismissing your servant in peace,
according to your word; 30 for my eyes have seen your salva-
tion, 31 which you have prepared in the presence of all peo-
ples, 32 a light for revelation to the Gentiles and for glory to
your people Israel."
33 And the child's father and mother were amazed at
what was being said about him. 34 Then Simeon blessed
them and said to his mother Mary, "This child is destined
for the falling and the rising of many in Israel, and to be a
sign that will be opposed 35 so that the inner thoughts of
many will be revealed—and a sword will pierce your own
soul too."
36 There was also a prophet, Anna the daughter of
Phanuel, of the tribe of Asher. She was of a great age, hav-
ing lived with her husband seven years after her marriage,
37 then as a widow to the age of eighty-four. She never left
the temple but worshiped there with fasting and prayer
night and day. 38 At that moment she came, and began to
praise God and to speak about the child to all who were
looking for the redemption of Jerusalem.
39 When they had finished everything required by the law
of the Lord, they returned to Galilee, to their own town of
Nazareth. 40 The child grew and became strong, filled with
wisdom; and the favor of God was upon him.

Notes:

Primary Hymns and Songs for the Day

62 "All Creatures of Our God and King" (Ps.) (O)
H-3 Handbell-44; Choir-21; Descant-66; Organ-73
S-1 #198-204. Various treatments

226 "My Master, See, the Time Has Come" (Luke)
H-3 Choir-139, 145; Descant-77
S-1 #241-42. Orff arrangement/descant

228 "He Is Born" ("Il Est Né") (Luke, Christmas)
H-3 Choir-92
S-1 #177. Orff instrument arrangement

249 "There's a Song in the Air" (Luke, Christmas) (C)
H-3 Choir-194
S-2 #40. Descant

Hymn Suggestions

240 "Hark! the Herald Angels Sing" (Isa., Gal.) (O)
612 "Deck Thyself, My Soul, with Gladness" (Isa.)
77 "How Great Thou Art" (Ps.)
151 "God Created Heaven and Earth" (Ps.)
2008 "Let All Things Now Living" (Ps.)
2248 "Baptized in Water" (Gal., Baptism)
150 "God Who Stretched the Spangled Heavens" (Gal.)
605 "Wash, O God, Our Sons and Daughters" (Gal.)
217 "Away in a Manger" (Luke, Christmas)
219 "What Child Is This" (Luke, Christmas)
237 "Sing We Now of Christmas" (Luke, Christmas)
250 "Once in Royal David's City" (Gal., Luke)
272 "Sing of Mary, Pure and Lowly" (Luke)
447 "Our Parent, by Whose Name" (Luke)
668 "Let Us Now Depart in Thy Peace" (Luke)
2092 "Like a Child" (Luke, Christmas)
2099 "Joseph Dearest, Joseph Mine" (Luke, Christmas)
2197 "Lord of All Hopefulness" (Luke)
671 "Lord, Dismiss Us with Thy Blessing" (Luke) (C)

Contemporary Suggestions

S2018 "Honor and Praise" (Ps.)
MM59 "Let Everything That Has Breath" (Ps.)
WY85
MM80 "God of Wonders" (Ps.)
WY14; V-3 p. 184 (vocal solo)
WG128 "The Doxology" (Ps.)
S2003 "Praise You" (Ps., Luke)
MM84
S2039 "Holy, Holy" (Gal., Communion)
R206, SP141
S2071 "Jesus, Name Above All Names" (Luke)
R26, SP76
S2098 "The Virgin Mary Had a Baby Boy" (Christmas)
UM665 "Go Now in Peace" (Luke)
R293, S-1 #146 Orff arrangement

Vocal Solos

"Sing a Song of Joy" (Ps.)
V-4 p. 2
"Abba Father" (Gal.)
V-3 p. 109
"Gentle Jesus, Meek and Mild" (Luke, Christmas)
V-1 p. 11

Anthems

"Sing We Now of Christmas" (Luke, Christmas)
Prentice/Barnett; Gentry Publication JG2283
SATB and harp or piano (JB0546 *a cappella*)

"Gather 'Round God's Temple Gladly" (Christmas)
Deborah Govenor; Brookfield Press 08745574
SATB with keyboard

Other Suggestions

Visuals:
O Wedding garments, crown, garland, spring garden
P Celestial imagery, nature imagery, all ages of people praising
E Clock, open manacles, children's toys
G Baby, elderly man/woman, Christ candle

Introit: UM244, sts. 2 and 4. " 'Twas in the Moon of Wintertime" (Christmas)
Introit: BOW213. "Christ Is Born" (Gal.)
Greeting: BOW274 (Isa., Ps.) or BOW275 (Luke)
Opening Prayer: BOW277 (Luke) or BOW463 (Gal.)
Canticle: UM225. "Canticle of Simeon" (Luke) (see S-1, p. 386)
Prayer: UM231 (Gal.)
Prayer: BOW316. Presentation of Jesus (Luke)
Prayer: BOW524. For Strength (Luke)
See Christmas Eve and Day for additional Christmas carols.

Ecclesiastes 3:1-13

1 For everything there is a season, and a time for every
matter under heaven: 2 a time to be born, and a time to
die; a time to plant, and a time to pluck up what is plant-
ed; 3 a time to kill, and a time to heal; a time to break
down, and a time to build up; 4 a time to weep, and a time
to laugh; a time to mourn, and a time to dance; 5 a time
to throw away stones, and a time to gather stones togeth-
er; a time to embrace, and a time to refrain from embrac-
ing; 6 a time to seek, and a time to lose; a time to keep,
and a time to throw away; 7 a time to tear, and a time to
sew; a time to keep silence, and a time to speak; 8 a time
to love, and a time to hate; a time for war, and a time for
peace.

9 What gain have the workers from their toil? 10 I have
seen the business that God has given to everyone to be
busy with. 11 He has made everything suitable for its time;
moreover he has put a sense of past and future into their
minds, yet they cannot find out what God has done from
the beginning to the end. 12 I know that there is nothing
better for them than to be happy and enjoy themselves as
long as they live; 13 moreover, it is God's gift that all
should eat and drink and take pleasure in all their toil.

Psalm 8

1 O LORD, our Sovereign, how majestic is your name
in all the earth! You have set your glory above the heav-
ens. 2 Out of the mouths of babes and infants you have
founded a bulwark because of your foes, to silence the
enemy and the avenger. 3 When I look at your heavens,
the work of your fingers, the moon and the stars that you
have established; 4 what are human beings that you are
mindful of them, mortals that you care for them? 5 Yet
you have made them a little lower than God, and
crowned them with glory and honor. 6 You have given
them dominion over the works of your hands; you have
put all things under their feet, 7 all sheep and oxen, and
also the beasts of the field, 8 the birds of the air, and the
fish of the sea, whatever passes along the paths of the seas.
9 O LORD, our Sovereign, how majestic is your name in all
the earth!

Revelation 21:1-6*a*

1 Then I saw a new heaven and a new earth; for the
first heaven and the first earth had passed away, and the
sea was no more. 2 And I saw the holy city, the new
Jerusalem, coming down out of heaven from God, pre-
pared as a bride adorned for her husband. 3 And I heard
a loud voice from the throne saying, "See, the home of
God is among mortals. He will dwell with them as their
God; they will be his peoples, and God himself will be
with them; 4 he will wipe every tear from their eyes. Death
will be no more; mourning and crying and pain will be no
more, for the first things have passed away."

5 And the one who was seated on the throne said,
"See, I am making all things new." Also he said, "Write
this, for these words are trustworthy and true." 6a Then he
said to me, "It is done! I am the Alpha and the Omega,
the beginning and the end."

Matthew 25:31-46

31 "When the Son of Man comes in his glory, and all
the angels with him, then he will sit on the throne of his
glory. 32 All the nations will be gathered before him, and
he will separate people one from another as a shepherd
separates the sheep from the goats, 33 and he will put the
sheep at his right hand and the goats at the left. 34 Then
the king will say to those at his right hand, 'Come, you
that are blessed by my Father, inherit the kingdom pre-
pared for you from the foundation of the world; 35 for I
was hungry and you gave me food, I was thirsty and you
gave me something to drink, I was a stranger and you wel-
comed me, 36 I was naked and you gave me clothing, I was
sick and you took care of me, I was in prison and you visit-
ed me.' 37 Then the righteous will answer him, 'Lord,
when was it that we saw you hungry and gave you food, or
thirsty and gave you something to drink? 38 And when was
it that we saw you a stranger and welcomed you, or naked
and gave you clothing? 39 And when was it that we saw you
sick or in prison and visited you?' 40 And the king will
answer them, 'Truly I tell you, just as you did it to one of
the least of these who are members of my family, you did
it to me.' 41 Then he will say to those at his left hand, 'You
that are accursed, depart from me into the eternal fire
prepared for the devil and his angels; 42 for I was hungry
and you gave me no food, I was thirsty and you gave me
nothing to drink, 43 I was a stranger and you did not wel-
come me, naked and you did not give me clothing, sick
and in prison and you did not visit me.' 44 Then they also
will answer, 'Lord, when was it that we saw you hungry or
thirsty or a stranger or naked or sick or in prison, and did
not take care of you?' 45 Then he will answer them, 'Truly
I tell you, just as you did not do it to one of the least of
these, you did not do it to me.' 46 And these will go away
into eternal punishment, but the righteous into eternal
life."

Notes:

Primary Hymns and Songs for the Day
2023 "How Majestic Is Your Name" (Ps.) (O)
R98, SP14
707 "Hymn of Promise" (Eccles.)
H-3 Choir-112; Organ-117
S-1 #270. Descant
383 "This Is a Day of New Beginnings" (Rev., Comm.)
H-3 Choir-196
192 "There's a Spirit in the Air" (Matt.)
S-2 #144. Orff instrument arrangement
569 "We've a Story to Tell to the Nations" (C) (Rev., Matt.)

Hymn Suggestions
117 "O God, Our Help in Ages Past" (Eccles.) (C)
77 "How Great Thou Art" (Ps.)
384 "Love Divine, All Loves Excelling" (Rev.)
388 "O Come and Dwell in Me" (Rev.)
510 "Come, Ye Disconsolate" (Rev.)
524 "Beams of Heaven as I Go" (Eccles., Rev.)
533 "We Shall Overcome" (Rev.)
722 "I Want to Be Ready" (Rev.)
726 "O Holy City, Seen of John" (Rev.)
727 "O What Their Joy and Their Glory Must Be" (Rev.)
2142 "Blessed Quietness" (Rev.)
2210 "Joy Comes with the Dawn" (Rev.)
2284 "Joy in the Morning" (Rev.)
428 "For the Healing of the Nations" (Rev.)
434 "Cuando El Pobre" ("When the Poor Ones") (Matt.)
591 "Rescue the Perishing" (Matt.)
2048 "God Weeps" (Matt.)
2094 "Carol of the Epiphany" (Matt.)
2095 "Star-Child" (Matt., New Year)
2126 "All Who Hunger" (Rev., Matt., Communion)
2175 "Together We Serve" (Matt., Covenant Renewal)
2178 "Here Am I" (Matt.)
2254 "In Remembrance of Me" (Matt., Communion)
2268 "As We Gather at Your Table" (Matt., Communion)

Contemporary Suggestions
S2203 "In His Time" (Eccles.)
MM63 "I Could Sing of Your Love Forever" (Eccles.)
WY44; V-3 p. 22 (vocal solo)
MM80 "God of Wonders" (Ps.)
WY14; V-3 p. 184 (vocal solo)
UM706 "Soon and Very Soon" (Rev.)
R276
S2087 "We Will Glorify" (Ps., Rev.)
SP68
S2194 "O Freedom" (Rev.)
UM347 "Spirit Song" (Rev.)
R248, SP134
UM171 "There's Something About That Name" (Rev.)
R26, SP89
M21 "Blessing, Honor and Glory" (Rev.)
R81
M23 "Hallelujah to the Lamb" (Rev.)
M27 "We Will Worship the Lamb of Glory" (Rev.)
M32 "Holy and Anointed One" (Rev.)
WO53
M55 "Jehovah Reigns" (Rev.)
WO72 "I See the Lord" (Rev., Matt.)
M31
SP60 "To Him Who Sits on the Throne" (Rev., Matt.)
R265, WG149
S2132 "You Who Are Thirsty" (Rev., Matt.)
S2244 "People Need the Lord" (Matt.)

Vocal Solos
"I Will Sing of Thy Great Mercies" (Eccles.)
V-4 p. 43
"Ocean" (Ps.)
V-3 p. 78
"For Those Tears I Died" (Rev., Matt.)
V-8 p. 242
"Reach Out to Your Neighbor" (Matt.)
V-8 p. 372

Anthems
"Now Is the Time" (Eccles.)
John Horman; Abingdon Press 0687503604
Unison (opt. two-part) with keyboard and instruments

"Lead Me, Lord" (Ps.)
Samuel Sebastian Wesley; Novello 29-0305
SATB with organ

Other Suggestions
Visuals:
O Clock, many images from text
P Infants, all ages, outer space, nature
E Butterfly, chrysalis, bride, portrait of Christ
G Shepherd, sheep, goats, ministries to others
Covenant Renewal Service: BOW288
Greeting: BOW294 (New Year)
Canticle: UM734. "Canticle of Hope" (Rev.)
Prayer of Confession: BOW494 (Matt.)
Prayer: UM607. A Covenant Prayer in the Wesleyan Tradition (New Year)
Prayer: BOW294 (New Year)
Prayer: BOW510. For Discernment (Eccles.)
Prayer: BOW519. For Others (Matt.)
Litany: BOW508. Psalm of the Woodlands (Ps., Matt.)
Prayer of Thanksgiving: BOW556 (Ps.)
Great Thanksgiving for New Year: BOW58
Blessing: BOW564 (Rev., Matt.)
Benediction: UM383, st. 4. "This Is a Day of New Beginnings" (Rev.)

Isaiah 60:1-6

1 Arise, shine; for your light has come, and the glory of the
LORD has risen upon you. 2 For darkness shall cover the earth,
and thick darkness the peoples; but the LORD will arise upon
you, and his glory will appear over you. 3 Nations shall come
to your light, and kings to the brightness of your dawn. 4 Lift
up your eyes and look around; they all gather together, they
come to you; your sons shall come from far away, and your
daughters shall be carried on their nurses' arms. 5 Then you
shall see and be radiant; your heart shall thrill and rejoice,
because the abundance of the sea shall be brought to you,
the wealth of the nations shall come to you. 6 A multitude of
camels shall cover you, the young camels of Midian and
Ephah; all those from Sheba shall come. They shall bring
gold and frankincense, and shall proclaim the praise of the
LORD.

Psalm 72:1-7, 10-14

1 Give the king your justice, O God, and your righteous-
ness to a king's son. 2 May he judge your people with righ-
teousness, and your poor with justice. 3 May the mountains
yield prosperity for the people, and the hills, in righteous-
ness. 4 May he defend the cause of the poor of the people,
give deliverance to the needy, and crush the oppressor.
5 May he live while the sun endures, and as long as the moon,
throughout all generations. 6 May he be like rain that falls on
the mown grass, like showers that water the earth.
7 In his days may righteousness flourish and peace abound,
until the moon is no more.

10 May the kings of Tarshish and of the isles render him
tribute, may the kings of Sheba and Seba bring gifts. 11 May
all kings fall down before him, all nations give him service.
12 For he delivers the needy when they call, the poor and
those who have no helper. 13 He has pity on the weak and the
needy, and saves the lives of the needy. 14 From oppression
and violence he redeems their life; and precious is their
blood in his sight.

Ephesians 3:1-12

1 This is the reason that I Paul am a prisoner for Christ
Jesus for the sake of you Gentiles— 2 for surely you have
already heard of the commission of God's grace that was
given me for you, 3 and how the mystery was made known to
me by revelation, as I wrote above in a few words, 4 a reading
of which will enable you to perceive my understanding of the
mystery of Christ. 5 In former generations this mystery was
not made known to humankind, as it has now been revealed
to his holy apostles and prophets by the Spirit: 6 that is, the
Gentiles have become fellow heirs, members of the same
body, and sharers in the promise in Christ Jesus through the
gospel.

7 Of this gospel I have become a servant according to the
gift of God's grace that was given me by the working of his
power. 8 Although I am the very least of all the saints, this
grace was given to me to bring to the Gentiles the news of
the boundless riches of Christ, 9 and to make everyone see
what is the plan of the mystery hidden for ages in God who
created all things; 10 so that through the church the wisdom
of God in its rich variety might now be made known to the
rulers and authorities in the heavenly places. 11 This was in
accordance with the eternal purpose that he has carried out
in Christ Jesus our Lord, 12 in whom we have access to God in
boldness and confidence through faith in him.

Matthew 2:1-12

1 In the time of King Herod, after Jesus was born in
Bethlehem of Judea, wise men from the East came to
Jerusalem, 2 asking, "Where is the child who has been born
king of the Jews? For we observed his star at its rising, and
have come to pay him homage." 3 When King Herod heard
this, he was frightened, and all Jerusalem with him; 4 and call-
ing together all the chief priests and scribes of the people, he
inquired of them where the Messiah was to be born. 5 They
told him, "In Bethlehem of Judea; for so it has been written
by the prophet: 6 'And you, Bethlehem, in the land of Judah,
are by no means least among the rulers of Judah; for from
you shall come a ruler who is to shepherd my people
Israel.' "

7 Then Herod secretly called for the wise men and learned
from them the exact time when the star had appeared.
8 Then he sent them to Bethlehem, saying, "Go and search
diligently for the child; and when you have found him, bring
me word so that I may also go and pay him homage." 9 When
they had heard the king, they set out; and there, ahead of
them, went the star that they had seen at its rising, until it
stopped over the place where the child was. 10 When they saw
that the star had stopped, they were overwhelmed with joy.
11 On entering the house, they saw the child with Mary his
mother; and they knelt down and paid him homage. Then,
opening their treasure chests, they offered him gifts of gold,
frankincense, and myrrh. 12 And having been warned in a
dream not to return to Herod, they left for their own country
by another road.

Notes:____________________

Primary Hymns and Songs for the Day

220 "Angels From the Realms of Glory" (Matt.) (O)
 H-3 Choir-30, 48, 62; Descant-89; Organ-121
 S-1 #280. Descant/harmonization
219 "What Child Is This" (Matt.)
 H-3 Handbell-102; Choir-210; Descant-46; Organ-47
 S-1 #150. Guitar chords
254 "We Three Kings" (Matt.)
 H-3 Choir-208; Organ-65
245 "The First Noel" (Matt.) (C)
 H-3 Handbell-95; Choir-182; Descant-100; Organ-161
 S-1 #328-30. Various treatments

Hymn Suggestions

187 "Rise, Shine, You People" (Isa.)
223 "Break Forth, O Beauteous Heavenly Light" (Isa.)
585 "This Little Light of Mine" (Isa.)
725 "Arise, Shine Out, Your Light Has Come" (Isa.)
2172 "We Are Called" (Isa., Ps.)
2236 "Gather Us In" (Isa.)
247 "O Morning Star, How Fair and Bright" (Isa., Matt.)
157 "Jesus Shall Reign" (Ps.)
203 "Hail to the Lord's Anointed" (Ps.)
2177 "Wounded World that Cries for Healing" (Ps.)
2178 "Here Am I" (Ps.)
2182 "When God Restored Our Common Life" (Ps.)
103 "Immortal, Invisible, God Only Wise" (Eph.)
421 "Make Me a Captive, Lord" (Eph.)
216 "Lo, How a Rose E'er Blooming" (Matt.)
237 "Sing We Now of Christmas" (Matt.)
243 "De Tierra Lejana Venimos" ("From a Distant Home") (Matt.)
248 "On This Day Earth Shall Ring" (Matt.)
256 "We Would See Jesus" (Matt.)
383 "This Is a Day of New Beginnings" (New Year, Communion)
2094 "Carol of the Epiphany" (Matt.)
2095 "Star-Child" (Matt.)
2096 "Rise Up, Shepherd, and Follow" (Matt.)
2098 "The Virgin Mary Had a Baby Boy" (Matt.)
251 "Go, Tell It on the Mountain" (Eph., Matt.) (C)

Contemporary Suggestions

S2005 "Arise, Shine" (Isa.)
 BOW216
SP176 "Arise Shine" (Isa.)
 R123
M4 "Let It Rise" (Isa.)
M19 "Shine on Us" (Isa., Epiphany)
UM63 "Blessed Be the Name" (Ps.)
 S2034 (different tune)
S2162 "Grace Alone" (Eph.)
 MM100
S2018 "Honor and Praise" (Matt., Epiphany)
S2069 "All Hail King Jesus" (Matt., Epiphany)
 SP63
SP103 "We Worship and Adore You" (Matt.)
M18 "Come and Behold Him" (Matt.)
UM186 "Alleluia" (Matt., Epiphany)
 R136, SP108; S-2 #3-4

Vocal Solos

"The People That Walked in Darkness" (Isa.)
V-2
"A Scottish Christmas Song" (Matt.)
V-4 p. 4

Anthems

"A Star That Shines for Us All" (Isa., Matt.)
Mark Burrows; Abingdon Press 0687492823
SATB (opt. two-part) with piano

"O Lux Beatissima" (Epiphany)
Howard Helvey; Hinshaw HMC1971
SATB *a cappella*

Other Suggestions

Note: Today may also be celebrated as 2nd Sunday After Christmas using the following readings: Jer. 31:7-14; Ps. 147:12-20; Eph. 1:3-14; and John 1:(1-9), 10-18. If using these readings, see December 25 for music ideas.

Visuals:
 O Light, gold, frankincense, crown
 P Deliverance, poor and needy being helped, sun, moon, rain, kings, gifts
 E Manacles, towel, bowl/pitcher (servant)
 G Kings, gold, frankincense, myrrh (gifts), star

Introit: BOW216. "Arise, Shine" (Isa.)
Introit: S2118. "Holy Spirit, Come to Us" (Ps.)
Introit: UM244, sts. 3 and 4. " 'Twas in the Moon of Wintertime" (Matt.)
Greeting: BOW296 (Epiphany), BOW304 (Isa.,) or BOW455 (Matt.)
Opening Prayer: BOW313 or BOW315 (Matt.)
Centering Words: BOW472 (Matt., 1 Cor., Epiphany)
Canticle: UM225. Canticle of Simeon (Matt.) (S-1, p. 386)
Prayer of Confession: BOW482 (Matt.)
Prayer: UM255 or BOW297 (Epiphany, Matt.)
Prayer: BOW510, BOW522, or BOW525 (Matt.)
Great Thanksgiving for Epiphany: BOW58
Blessing: BOW562 (Matt., Epiphany)
For additional ideas, see *The Abingdon Worship Annual 2009.*

JANUARY 11, 2009

Genesis 1:1-5
1 In the beginning when God created the heavens and
the earth, 2 the earth was a formless void and darkness cov-
ered the face of the deep, while a wind from God swept over
the face of the waters. 3 Then God said, "Let there be light";
and there was light. 4 And God saw that the light was good;
and God separated the light from the darkness. 5 God called
the light Day, and the darkness he called Night. And there
was evening and there was morning, the first day.

Psalm 29
1 Ascribe to the LORD, O heavenly beings, ascribe to the
LORD glory and strength. 2 Ascribe to the LORD the glory of
his name; worship the LORD in holy splendor. 3 The voice of
the LORD is over the waters; the God of glory thunders, the
LORD, over mighty waters. 4 The voice of the LORD is power-
ful; the voice of the LORD is full of majesty. 5 The voice of the
LORD breaks the cedars; the Lord breaks the cedars of
Lebanon. 6 He makes Lebanon skip like a calf, and Sirion
like a young wild ox. 7 The voice of the LORD flashes forth
flames of fire. 8 The voice of the LORD shakes the wilderness;
the LORD shakes the wilderness of Kadesh. 9 The voice of the
LORD causes the oaks to whirl, and strips the forest bare;
and in his temple all say, "Glory!"
10 The LORD sits enthroned over the flood; the LORD sits
enthroned as king forever. 11 May the LORD give strength to
his people! May the LORD bless his people with peace!

Acts 19:1-7
1 While Apollos was in Corinth, Paul passed through the
interior regions and came to Ephesus, where he found
some disciples. 2 He said to them, "Did you receive the Holy
Spirit when you became believers?" They replied, "No, we
have not even heard that there is a Holy Spirit." 3 Then he
said, "Into what then were you baptized?" They answered,
"Into John's baptism." 4 Paul said, "John baptized with the
baptism of repentance, telling the people to believe in the
one who was to come after him, that is, in Jesus." 5 On hear-
ing this, they were baptized in the name of the Lord Jesus.
6 When Paul had laid his hands on them, the Holy Spirit
came upon them, and they spoke in tongues and prophe-
sied— 7 altogether there were about twelve of them.

Mark 1:4-11
4 John the baptizer appeared in the wilderness, proclaim-
ing a baptism of repentance for the forgiveness of sins.
5 And people from the whole Judean countryside and all the
people of Jerusalem were going out to him, and were bap-
tized by him in the river Jordan, confessing their sins. 6 Now
John was clothed with camel's hair, with a leather belt
around his waist, and he ate locusts and wild honey. 7 He
proclaimed, "The one who is more powerful than I is com-
ing after me; I am not worthy to stoop down and untie the
thong of his sandals. 8 I have baptized you with water; but he
will baptize you with the Holy Spirit."

9 In those days Jesus came from Nazareth of Galilee and
was baptized by John in the Jordan. 10 And just as he was
coming up out of the water, he saw the heavens torn apart
and the Spirit descending like a dove on him. 11 And a voice
came from heaven, "You are my Son, the Beloved; with you
I am well pleased."

Notes:

Primary Hymns and Songs for the Day

152 "I Sing the Almighty Power of God" (Gen., Ps.) (O)
H-3 Handbell-44; Choir-21; Descant-40; Organ-40
S-1 #131-32. Introduction/descant
252 "When Jesus Came to Jordan" (Mark)
H-3 Choir-211
347 "Spirit Song" (Mark)
R248, SP134
2250 "I've Just Come from the Fountain" (Acts, Mark, Baptism) (C)

Hymn Suggestions

122 "God of the Sparrow, God of the Whale" (Gen.)
145 "Morning Has Broken" (Gen.)
151 "God Created Heaven and Earth" (Gen.)
443 "O God Who Shaped Creation" (Gen.)
538 "Wind Who Makes All Winds That Blow" (Gen.)
688 "God, That Madest Earth and Heaven" (Gen.)
2046 "Womb of Life" (Gen.)
2050 "Mothering God, You Gave Me Birth" (Gen, Baptism)
2060 "God the Sculptor of the Mountains" (Gen.)
2117 "Spirit of God" (Gen., Mark)
2120 "Spirit, Spirit of Gentleness" (Gen., Mark)
2122 "She Comes Sailing on the Wind" (Gen., Mark)
2123 "Loving Spirit" (Gen., Mark, Baptism)
604 "Praise and Thanksgiving Be to God" (Ps., Acts, Mark)
331 "Holy Spirit, Come, Confirm Us" (Acts)
605 "Wash, O God, Our Sons and Daughters" (Acts,)
606 "Come, Let Us Use the Grace Divine" (Acts)
608 "This Is the Spirit's Entry Now" (Acts, Mark)
651 "Come, Holy Ghost, Our Souls Inspire" (Acts, Mark)
2247 "Wonder of Wonders" (Acts, Mark, Baptism)
2248 "Baptized in Water" (Acts, Mark, Baptism)
193 "Jesus! the Name High over All" (Mark)
209 "Blessed Be the God of Israel" (Mark)
267 "O Love, How Deep" (Mark)
609 "You Have Put on Christ" (Mark, Baptism)
723 "Shall We Gather at the River" (Mark, Baptism)
2089 "Wild and Lone the Prophet's Voice" (Mark)
2114 "At the Font We Start Our Journey" (Mark)

Contemporary Suggestions

S2041 "Thou Art Worthy" (Gen., Mark)
R34, SP5
S2118 "Holy Spirit, Come to Us" (Gen., Baptism)
SP2 "Ah, Lord God" (Gen.)
R254
MM80 "God of Wonders" (Gen., Ps.)
WY14; V-3 p. 184 (vocal solo)
S2154 "Please Enter My Heart, Hosanna" (Acts)
S2229 "We Are One in Christ Jesus" (Acts)
S2273 "Jesus, We Are Here" ("Jesu Tawa Pano") (Acts)
BOW187
S2071 "Jesus, Name Above All Names" (Mark)
R26, SP76
S2253 "Water, River, Spirit, Grace" (Mark)
M11 "Great and Mighty Is He" (Mark)
SP4

Vocal Solos

"Who Are You to Disagree?" (Gen.)
V-8 p. 330
"Spirit of Faith Come Down" (Mark)
V-1 p. 43
"Consume Me" (Mark, Baptism)
V-3 p. 148
"This Is De Healin' Water" (Baptism)
V-7 p. 52

Anthems

"The Journey Was Chosen" (Mark)
Linda Cable Shute; Kjos 9046
SATB *divisi* with piano

"Down to the River to Pray" (Mark)
Arr. Sheldon Curry; Daybreak Music 08743261
SATB with keyboard

Other Suggestions

Note: Today is an excellent day to celebrate baptisms or baptism renewal using Baptismal Covenant IV (UM, p. 50). See BOW, pp. 81-114 for a full range of baptismal covenants.

Visuals:
O Light/darkness, water, wind, evening/morning
P Water, cedar, skipping calf, wind (bent trees), Ps. 29:2*b*, 11*a*, *b*
E Dove, symbols of the Holy Spirit, water, baptism
G Sandals, water, dove, Mark 1:8, 11*b*

Introit: UM145, st. 1. "Morning Has Broken" (Gen.)
Greeting: BOW300 (Baptism, Ps.) or BOW458 (Gen.)
Opening Prayer: BOW459 (Gen.)
Litany: BOW507. For Creation (Gen.)
Prayer of Confession: BOW487 (Gen.)
Prayer: UM146, UM253, or BOW301 (Baptism, Mark)
Call to Baptism: S2252, BOW173. "Come, Be Baptized"
Baptism Response: S2249, BOW175. "God Claims You" (Acts, Mark)
Baptism Responses: BOW173 or BOW174 (Acts, Mark)
Response: UM334. "Sweet, Sweet Spirit" (Acts, Mark)
Prayer: BOW509. In Time of Natural Disaster (Gen.)
Prayer of Thanksgiving: BOW556 (Gen.)
Response: BOW179. "For the Gift of Creation" (Gen.)
Blessing: BOW561 (Acts, Mark)

1 Samuel 3:1-10 (11-20)

[1] Now the boy Samuel was ministering to the LORD under
Eli. The word of the LORD was rare in those days; visions
were not widespread.
[2] At that time Eli, whose eyesight had begun to grow dim
so that he could not see, was lying down in his room;
[3] the lamp of God had not yet gone out, and Samuel was
lying down in the temple of the LORD, where the ark of God
was. [4] Then the LORD called, "Samuel! Samuel!" and he said,
"Here I am!" [5] and ran to Eli, and said, "Here I am, for you
called me." But he said, "I did not call; lie down again." So
he went and lay down. [6] The LORD called again, "Samuel!"
Samuel got up and went to Eli, and said, "Here I am, for
you called me." But he said, "I did not call, my son; lie down
again." [7] Now Samuel did not yet know the LORD, and the
word of the LORD had not yet been revealed to him. [8] The
LORD called Samuel again, a third time. And he got up and
went to Eli, and said, "Here I am, for you called me." Then
Eli perceived that the LORD was calling the boy. [9] Therefore
Eli said to Samuel, "Go, lie down; and if he calls you, you
shall say, 'Speak, LORD, for your servant is listening.' " So
Samuel went and lay down in his place.
[10] Now the LORD came and stood there, calling as before,
"Samuel! Samuel!" And Samuel said, "Speak, for your ser-
vant is listening." [11] Then the LORD said to Samuel, "See, I
am about to do something in Israel that will make both ears
of anyone who hears of it tingle. [12] On that day I will fulfill
against Eli all that I have spoken concerning his house,
from beginning to end. [13] For I have told him that I am
about to punish his house forever, for the iniquity that he
knew, because his sons were blaspheming God, and he did
not restrain them. [14] Therefore I swear to the house of Eli
that the iniquity of Eli's house shall not be expiated by sacri-
fice or offering forever."
[15] Samuel lay there until morning; then he opened the
doors of the house of the LORD. Samuel was afraid to tell
the vision to Eli. [16] But Eli called Samuel and said, "Samuel,
my son." He said, "Here I am." [17] Eli said, "What was it that
he told you? Do not hide it from me. May God do so to you
and more also, if you hide anything from me of all that he
told you." [18] So Samuel told him everything and hid nothing
from him. Then he said, "It is the LORD; let him do what
seems good to him."
[19] As Samuel grew up, the LORD was with him and let
none of his words fall to the ground. [20] And all Israel from
Dan to Beer-sheba knew that Samuel was a trustworthy
prophet of the LORD.

Psalm 139:1-6, 13-18

[1] O LORD, you have searched me and known me. [2] You
know when I sit down and when I rise up; you discern my
thoughts from far away. [3] You search out my path and my
lying down, and are acquainted with all my ways. [4] Even
before a word is on my tongue, O LORD, you know it com-
pletely. [5] You hem me in, behind and before, and lay your
hand upon me. [6] Such knowledge is too wonderful for me; it
is so high that I cannot attain it.
[13] For it was you who formed my inward parts; you knit
me together in my mother's womb. [14] I praise you, for I am
fearfully and wonderfully made. Wonderful are your works;
that I know very well. [15] My frame was not hidden from you,
when I was being made in secret, intricately woven in the
depths of the earth. [16] Your eyes beheld my unformed sub-
stance. In your book were written all the days that were
formed for me, when none of them as yet existed. [17] How
weighty to me are your thoughts, O God! How vast is the
sum of them! [18] I try to count them—they are more than the
sand; I come to the end—I am still with you.

---

1 Corinthians 6:12-20

[12] "All things are lawful for me," but not all things are
beneficial. "All things are lawful for me," but I will not be
dominated by anything. [13] "Food is meant for the stomach
and the stomach for food," and God will destroy both one
and the other. The body is meant not for fornication but for
the Lord, and the Lord for the body. [14] And God raised the
Lord and will also raise us by his power. [15] Do you not know
that your bodies are members of Christ? Should I therefore
take the members of Christ and make them members of a
prostitute? Never! [16] Do you not know that whoever is united
to a prostitute becomes one body with her? For it is said,
"The two shall be one flesh." [17] But anyone united to the
Lord becomes one spirit with him. [18] Shun fornication!
Every sin that a person commits is outside the body; but the
fornicator sins against the body itself. [19] Or do you not know
that your body is a temple of the Holy Spirit within you,
which you have from God, and that you are not your own?
[20] For you were bought with a price; therefore glorify God in
your body.

John 1:43-51

[43] The next day Jesus decided to go to Galilee. He found
Philip and said to him, "Follow me." [44] Now Philip was from
Bethsaida, the city of Andrew and Peter. [45] Philip found
Nathanael and said to him, "We have found him about
whom Moses in the law and also the prophets wrote, Jesus
son of Joseph from Nazareth." [46] Nathanael said to him,
"Can anything good come out of Nazareth?" Philip said to
him, "Come and see." [47] When Jesus saw Nathanael coming
toward him, he said of him, "Here is truly an Israelite in
whom there is no deceit!" [48] Nathanael asked him, "Where
did you get to know me?" Jesus answered, "I saw you under
the fig tree before Philip called you." [49] Nathanael replied,
"Rabbi, you are the Son of God! You are the King of Israel!"
[50] Jesus answered, "Do you believe because I told you that I
saw you under the fig tree? You will see greater things than
these." [51] And he said to him, "Very truly, I tell you, you will
see heaven opened and the angels of God ascending and
descending upon the Son of Man."

Primary Hymns and Songs for the Day

454 "Open My Eyes, That I May See" (1 Sam.) (O)
H-3 Choir-157; Organ-108
419 "I Am Thine, O Lord" (1 Sam., John)
2052 "The Lone, Wild Bird" (Ps.)
2127 "Come and See" ("Kyrie") (John)
463 "Lord, Speak to Me" (1 Sam.. John) (C)
H-3 Handbell-75; Choir-131; Descant-22; Organ-18
S-1 #52. Descant

Hymn Suggestions

400 "Come, Thou Fount of Every Blessing" (1 Sam.)
508 "Faith, While Trees Are Still in Blossom" (1 Sam.)
593 "Here I Am, Lord" (1 Sam.)
451 "Be Thou My Vision" (1 Sam., 1 Cor., John)
579 "Lord God, Your Love Has Called Us Here" (1 Cor.)
582 "Whom Shall I Send?" (1 Sam., John)
139 "Praise to the Lord, the Almighty" (Ps.)
411 "Dear Lord, Lead Me Day by Day" (Ps.)
474 "Precious Lord, Take My Hand" (Ps., Martin Luther King Jr. Day)
2046 "Womb of Life" (Ps.)
2050 "Mothering God, You Gave Me Birth" (Ps.)
2051 "I Was There to Hear Your Borning Cry" (Ps.)
2117 "Spirit of God" (Ps.)
2123 "Loving Spirit" (Ps.)
2208 "Guide My Feet" (Ps., Martin Luther King Jr. Day)
2214 "Lead Me, Guide Me" (Ps.)
98 "To God Be the Glory" (1 Cor.)
382 "Have Thine Own Way, Lord" (1 Cor.)
413 "A Charge to Keep I Have" (1 Cor.)
2084 "Come, Let Us with Our Lord Arise" (1 Cor.)
128 "He Leadeth Me: O Blessed Thought" (John)
256 "We Would See Jesus" (John)
300 "O The Lamb" (John)
2101 "Two Fishermen" (John)
2137 "Would I Have Answered When You Called" (John)
733 "Marching to Zion" (Human Relations Day)
2135 "When Cain Killed Abel" (Human Relations Day)
2170 "God Made from One Blood" (Human Relations Day)
2181 "We Need a Faith" (Human Relations, Martin Luther King Jr. Day)
584 "Lord, You Give the Great Commission" (1 Sam., John) (C)

Contemporary Suggestions

S2139 "Oh, I Know the Lord's Laid His Hands on Me" (1 Sam., Ps., Martin Luther King Jr. Day)
MM105 "Let My Words Be Few" (1 Sam.)
MM108 "Lead Me, Lord" (1 Sam., John)
MM109 "He Knows My Name" (1 Sam., Ps.)
M38 "In the Secret" ("I Want to Know You") (Ps.)
WO103; V-3 p. 36 (vocal solo)
MM85 "The Potter's Hand" (Ps.)
MM101 "These Hands" (Ps.)
S2164 "Sanctuary" (1 Cor.)
S2150 "Lord, Be Glorified" (1 Cor.)
M13 "Be Glorified" (1 Cor.)
S2165 "Cry of My Heart" (John)
M39, WG32
S2218 "You Are Mine" (John)
M47 "Come Just As You Are" (John)
WG26
M51 "Step By Step" (John)
WY104

Vocal Solos

"Lord Over All" (1 Sam., John)
V-3 p. 84
"Be Thou My Vision" (1 Sam., 1 Cor., John)
V-6 p. 13
"Here I Am" (1 Sam., John)
V-9 p. 19
"Sing a Song of Joy" (Ps.)
V-4 p. 2
"Gospel Train" (John)
V-7 p. 74

Anthems

"Here I Am, Lord" (1 Sam.)
Schutte/Mayfield; Daybreak Music 08743186
SATB with keyboard

"Search Me, Lord" (Ps.)
Timothy Broege; Hal Leonard 48019113
SATB with piano (opt. cello)

Other Suggestions

Visuals:

O Listening, service to others, 1 Sam. 3:4*b*, 5*b*, 9*b*
P Hand, newborn child, hour glass
E Unity, various body shapes and sizes, circle of hands, 1 Cor. 6:19
G John 1:43*c*, "Come and see," invitation, fig tree, mission

Greeting: BOW307 (Human Relations, Epiphany)
Opening Prayer: BOW313 (1 Sam.) or BOW315 (Human Relations)
Opening Litany: BOW423 (Human Relations Day)
Call to Prayer: BOW196. "Call to Prayer" (Ps.)
Prayer of Confession: BOW478 (1 Sam.) or BOW480 (Ps.)
Prayer of Confession: BOW492 (Human Relations)
Prayer: UM403. For True Life (1 Sam.)
Prayer: UM570. Prayer of Ignatius (Human Relations)
Prayer: BOW435 or BOW544 (John, Martin Luther King Jr. Day)
Prayer: BOW510. For Discernment (1 Sam.)
Prayer: BOW519, BOW526, or BOW547 (Human Relations)
Response: S2072. "Amen, Amen" (John, Martin Luther King Jr. Day)

Jonah 3:1-5, 10

[1]The word of the LORD came to Jonah a second time, saying, [2]"Get up, go to Nineveh, that great city, and proclaim to it the message that I tell you." [3]So Jonah set out and went to Nineveh, according to the word of the LORD. Now Nineveh was an exceedingly large city, a three days' walk across. [4]Jonah began to go into the city, going a day's walk. And he cried out, "Forty days more, and Nineveh shall be overthrown!" [5]And the people of Nineveh believed God; they proclaimed a fast, and everyone, great and small, put on sackcloth.

[10]When God saw what they did, how they turned from their evil ways, God changed his mind about the calamity that he had said he would bring upon them; and he did not do it.

Psalm 62:5-12

[5]For God alone my soul waits in silence, for my hope is from him. [6]He alone is my rock and my salvation, my fortress; I shall not be shaken. [7]On God rests my deliverance and my honor; my mighty rock, my refuge is in God. [8]Trust in him at all times, O people; pour out your heart before him; God is a refuge for us. [9]Those of low estate are but a breath, those of high estate are a delusion; in the balances they go up; they are together lighter than a breath. [10]Put no confidence in extortion, and set no vain hopes on robbery; if riches increase, do not set your heart on them. [11]Once God has spoken; twice have I heard this: that power belongs to God, [12]and steadfast love belongs to you, O Lord. For you repay to all according to their work.

1 Corinthians 7:29-31

[29]I mean, brothers and sisters, the appointed time has grown short; from now on, let even those who have wives be as though they had none, [30]and those who mourn as though they were not mourning, and those who rejoice as though they were not rejoicing, and those who buy as though they had no possessions, [31]and those who deal with the world as though they had no dealings with it. For the present form of this world is passing away.

Mark 1:14-20

[14]Now after John was arrested, Jesus came to Galilee, proclaiming the good news of God, [15]and saying, "The time is fulfilled, and the kingdom of God has come near; repent, and believe in the good news."

[16]As Jesus passed along the Sea of Galilee, he saw Simon and his brother Andrew casting a net into the sea—for they were fishermen. [17]And Jesus said to them, "Follow me and I will make you fish for people." [18]And immediately they left their nets and followed him. [19]As he went a little farther, he saw James son of Zebedee and his brother John, who were in their boat mending the nets. [20]Immediately he called them; and they left their father Zebedee in the boat with the hired men, and followed him.

Notes:

Primary Hymns and Songs for the Day

261 "Lord of the Dance" (Mark) (O)
H-3 Choir-106; Organ-81

344 "Tú Has Venido a la Orilla" ("Lord, You Have Come to the Lakeshore") (Mark)
H-3 Choir-133; Organ-114

358 "Dear Lord and Father of Mankind" (Jon., Mark) (alternate text: "Parent of Us All")
H-3 Handbell-56; Choir-61; Organ-124
S-2 #151. Introduction
#152. Violin descant

2101 "Two Fishermen" (Mark)

2129 "I Have Decided to Follow Jesus" (Mark)

398 "Jesus Calls Us" (Mark) (C)
H-3 Choir-115
S-2 #65. Harmonization

Hymn Suggestions

209 "Blessed Be the God of Israel" (Jon., Mark) (O)
120 "Your Love, O God" (Jon.)
350 "Come, All of You" (Jon., Mark)
352 "It's Me, It's Me, O Lord" (Jon., 1 Cor.)
355 "Depth of Mercy" (Jon., Mark)
361 "Rock of Ages, Cleft for Me" (Jon., Ps.)
365 "Grace Greater Than Our Sin" (Jon.)
428 "For the Healing of the Nations" (Jon.)
578 "God of Love and God of Power" (Jon., Mark)
579 "Lord God, Your Love Has Called Us Here" (Jon., Mark)
2009 "O God Beyond All Praising" (Jon.)
2267 "Taste and See" (Ps., Communion)
178 "Hope of the World" (Ps.)
523 "Saranam, Saranam" ("Refuge") (Ps.)
411 "Dear Lord, Lead Me Day by Day" (1 Cor.)
577 "God of Grace and God of Glory" (1 Cor., Mark)
256 "We Would See Jesus" (Mark)
348 "Softly and Tenderly Jesus Is Calling" (Mark)
396 "O Jesus, I Have Promised" (Mark)
582 "Whom Shall I Send" (Mark)
2127 "Come and See" ("Kyrie") (Mark)
2130 "The Summons" (Mark)
2137 "Would I Have Answered When You Called" (Mark)
438 "Forth in Thy Name, O Lord" (1 Cor., Mark) (C)

Contemporary Suggestions

S2002 "I Will Call Upon the Lord" (Jon., Ps.)
R15, SP224

MM93 "Rock of Ages" (Ps.)
WO125

S2036 "Give Thanks" (Ps.)
R266, SP170

S2066 "Praise the Name of Jesus" (Ps., Mark)
R7, SP87

S2072 "Amen, Amen" (Mark)

S2218 "You Are Mine" (Mark)

S2165 "Cry of My Heart" (Mark)
M39, WG32

M41 "You're Worthy of My Praise" (Mark)
WG178

M51 "Step By Step" (Mark)
WY104

Vocal Solos

"My Father's Heart" (Jon., Mark)
V-3 p. 134
"Keep A-Inchin' Along" (Jon., Mark)
V-7 p. 32
"Patiently Have I Waited for the Lord" (Ps.)
V-4 p. 24
"I Surrender All" (Mark)
V-10 (90) p. 173

Anthems

"O For a Closer Walk with God" (Jon., Mark)
Mark Burrows; Abingdon Press 068732520X
SATB with piano

"Step By Step" (Mark)
Arr. Larry Shackley; Hope Publishing C-5290
SATB with piano

Other Suggestions

Visuals:
- **O** Sackcloth, empty plate, no. 40
- **P** Large rock, refuge, symbols of power, Ps. 62:11
- **E** Ticking alarm clock
- **G** Sackcloth, fish/net, fishing, nets left behind, discipling, multiple images of people

Greeting: BOW307 (Epiphany)
Opening Prayer: BOW309 (Mark) or BOW312 (Jon.)
Call to Confession: UM366. For Guidance
Prayer of Confession: BOW492 or BOW493 (Jon.)
Prayer: BOW519 (Jon., 1 Cor.)
Prayer of Thanksgiving: BOW551 (Jon., Mark)
Response: UM587. "Bless Thou the Gifts" (Jon., Mark)
Response: S2072. "Amen, Amen" (Mark)
See *The Abingdon Worship Annual 2009* for additional worship resources.

Deuteronomy 18:15-20

[15] The LORD your God will raise up for you a prophet
like me from among your own people; you shall heed
such a prophet. [16] This is what you requested of the LORD
your God at Horeb on the day of the assembly when you
said: "If I hear the voice of the LORD my God any more, or
ever again see this great fire, I will die." [17] Then the LORD
replied to me: "They are right in what they have said. [18] I
will raise up for them a prophet like you from among
their own people; I will put my words in the mouth of the
prophet, who shall speak to them everything that I com-
mand. [19] Anyone who does not heed the words that the
prophet shall speak in my name, I myself will hold
accountable. [20] But any prophet who speaks in the name
of other gods, or who presumes to speak in my name a
word that I have not commanded the prophet to speak—
that prophet shall die."

Psalm 111

[1] Praise the LORD! I will give thanks to the LORD with my
whole heart, in the company of the upright, in the con-
gregation. [2] Great are the works of the LORD, studied by all
who delight in them. [3] Full of honor and majesty is his
work, and his righteousness endures forever. [4] He has
gained renown by his wonderful deeds; the LORD is gra-
cious and merciful. [5] He provides food for those who fear
him; he is ever mindful of his covenant. [6] He has shown
his people the power of his works, in giving them the her-
itage of the nations. [7] The works of his hands are faithful
and just; all his precepts are trustworthy. [8] They are estab-
lished forever and ever, to be performed with faithfulness
and uprightness. [9] He sent redemption to his people; he
has commanded his covenant forever. Holy and awesome
is his name. [10] The fear of the LORD is the beginning of
wisdom; all those who practice it have a good understand-
ing. His praise endures forever.

---

1 Corinthians 8:1-13

[1] Now concerning food sacrificed to idols: we know that
"all of us possess knowledge." Knowledge puffs up, but
love builds up. [2] Anyone who claims to know something
does not yet have the necessary knowledge; [3] but anyone
who loves God is known by him.

[4] Hence, as to the eating of food offered to idols, we
know that "no idol in the world really exists," and that
"there is no God but one." [5] Indeed, even though there
may be so-called gods in heaven or on earth—as in fact
there are many gods and many lords— [6] yet for us there is
one God, the Father, from whom are all things and for
whom we exist, and one Lord, Jesus Christ, through
whom are all things and through whom we exist.

[7] It is not everyone, however, who has this knowledge.
Since some have become so accustomed to idols until
now, they still think of the food they eat as food offered to
an idol; and their conscience, being weak, is defiled.
[8] "Food will not bring us close to God." We are no worse
off if we do not eat, and no better off if we do. [9] But take
care that this liberty of yours does not somehow become a
stumbling block to the weak. [10] For if others see you, who
possess knowledge, eating in the temple of an idol, might
they not, since their conscience is weak, be encouraged to
the point of eating food sacrificed to idols? [11] So by your
knowledge those weak believers for whom Christ died are
destroyed. [12] But when you thus sin against members of
your family, and wound their conscience when it is weak,
you sin against Christ. [13] Therefore, if food is a cause of
their falling, I will never eat meat, so that I may not cause
one of them to fall.

Mark 1:21-28

[21] They went to Capernaum; and when the sabbath
came, he entered the synagogue and taught. [22] They were
astounded at his teaching, for he taught them as one hav-
ing authority, and not as the scribes. [23] Just then there was
in their synagogue a man with an unclean spirit, [24] and he
cried out, "What have you to do with us, Jesus of
Nazareth? Have you come to destroy us? I know who you
are, the Holy One of God." [25] But Jesus rebuked him, say-
ing, "Be silent, and come out of him!" [26] And the unclean
spirit, convulsing him and crying with a loud voice, came
out of him. [27] They were all amazed, and they kept on ask-
ing one another, "What is this? A new teaching—with
authority! He commands even the unclean spirits, and
they obey him." [28] At once his fame began to spread
throughout the surrounding region of Galilee.

Notes:

Primary Hymns and Songs for the Day

108 "God Hath Spoken By the Prophets" (Deut.) (O)
  H-3 Choir-53; Organ-33
  S-1 #109-10. Descant/harmonization
561 "Jesus, United By Thy Grace" (1 Cor.)
  H-3 Handbell-66, 73; Choir-90; Descant-92; Organ-131
  S-1 #291-92. Descant/harmonization
264 "Silence, Frenzied, Unclean Spirit" (Mark)
  (Alternate tunes: EBENEZER or HYMN TO JOY)
  H-3 Choir-171
557 "Blest Be the Tie That Binds" (1 Cor.) (C)
  H-3 Handbell-49; Choir-14; Descant-27; Organ-25

Hymn Suggestions

62 "All Creatures of Our God and King" (1 Cor.) (O)
127 "Guide Me, O Thou Great Jehovah" (Deut.)
463 "Lord, Speak to Me" (Deut.)
2001 "We Sing to You, O God" (Deut.)
2011 "We Sing of Your Glory" (Deut.)
67 "We, Thy People, Praise Thee" (Ps.)
96 "Praise the Lord Who Reigns Above" (Ps.)
85 "We Believe in One True God" (1 Cor.)
188 "Christ Is the World's Light" (1 Cor.)
390 "Forgive Our Sins as We Forgive" (1 Cor.)
451 "Be Thou My Vision" (1 Cor.)
554 "All Praise to Our Redeeming Lord" (1 Cor.)
562 "Jesus, Lord, We Look to Thee" (1 Cor.)
616 "Come, Sinners, to the Gospel Feast" (1 Cor., Communion)
629 "You Satisfy the Hungry Heart" (Communion)
2170 "God Made from One Blood" (1 Cor.)
2175 "Together We Serve" (1 Cor.)
2187 "Now It Is Evening" (1 Cor.)
2248 "Baptized in Water" (1 Cor., Baptism)
265 "O Christ, the Healer" (1 Cor., Mark)
632 "Draw Us in the Spirit's Tether" (1 Cor., Comm.)
173 "Christ, Whose Glory Fills the Skies" (Mark)
187 "Rise, Shine, You People" (Mark)
262 "Heal Me, Hands of Jesus" (Mark)
263 "When Jesus the Healer Passed Through Galilee" (Mark)
267 "O Love, How Deep" (Mark)
2104 "An Outcast among Outcasts" (Mark)
2177 "Wounded World that Cries for Healing" (Mark)

Contemporary Suggestions

S2040 "Awesome God" (Deut., Ps., Mark)
  R245, SP11, WO9, WY3; V-10 (90) p. 21 (Vocal solo)
UM176 "Majesty" (Deut., Mark)
  R63, SP73, WY33
UM84 "Thank You, Lord" (Ps.)
S2022 "Great Is the Lord" (Ps.)
  R22, SP30, WG59
S2023 "How Majestic Is Your Name" (Ps.)
  R98, SP14
S2195 "In the Lord I'll Be Ever Thankful" (Ps.)
S2021 "What a Mighty God We Serve" (Ps., Mark)
UM507 "Through It All" (Ps., Mark)
M3 "Jesus, Your Name" (Mark)
MM104 "There Is None Like You" (Mark)
  WO137

Vocal Solos

"Where Shall My Wondering Soul Begin?" (Mark)
V-1 p. 59
"Jesus Is Lord of All" (Mark)
V-8 p. 254
"In Jesus' Name" (Mark)
V-8 p. 188

Anthems

"Song of Moses" (Deut.)
John Ness Beck; G Schirmer 11992
SATB with keyboard

"Follow Me" (Mark)
Cox/Hench; Abingdon Press 098947
SAB with keyboard

Other Suggestions

Visuals:
- **O** Bust or painting of Moses, fire, prophets, pulpit, open Bible
- **P** Praise, food, hands, justice, Ps. 111:9*c*, 10*a*, *c*
- **E** Building, no. 1 (God, Lord), 1 Cor. 8:1*b*, food, stumbling blocks, books, healing, Christ, love
- **G** Christ sitting and teaching, healing, others teaching, healing, Mark 1:24*b*, open Bible

Introit: S2271, BOW199. "Come! Come! Everybody Worship" (Ps.)
Greeting: BOW303 or BOW451 (Ps., Epiphany)
Opening Prayer: BOW308 (Mark, Epiphany)
Prayer of Confession: BOW477 (1 Cor.)
Prayer: UM564. For the Unity of Christ's Body (1 Cor.)
Prayer: BOW312, BOW500, BOW518, or BOW546 (Mark, 1 Cor.)
Prayer: BOW525. For Wisdom (Ps.)
Song of Preparation: UM264. "Silence, Frenzied, Unclean Spirit." For congregational singing, consider alternate tunes in 87.87D meter, such as EBENEZER or HYMN TO JOY (Mark)
Prayer of Thanksgiving: BOW551 (Deut., Ps.)
Response: UM84. "Thank You, Lord" (Ps.)
Great Thanksgiving for Epiphany: BOW58
Blessing: BOW564 (Ps., 1 Cor.)
February is Black History Month and can be reflected in your choice of music and liturgy.

Isaiah 40:21-31

21 Have you not known? Have you not heard? Has it not
been told you from the beginning? Have you not under-
stood from the foundations of the earth? 22 It is he who
sits above the circle of the earth, and its inhabitants are
like grasshoppers; who stretches out the heavens like a
curtain, and spreads them like a tent to live in; 23 who
brings princes to naught, and makes the rulers of the
earth as nothing. 24 Scarcely are they planted, scarcely
sown, scarcely has their stem taken root in the earth,
when he blows upon them, and they wither, and the tem-
pest carries them off like stubble. 25 To whom then will
you compare me, or who is my equal? says the Holy One.
26 Lift up your eyes on high and see: Who created these?
He who brings out their host and numbers them, calling
them all by name; because he is great in strength, mighty
in power, not one is missing. 27 Why do you say, O Jacob,
and speak, O Israel, "My way is hidden from the LORD,
and my right is disregarded by my God"? 28 Have you not
known? Have you not heard? The LORD is the everlasting
God, the Creator of the ends of the earth. He does not
faint or grow weary; his understanding is unsearchable.
29 He gives power to the faint, and strengthens the power-
less. 30 Even youths will faint and be weary, and the young
will fall exhausted; 31 but those who wait for the LORD
shall renew their strength, they shall mount up with wings
like eagles, they shall run and not be weary, they shall
walk and not faint.

Psalm 147:1-11, 20*c*

1 Praise the LORD! How good it is to sing praises to our
God; for he is gracious, and a song of praise is fitting.

2 The LORD builds up Jerusalem; he gathers the outcasts
of Israel. 3 He heals the brokenhearted, and binds up
their wounds. 4 He determines the number of the stars; he
gives to all of them their names. 5 Great is our LORD, and
abundant in power; his understanding is beyond measure.
6 The LORD lifts up the downtrodden; he casts the wicked
to the ground. 7 Sing to the LORD with thanksgiving; make
melody to our God on the lyre. 8 He covers the heavens
with clouds, prepares rain for the earth, makes grass grow
on the hills. 9 He gives to the animals their food, and to
the young ravens when they cry. 10 His delight is not in the
strength of the horse, nor his pleasure in the speed of a
runner; 11 but the LORD takes pleasure in those who fear
him, in those who hope in his steadfast love.

20c Praise the LORD!

---

1 Corinthians 9:16-23

16 If I proclaim the gospel, this gives me no ground for
boasting, for an obligation is laid on me, and woe to me
if I do not proclaim the gospel! 17 For if I do this of my
own will, I have a reward; but if not of my own will, I am
entrusted with a commission. 18 What then is my reward?
Just this: that in my proclamation I may make the gospel
free of charge, so as not to make full use of my rights in
the gospel.

19 For though I am free with respect to all, I have made
myself a slave to all, so that I might win more of them.
20 To the Jews I became as a Jew, in order to win Jews. To
those under the law I became as one under the law
(though I myself am not under the law) so that I might
win those under the law. 21 To those outside the law I
became as one outside the law (though I am not free
from God's law but am under Christ's law) so that I might
win those outside the law. 22 To the weak I became weak,
so that I might win the weak. I have become all things to
all people, that I might by all means save some. 23 I do it
all for the sake of the gospel, so that I may share in its
blessings.

Mark 1:29-39

29 As soon as they left the synagogue, they entered the
house of Simon and Andrew, with James and John. 30 Now
Simon's mother-in-law was in bed with a fever, and they
told him about her at once. 31 He came and took her by
the hand and lifted her up. Then the fever left her, and
she began to serve them.

32 That evening, at sundown, they brought to him all
who were sick or possessed with demons. 33 And the whole
city was gathered around the door. 34 And he cured many
who were sick with various diseases, and cast out many
demons; and he would not permit the demons to speak,
because they knew him.

35 In the morning, while it was still very dark, he got up
and went out to a deserted place, and there he prayed.
36 And Simon and his companions hunted for him.
37 When they found him, they said to him, "Everyone is
searching for you." 38 He answered, "Let us go on to the
neighboring towns, so that I may proclaim the message
there also; for that is what I came out to do." 39 And he
went throughout Galilee, proclaiming the message in
their synagogues and casting out demons.

Notes:

Primary Hymns and Songs for the Day

139 "Praise to the Lord, the Almighty" (Isa., Ps.) (O)
H-3 Handbell-89; Choir-163; Descant-69; Organ-79
S-1 #218-22. Various treatments

263 "When Jesus the Healer Passed Through Galilee" (Mark)
S-2 #76. Flute/recorder descant

474 "Precious Lord, Take My Hand" (Mark, Black History)
H-3 Choir-164; Organ-116

421 "Make Me a Captive, Lord" (1 Cor.) (C)
H-3 Handbell-61; Choir-71; Descant-93; Organ-133

Hymn Suggestions

57 "O For a Thousand Tongues to Sing" (Ps.) (O)
126 "Sing Praise to God Who Reigns Above" (Isa., Ps.)
132 "All My Hope Is Firmly Grounded" (Isa., Ps.)
709 "Come, Let Us Join Our Friends Above" (Isa., Communion)
2001 "We Sing to You, O God" (Isa.)
2077 "You Alone Are Holy" ("Solo Tú Eres Santo") (Isa.)
2117 "Spirit of God" (Isa., Communion)
2121 "O Holy Spirit, Root of Life" (Isa.)
2238 "In the Midst of New Dimensions" (Isa.)
160 "Rejoice, Ye Pure in Heart" (Ps.)
161 "Rejoice, Ye Pure in Heart" (Ps.)
333 "I'm Goin'a Sing When the Spirit Says Sing" (Ps., Black History)
410 "I Want a Principle Within" (1 Cor.)
413 "A Charge to Keep I Have" (1 Cor.)
261 "Lord of the Dance" (1 Cor., Mark)
262 "Heal Me, Hands of Jesus" (Mark)
265 "O Christ, the Healer" (Mark)
266 "Heal Us, Emmanuel, Hear Our Prayer" (Mark)
267 "O Love, How Deep" (Mark)
367 "He Touched Me" (Mark)
375 "There Is a Balm in Gilead" (Mark, Black History)
395 "Take Time to Be Holy" (Mark)
2151 "I'm So Glad Jesus Lifted Me" (Mark, Black History)

Contemporary Suggestions

UM143 "On Eagle's Wings" (Isa.)
R112, S-2 #143 (stanzas for soloist)
M26 "The Power of Your Love" (Isa.)
WG133
MM99 "Shout to the North" (Isa.)
WG114
SP220 "You Are My All in All" (Isa.)
WY39
SP4 "Great and Mighty Is He" (Isa., Ps.)
M11
SP102 "Great Are You, Lord" (Isa., Ps.)
R69
MM103 "How Great Are You, Lord" (Isa., Ps.)
WG54 "Good to Me" (Isa., Mark)
WG163 "Unashamed Love" (Isa., 1 Cor.)
S2244 "People Need the Lord" (Isa., Mark)
S2022 "Great Is the Lord" (Ps.)
R22, SP30, WG59
S2144 "Why We Sing" (Ps., Black History)
S2064 "Oh Lord, You're Beautiful" (Mark)
WY207
S2072 "Amen, Amen" (Mark, Black History)
S2139 "Oh, I Know the Lord's Laid His Hands on Me" (Mark, Black History)
MM73 "My Redeemer Lives" (Mark)
WG98

Vocal Solos

"Wings Like Eagles" (Isa.)
V-9 p. 9
"Your Love, Oh Lord" (Isa.)
WY118
"O For a Thousand Tongues to Sing" (Ps.)
V-1 p. 32
"Sing a Song of Joy" (Ps.)
V-4 p. 2
"A Song of Joy" (Ps.)
V-9 p. 2

Anthems

"With Wings as Eagles" (Isa.)
Donald McCullough; Hinshaw HMC-1961
SATB with piano and flute

"O Christ the Healer, We Have Come " (Mark)
Richard Gieseke; Concordia 98-2815
SAB with keyboard

Other Suggestions

Visuals:
O Helping the powerless, exhausted youth, Isa. 40:31
P Praising, singing, healing, stars, stringed instruments (lyre), rain clouds, grass, birds, love
E Proclamation, ordination certificate, manacles (slave)
G Helping older woman up, healing, sundown/early dawn

Greeting: BOW307 (Mark)
Opening Prayer: UM466. An Invitation to Christ (Mark)
Call to Prayer: UM265, st. 1. "O Christ, the Healer" (Mark)
Intercessory Prayer: UM457. For the Sick (Mark)
Prayer: BOW314 (1 Cor.) or BOW524 (Isa.)
Prayer: BOW436 (Scout Sunday)
Scripture Response: UM382, st. 3. "Have Thine Own Way, Lord" (Ps., Mark)
Service of Healing: BOW615 (Mark)
Response: S2067, BOW177. "Amen, We Praise Your Name, O God" ("Amen Siakudumisa") (Ps., Black History)
Benediction: S2281. "May You Run and Not Be Weary" (Isa.)

2 Kings 5:1-14

[1]Naaman, commander of the army of the king of Aram, was a great man and in high favor with his master, because by him the LORD had given victory to Aram. The man, though a great warrior, suffered from leprosy. [2]Now the Arameans on one of the their raids had taken a young girl captive from the land of Israel, and she served Naaman's wife. [3]She said to her mistress, "If only my lord were with the prophet who is in Samaria! He would cure him of his leprosy." [4]So Naaman went in and told his lord just what the girl from the land of Israel said. [5]And the king of Aram said, "Go then, and I will send along a letter to the king of Israel."

He went, taking with him ten talents of silver, six thousand shekels of gold, and ten sets of garments. [6]He brought the letter to the king of Israel, which read, "When this letter reaches you, know that I have sent to you my servant Naaman, that you may cure him of his leprosy." [7]When the king of Israel read the letter, he tore his clothes and said, "Am I God, to give death or life, that this man sends word to me to cure a man of his leprosy? Just look and see how he is trying to pick a quarrel with me."

[8]But when Elisha the man of God heard that the king of Israel had torn his clothes, he sent a message to the king, "Why have you torn your clothes? Let him come to me, that he may learn that there is a prophet in Israel." [9]So Naaman came with his horses and chariots, and halted at the entrance of Elisha's house. [10]Elisha sent a messenger to him, saying, "Go, wash in the Jordan seven times, and your flesh shall be restored and you shall be clean." [11]But Naaman became angry and went away, saying, "I thought that for me he would surely come out, and stand and call on the name of the LORD his God, and would wave his hand over the spot, and cure the leprosy! [12]Are not Abana and Pharpar, the rivers of Damascus, better than all the waters of Israel? Could I not wash in them, and be clean?" He turned and went away in a rage. [13]But his servants approached and said to him, "Father, if the prophet commanded you to do something difficult, would you not have done it? How much more, when all he said to you was, 'Wash, and be clean'?" [14]So he went down and immersed himself seven times in the Jordan, according to the word of the man of God; his flesh was restored like the flesh of a young boy, and he was clean.

Psalm 30

[1]I will extol you, O LORD, for you have drawn me up, and did not let my foes rejoice over me. [2]O LORD my God, I cried to you for help, and you have healed me. [3]O LORD, you brought up my soul from Sheol, restored me to life from among those gone down to the Pit. [4]Sing praises to the LORD, O you his faithful ones, and give thanks to his holy name. [5]For his anger is but for a moment; his favor is for a lifetime. Weeping may linger for the night, but joy comes with the morning. [6]As for me, I said in my prosperity, "I shall never be moved." [7]By your favor, O LORD, you had established me as a strong mountain; you hid your face; I was dismayed. [8]To you, O LORD, I cried, and to the LORD I made supplication: [9]"What profit is there in my death, if I go down to the Pit? Will the dust praise you? Will it tell of your faithfulness? [10]Hear, O LORD, and be gracious to me! O LORD, be my helper!" [11]You have turned my mourning into dancing; you have taken off my sackcloth and clothed me with joy, [12]so that my soul may praise you and not be silent. O LORD my God, I will give thanks to you forever.

1 Corinthians 9:24-27

[24]Do you not know that in a race the runners all compete, but only one receives the prize? Run in such a way that you may win it. [25]Athletes exercise self-control in all things; they do it to receive a perishable wreath, but we an imperishable one. [26]So I do not run aimlessly, nor do I box as though beating the air; [27]but I punish my body and enslave it, so that after proclaiming to others I myself should not be disqualified.

Mark 1:40-45

[40]A leper came to him begging him, and kneeling he said to him, "If you choose, you can make me clean." [41]Moved with pity, Jesus stretched out his hand and touched him, and said to him, "I do choose. Be made clean!" [42]Immediately the leprosy left him, and he was made clean. [43]After sternly warning him he sent him away at once, [44]saying to him, "See that you say nothing to anyone; but go, show yourself to the priest, and offer for your cleansing what Moses commanded, as a testimony to them." [45]But he went out and began to proclaim it freely, and to spread the word, so that Jesus could no longer go into a town openly, but stayed out in the country; and people came to him from every quarter.

Notes:

Primary Hymns and Songs for the Day

733 "Marching to Zion" (Ps., Black History) (O)
H-3 Choir-298
357 "Just As I Am" (Mark)
H-3 Choir-120; Organ-186
367 "He Touched Me" (Mark)
2064 "Oh Lord, You're Beautiful" (Mark)
WY207
2208 "Guide My Feet" (1 Cor., Black History) (C)

Hymn Suggestions

66 "Praise, My Soul, the King of Heaven" (2 Kings, Ps., Mark) (O)
139 "Praise to the Lord, the Almighty" (2 Kings, Ps.)
383 "This Is a Day of New Beginnings" (2 Kings, Mark)
605 "Wash, O God, Our Sons and Daughters" (2 Kings, Mark)
2253 "Water, River, Spirit, Grace" (2 Kings, Baptism)
579 "Lord God, Your Love Has Called Us Here" (2 Kings)
142 "If Thou But Suffer God to Guide Thee" (2 Kings)
707 "Hymn of Promise" (Ps.)
732 "Come, We That Love the Lord" (Ps.)
2195 "In the Lord I'll Be Ever Thankful" (Ps.)
2210 "Joy Comes with the Dawn" (Ps.)
2211 "Faith Is Patience in the Night" (Ps., 1 Cor.)
2282 "I'll Fly Away" (Ps.)
2284 "Joy in the Morning" (Ps.)
206 "I Want to Walk as a Child of the Light" (1 Cor.)
701 "When We All Get to Heaven" (1 Cor.)
709 "Come, Let Us Join Our Friends Above" (1 Cor.)
263 "When Jesus the Healer Passed Through Galilee" (Mark)
265 "O Christ, the Healer" (Mark)
266 "Heal Us, Emmanuel, Hear Our Prayer" (Mark)
362 "Nothing But the Blood" (Mark)
391 "O Happy Day, That Fixed My Choice" (Mark)
368 "My Hope Is Built" (Mark) (C)

Contemporary Suggestions

S2036 "Give Thanks" (Ps.)
R266, SP170
SP18 "I Exalt You" (Ps.)
R44
SP78 "I Extol You" (Ps.)
M5 "The River Is Here" (Ps.)
MM63 "I Could Sing of Your Love Forever" (Ps.)
WY44; V-3 p. 22 (vocal solo)
MM75 "Trading My Sorrows" (Ps.)
WG155
S2144 "Why We Sing" (Ps., Black History)
S2194 "O Freedom" (Ps., Black History)
UM706 "Soon and Very Soon" (Ps., Black History)
R276
S2163 "He Who Began a Good Work in You" (1 Cor.)
SP180, R134
M34 "I Will Never Be" (the Same Again) (1 Cor.)
M38 "In the Secret" ("I Want to Know You") (1 Cor.)
WO103; V-3 p. 36 (vocal solo)
M53 "Let It Be Said of Us" (1 Cor.)
UM349 "Turn Your Eyes upon Jesus" (1 Cor., Mark)
SP218
UM507 "Through It All" (Mark)
S2244 "People Need the Lord" (Mark)
M35 "White as Snow" (Mark)

Vocal Solos

"Praise to the Lord, the Almighty" (1 Kings, Ps.)
V-6 p. 18
"Ev'ry Time I Feel De Spirit" (1 Kings)
V-7 p. 78
"Clean Before My Lord" (1 Kings, Mark)
V-8 p. 233
"I Surrender All" (1 Cor.)
V-10 p. 173

Anthems

"Exaltabo Te" (Ps., Mark)
Orlando di Lasso; Lawson-Gould 52909
SATB *a cappella*

"You Can Make Me Whole" (Mark)
David Haas; GIA G-6155
SATB with keyboard

Other Suggestions

Visuals:
O Leper, young girl, riches/gold, letter, torn clothes, no. 7
P Praying hands, healing, singing, Ps. 30:5*b* (weeping/joy)
E Runners/race, trophy, athletes training, laurel wreath, boxer
G Leper, kneeling, outstretched hand, offering, Mark 1:44

Introit: S2271, BOW199. "Come! Come! Everybody Worship" (Ps.)
Greeting: BOW453 (Ps.)
Opening Prayer: BOW473 (Winter)
Prayer of Confession: BOW483 (1 Cor.)
Prayer: BOW314 (1 Cor., Mark)
Response: BOW186. "An Indian Blessing" (Mark)
Offering Response: S2195. "In the Lord I'll Be Ever Thankful" (Ps.)
Blessing: BOW559 (1 Cor.)
Response: MM87. "Let the Peace of God Reign" (1 Cor.)
Additional prayers can be found in *The Abingdon Worship Annual 2009.*

2 Kings 2:1-12

1 Now when the LORD was about to take Elijah up to heaven by a whirlwind, Elijah and Elisha were on their way from Gilgal. 2 Elijah said to Elisha, "Stay here; for the LORD has sent me as far as Bethel." But Elisha said, "As the LORD lives, and as you yourself live, I will not leave you." So they went down to Bethel. 3 The company of prophets who were in Bethel came out to Elisha, and said to him, "Do you know that today the LORD will take your master away from you?" And he said, "Yes, I know; keep silent."

4 Elijah said to him, "Elisha, stay here; for the LORD has sent me to Jericho." But he said, "As the LORD lives, and as you yourself live, I will not leave you." So they came to Jericho. 5 The company of prophets who were at Jericho drew near to Elisha, and said to him, "Do you know that today the LORD will take your master away from you?" And he answered, "Yes, I know; be silent."

6 Then Elijah said to him, "Stay here; for the LORD has sent me to the Jordan." But he said, "As the LORD lives, and as you yourself live, I will not leave you." So the two of them went on. 7 Fifty men of the company of prophets also went, and stood at some distance from them, as they both were standing by the Jordan. 8 Then Elijah took his mantle and rolled it up, and struck the water; the water was parted to the one side and to the other, until the two of them crossed on dry ground.

9 When they had crossed, Elijah said to Elisha, "Tell me what I may do for you, before I am taken from you." Elisha said, "Please let me inherit a double share of your spirit." 10 He responded, "You have asked a hard thing; yet, if you see me as I am being taken from you, it will be granted you; if not, it will not." 11 As they continued walking and talking, a chariot of fire and horses of fire separated the two of them, and Elijah ascended in a whirlwind into heaven. 12 Elisha kept watching and crying out, "Father, father! The chariots of Israel and its horsemen!" But when he could no longer see him, he grasped his own clothes and tore them in two pieces.

Psalm 50:1-6

1 The mighty one, God the LORD, speaks and summons the earth from the rising of the sun to its setting. 2 Out of Zion, the perfection of beauty, God shines forth. 3 Our God comes and does not keep silence, before him is a devouring fire, and a mighty tempest all around him. 4 He calls to the heavens above and to the earth, that he may judge his people: 5 "Gather to me my faithful ones, who made a covenant with me by sacrifice!" 6 The heavens declare his righteousness, for God himself is judge.

2 Corinthians 4:3-6

3 And even if our gospel is veiled, it is veiled to those who are perishing. 4 In their case the god of this world has blinded the minds of the unbelievers, to keep them from seeing the light of the gospel of the glory of Christ, who is the image of God. 5 For we do not proclaim ourselves; we proclaim Jesus Christ as Lord and ourselves as your slaves for Jesus' sake. 6 For it is the God who said, "Let light shine out of darkness," who has shone in our hearts to give the light of the knowledge of the glory of God in the face of Jesus Christ.

Mark 9:2-9

2 Six days later, Jesus took with him Peter and James and John, and led them up a high mountain apart, by themselves. And he was transfigured before them, 3 and his clothes became dazzling white, such as no one on earth could bleach them. 4 And there appeared to them Elijah with Moses, who were talking with Jesus. 5 Then Peter said to Jesus, "Rabbi, it is good for us to be here; let us make three dwellings, one for you, one for Moses, and one for Elijah." 6 He did not know what to say, for they were terrified. 7 Then a cloud overshadowed them, and from the cloud there came a voice, "This is my Son, the Beloved; listen to him!" 8 Suddenly when they looked around, they saw no one with them any more, but only Jesus.

9 As they were coming down the mountain, he ordered them to tell no one about what they had seen, until after the Son of Man had risen from the dead.

Notes:

Primary Hymns and Songs for the Day

173 "Christ, Whose Glory Fills the Skies" (Mark) (O)
H-3 Handbell-51; Choir-206; Descant-89; Organ-120
S-1 #278-79. Harmonizations

258 "O Wondrous Sight! O Vision Fair" (Mark)
S-2 #191. Harmonization

2103 "We Have Come at Christ's Own Bidding" (Mark)
H-3 Handbell-46; Choir-26, 134; Descant-53; Organ-56
S-1 #168-71. Various treatments

2173 "Shine, Jesus, Shine" (2 Cor., Mark)
H-3 Choir-171

703 "Swing Low, Sweet Chariot" (2 Kings, Black History) (C)
H-3 Choir-177

Hymn Suggestions

203 "Hail to the Lord's Anointed" (2 Kings, Mark) (O)
113 "Source and Sovereign, Rock and Cloud" (2 Kings, Ps., 2 Cor., John)
704 "Steal Away to Jesus" (2 Kings, Mark, Black History)
124 "Seek the Lord" (Ps.)
206 "I Want to Walk as a Child of the Light" (2 Cor.)
451 "Be Thou My Vision" (2 Cor.)
454 "Open My Eyes, That I May See" (2 Cor.)
585 "This Little Light of Mine" (2 Cor.)
2166 "Christ Beside Me" (2 Cor.)
2204 "Light of the World" (2 Cor.)
2218 "You Are Mine" (2 Cor.)
2237 "As a Fire Is Meant for Burning" (2 Cor.)
188 "Christ Is the World's Light" (2 Cor., Mark) (C)
157 "Jesus Shall Reign" (Mark)
260 "Christ, Upon the Mountain Peak" (Mark)
371 "I Stand Amazed in the Presence" (Mark)
636 "Christian People, Raise Your Song" (Mark, Comm.)
638 "This Is the Feast of Victory" (Mark, Communion)
717 "Mine Eyes Have Seen the Glory" (Mark, Transfiguration)
2077 "You Alone Are Holy" (Mark)
2084 "Come, Let Us with Our Lord Arise" (Mark)
2102 "Swiftly Pass the Clouds of Glory" (Mark)
2202 "Come Away with Me" (Mark)
2268 "As We Gather at Your Table" (Mark, Communion)

Contemporary Suggestions

S2029 "Praise to the Lord" (Ps.)
S2024 "From the Rising of the Sun" (Ps.)
S2049 "God Is Here Today" (Ps., Transfiguration)
MM68 "Forever" (Ps.)
WY57
M19 "Shine on Us" (2 Cor.)
WY145 "In Christ Alone" (2 Cor.)
UM349 "Turn Your Eyes upon Jesus" (Mark)
SP218
S2273 "Jesus, We Are Here" ("Jesu Tawa Pano") (Mark)
BOW187
S2272 "Holy Ground" (Mark)
SP86, WO57
S2070 "He Is Exalted" (Mark, Transfiguration)
R238, SP66, WY198, WG71
S2069 "All Hail King Jesus" (Transfiguration)
SP63
WO162 "When I Look Into Your Holiness" (Mark, Transfiguration)
M11 "Great and Mighty Is He" (Transfiguration)
SP4
M36 "Awesome in this Place" (Transfiguration)
WG14
M43 "We Declare Your Majesty" (Mark, Transfiguration)
S2018 "Honor and Praise" (Transfiguration)

Vocal Solos

"I Saw the Lord, and All Beside Was Darkness" (Mark)
V-8 p. 268
"Show Me Your Glory" (Mark, Transfiguration)
V-3 p. 178

Anthems

"This Little Light of Mine" (2 Cor.)
Arr. David L. Bone; Hinshaw HMC1966
SSAATTBB *a cappella*

"Christ Is the World's Light" (2 Cor., Mark)
K. Lee Scott; Concordia 98-3776
SATB with organ (opt. brass, timpani, congregation)

Other Suggestions

Visuals:
O Light, whirlwind, fire, mantle/stole, generations
P Sunrise/set, fire, scales of justice, Ps. 50:6*a*
E Manacles, light/darkness, Christ
G White robe, cloud, transfigured Christ, Elijah, Moses

Introit: S2005, BOW216. "Arise, Shine" (2 Kings, Mark)
Greeting: BOW306 (2 Cor.) or BOW318 (2 Kings, Mark)
Opening Prayer: BOW308 or BOW310 (Mark)
Canticle: UM652. "Canticle of Remembrance" (1 Kings)
Call to Prayer: S2202. "Come Away with Me" (Mark)
Prayer of Confession: BOW478 (Mark)
Words of Assurance: BOW476 (1 Cor.)
Prayer: UM259. Transfiguration (1 Cor, Mark)
Prayer: UM489 or BOW525 (1 Cor.)
Prayer: BOW319, BOW500, or BOW529 (1 Kings, Mark)
Prayer of Thanksgiving: BOW556 (Transfiguration)
Blessing: BOW560 (Transfiguration)

Joel 2:1-2, 12-17

1 Blow the trumpet in Zion; sound the alarm on my holy
mountain! Let all the inhabitants of the land tremble, for
the day of the LORD is coming, it is near— 2 a day of dark-
ness and gloom, a day of clouds and thick darkness! Like
blackness spread upon the mountains a great and power-
ful army comes; their like has never been from of old, nor
will be again after them in ages to come.

12 Yet even now, says the LORD, return to me with all
your heart, with fasting, with weeping, and with mourn-
ing; 13 rend your hearts and not your clothing. Return to
the LORD, your God, for he is gracious and merciful, slow
to anger, and abounding in steadfast love, and relents
from punishing. 14 Who knows whether he will not turn
and relent, and leave a blessing behind him, a grain offer-
ing and a drink offering for the LORD, your God? 15 Blow
the trumpet in Zion; sanctify a fast; call a solemn assem-
bly; 16 gather the people. Sanctify the congregation; assem-
ble the aged; gather the children, even infants at the
breast. Let the bridegroom leave his room, and the bride
her canopy. 17 Between the vestibule and the altar let the
priests, the ministers of the LORD, weep. Let them say,
"Spare your people, O LORD, and do not make your her-
itage a mockery, a byword among the nations. Why should
it be said among the peoples, 'Where is their God?' "

Psalm 51:1-17

1 Have mercy on me, O God, according to your steadfast
love; according to your abundant mercy blot out my trans-
gressions. 2 Wash me thoroughly from my iniquity, and
cleanse me from my sin. 3 For I know my transgressions,
and my sin is ever before me. 4 Against you, you alone,
have I sinned, and done what is evil in your sight, so that
you are justified in your sentence and blameless when you
pass judgment. 5 Indeed, I was born guilty, a sinner when
my mother conceived me. 6 You desire truth in the inward
being; therefore teach me wisdom in my secret heart.
7 Purge me with hyssop, and I shall be clean; wash me, and
I shall be whiter than snow. 8 Let me hear joy and glad-
ness; let the bones that you have crushed rejoice. 9 Hide
your face from my sins, and blot out all my iniquities.
10 Create in me a clean heart, O God, and put a new and
right spirit within me. 11 Do not cast me away from your
presence, and do not take your holy spirit from me.
12 Restore to me the joy of your salvation, and sustain in
me a willing spirit. 13 Then I will teach transgressors your
ways, and sinners will return to you. 14 Deliver me from
bloodshed, O God, O God of my salvation, and my tongue
will sing aloud of your deliverance. 15 O Lord, open my
lips, and my mouth will declare your praise. 16 For you
have no delight in sacrifice; if I were to give a burnt offer-
ing, you would not be pleased. 17 The sacrifice acceptable
to God is a broken spirit; a broken and contrite heart, O
God, you will not despise.

2 Corinthians 5:20*b*–6:10

20b We entreat you on behalf of Christ, be reconciled to
God. 21 For our sake he made him to be sin who knew no
sin, so that in him we might become the righteousness of
God.

1 As we work together with him, we urge you also not to
accept the grace of God in vain. 2 For he says, "At an accept-
able time I have listened to you, and on a day of salvation I
have helped you." See, now is the acceptable time; see, now
is the day of salvation! 3 We are putting no obstacle in any-
one's way, so that no fault may be found with our ministry,
4 but as servants of God we have commended ourselves in
every way: through great endurance, in afflictions, hardships,
calamities, 5 beatings, imprisonments, riots, labors, sleepless
nights, hunger; 6 by purity, knowledge, patience, kindness,
holiness of spirit, genuine love, 7 truthful speech, and the
power of God; with the weapons of righteousness for the
right hand and for the left; 8 in honor and dishonor, in ill
repute and good repute. We are treated as impostors, and
yet are true; 9 as unknown, and yet are well known; as dying,
and see—we are alive; as punished, and yet not killed; 10 as
sorrowful, yet always rejoicing; as poor, yet making many
rich; as having nothing, and yet possessing everything.

Matthew 6:1-6, 16-21

1 "Beware of practicing your piety before others in
order to be seen by them; for then you have no reward
from your Father in heaven.

2 "So whenever you give alms, do not sound a trumpet
before you, as the hypocrites do in the synagogues and in
the streets, so that they may be praised by others. Truly I
tell you, they have received their reward. 3 But when you
give alms, do not let your left hand know what your right
hand is doing, 4 so that your alms may be done in secret;
and our Father who sees in secret will reward you.

5 "And whenever you pray, do not be like the hypocrites;
for they love to stand and pray in the synagogues and at
the street corners, so that they may be seen by others.
Truly I tell you, they have received their reward. 6 But
whenever you pray, go into your room and shut the door
and pray to your Father who is in secret; and your Father
who sees in secret will reward you.

16 "And whenever you fast, do not look dismal, like the
hypocrites, for they disfigure their faces so as to show oth-
ers that they are fasting. Truly I tell you, they have
received their reward. 17 But when you fast, put oil on
your head and wash your face, 18 so that your fasting may
be seen not by others but by your Father who is in secret;
and your Father who sees in secret will reward you.

19 "Do not store up for yourselves treasures on earth,
where moth and rust consume and where thieves break in
and steal; 20 but store up for yourselves treasures in heav-
en, where neither moth not rust consumes and where
thieves do not break in and steal. 21 For where your trea-
sure is, there your heart will be also."

Primary Hymns and Songs for the Day

269 "Lord, Who Throughout These Forty Days" (O) (Matt.)
  H-3 Handbell-129; Choir-106; Descant-65; Organ-72
  S-2 #105. Flute/violin descant
   #106. Harmonization
453 "More Love to Thee, O Christ" (Matt.)
  H-3 Organ-94
2128 "Come and Find the Quiet Center" (Matt.)
2138 "Sunday's Palms Are Wednesday's Ashes" (Ash Wednesday)
  H-3 Handbell-14, 64; Choir-132, 203
  S-2 #22. Descant

(Note that 2128 and 2138 use the same tune.)

402 "Lord, I Want to Be a Christian" (Joel, Matt.) (C)
  H-3 Choir-130

Hymn Suggestions

384 "Love Divine, All Loves Excelling" (2 Cor., Matt.) (O)
379 "Blow Ye the Trumpet, Blow" (Joel)
121 "There's a Wideness in God's Mercy" (Joel)
296 "Sing My Tongue, the Glorious Battle" (Joel)
2206 "Without Seeing You" (Joel, Ash Wednesday)
355 "Depth of Mercy" (Ps.)
2133 "Give Me a Clean Heart" (Ps.)
2134 "Forgive Us, Lord" ("Perdón, Señor") (Ps.)
294 "Alas! and Did My Savior Bleed" (2 Cor.)
359 "Alas! and Did My Savior Bleed" (2 Cor.)
450 "Creator of the Earth and Skies" (2 Cor.)
580 "Lead On, O King Eternal" (2 Cor.)
627 "O the Depth of Love Divine" (2 Cor., Communion)
2234 "Lead On, O Cloud of Presence" (2 Cor., Lent)
2255 "In the Singing" (2 Cor., Communion)
2278 "The Lord's Prayer" (Matt.)
352 "It's Me, It's Me, O Lord" (Matt., Black History)
357 "Just as I Am, Without One Plea" (Matt.)
395 "Take Time to Be Holy" (Matt.)
472 "Near to the Heart of God" (Matt.)
492 "Prayer Is the Soul's Sincere Desire" (Matt.)
496 "Sweet Hour of Prayer" (Matt.)
2202 "Come Away with Me" (Matt.)
2205 "The Fragrance of Christ" (Matt.)
2262 "Let Us Offer to the Father" (Matt.)
292 "What Wondrous Love Is This" (2 Cor.) (C)

Contemporary Suggestions

S2086 "Open Our Eyes, Lord" (Ps.)
S2133 "Give Me a Clean Heart" (Ps.)
S2152 "Change My Heart, O God" (Ps.)
S2154 "Please Enter My Heart, Hosanna" (Ps.)
S2157 "Come and Fill Our Hearts" (Ps.)
S2277 "Lord, Have Mercy" (Ps.)
M50 "Refiner's Fire" (Ps.)
M26 "The Power of Your Love" (Ps.)
  WG133
M35 "White as Snow" (Ps.)
MM97 "I Give You My Heart" (Ps.)
  WY71
MM90 "Purify My Heart" (Ps.)
  R187
S2055 "You Are My Hiding Place" (Ps., Matt.)
SP158 "The Battle Belongs to the Lord" (2 Cor.)
  R244
MM94 "That's Why We Praise Him" (2 Cor.)
  WG122
WO78 "I Walk By Faith" (2 Cor.)
S2193 "Lord, Listen to Your Children Praying" (Matt.)
M38 "I Want to Know You" ("In the Secret") (Matt.)
  WO103; V-3 p. 36 (vocal solo)
SP220 "You Are My All in All" (Matt.)

Vocal Solos

"A Contrite Heart" (Ps.)
V-4 p. 10
"Clean Before My Lord" (Ps.)
V-8 p. 233
"If With All Your Hearts" (Joel)
V-8 p. 277
"When It's All Been Said and Done" (Matt.)
MM115

Anthems

"O My God, Bestow Thy Tender Mercy" (Ps.)
Pergolesi/Hopson; Carl Fisher CM7974
Two-part mixed with keyboard

"The Lord's Prayer" (Matt.)
Mark A. Miller; Abingdon Press 0687491444
SATB with piano

Other Suggestions

Visuals:
 O Black cloth, grain, wine, trumpet, empty plate
 P Water, snow, rejoicing, heart, Ps. 51:10, 15, 17
 E Clock, calendar with today's date, rejoicing, black/gold
 G Praying hands, oil/water, closed door, empty plate, rust

Introit: S2273, BOW187. "Jesus, We Are Here" (Matt.)
Greeting: BOW321 or BOW328 (Joel) or BOW243 (2 Cor.)
Opening Prayer: BOW460 (Matt.)
Call to Prayer: S2200. "O Lord, Hear My Prayer" (Matt.)
Prayer of Confession: BOW475 (Joel, Ps.)
Response: S2275. "Kyrie" (Ps.)
Words of Assurance: BOW158. Words of Grace (Ash Wednesday)
Prayer: UM353. Ash Wednesday (Ps.)
Response: BOW217 "Remember that You Are Dust" (Joel, Ash Wednesday)
Prayer of Thanksgiving: BOW552 (Joel)

Genesis 9:8-17

8 Then God said to Noah and to his sons with him, 9 "As
for me, I am establishing my covenant with you and your
descendants after you, 10 and with every living creature
that is with you, the birds, the domestic animals, and
every animal of the earth with you, as many as came out of
the ark. 11 I establish my covenant with you, that never
again shall all flesh be cut off by the waters of a flood, and
never again shall there be a flood to destroy the earth."
12 God said, "This is the sign of the covenant that I make
between me and you and every living creature that is with
you, for all future generations: 13 I have set my bow in the
clouds, and it shall be a sign of the covenant between me
and the earth. 14 When I bring clouds over the earth and
the bow is seen in the clouds, 15 I will remember my
covenant that is between me and you and every living
creature of all flesh; and the waters shall never again
become a flood to destroy all flesh. 16 When the bow is in
the clouds, I will see it and remember the everlasting
covenant between God and every living creature of all
flesh that is on the earth." 17 God said to Noah, "This is
the sign of the covenant that I have established between
me and all flesh that is on the earth."

Psalm 25:1-10

1 To you, O LORD, I lift up my soul. 2 O my God, in you I
trust; do not let me be put to shame; do not let my ene-
mies exult over me. 3 Do not let those who wait for you be
put to shame; let them be ashamed who are wantonly
treacherous. 4 Make me to know your ways, O LORD; teach
me your paths. 5 Lead me in your truth, and teach me, for
you are the God of my salvation; for you I wait all day
long. 6 Be mindful of your mercy, O LORD, and of your
steadfast love, for they have been from of old. 7 Do not
remember the sins of my youth or my transgressions;
according to your steadfast love remember me, for your
goodness' sake, O LORD! 8 Good and upright is the LORD;
therefore he instructs sinners in the way. 9 He leads the
humble in what is right, and teaches the humble his way.
10 All the paths of the LORD are steadfast love and faithful-
ness, for those who keep his covenant and his decrees.

1 Peter 3:18-22

18 For Christ also suffered for sins once for all, the righ-
teous for the unrighteous, in order to bring you to God.
He was put to death in the flesh, but made alive in the
spirit, 19 in which also he went and made a proclamation to
the spirits in prison, 20 who in former times did not obey,
when God waited patiently in the days of Noah, during
the building of the ark, in which a few, that is, eight per-
sons, were saved through water. 21 And baptism, which this
prefigured, now saves you—not as a removal of dirt from
the body, but as an appeal to God for a good conscience,
through the resurrection of Jesus Christ, 22 who has gone
into heaven and is at the right hand of God, with angels,
authorities, and powers made subject to him.

Mark 1:9-15

9 In those days Jesus came from Nazareth of Galilee and
was baptized by John in the Jordan. 10 And just as he was
coming up out of the water, he saw the heavens torn apart
and the Spirit descending like a dove on him. 11 And a
voice came from heaven, "You are my Son, the Beloved;
with you I am well pleased."
12 And the Spirit immediately drove him out into the
wilderness. 13 He was in the wilderness forty days, tempted
by Satan; and he was with the wild beasts; and the angels
waited on him.
14 Now after John was arrested, Jesus came to Galilee,
proclaiming the good news of God, 15 and saying, "The
time is fulfilled, and the kingdom of God has come near;
repent, and believe in the good news."

Notes:

Primary Hymns and Songs for the Day

269 "Lord, Who Throughout These Forty Days" (O) (Mark)
H-3 Handbell-129; Choir-106; Descant-65; Organ-72
S-2 #105. Flute/violin descant
#106. Harmonization
2238 "In the Midst of New Dimensions" (Gen.)
2165 "Cry of My Heart" (Ps.)
M39, WG32
252 "When Jesus Came to Jordan" (Mark)
347 "Spirit Song" (1 Pet., Mark)
R248, SP134
502 "Thy Holy Wings, O Savior" (Gen., 1 Pet.) (C)
S-1 #47-49. Various treatments

Hymn Suggestions

122 "God of the Sparrow" (Gen.)
480 "O Love That Wilt Not Let Me Go" (Gen.)
508 "Faith, While Trees Are Still in Blossom" (Gen.)
2170 "God Made from One Blood" (Gen.)
2237 "As a Fire Is Meant for Burning" (Gen.)
411 "Dear Lord, Lead Me Day by Day" (Ps.) (O)
473 "Lead Me, Lord" (Ps.)
2214 "Lead Me, Guide Me" (Ps.)
2254 "In Remembrance of Me" (Ps., Communion)
289 "Ah, Holy Jesus" (1 Pet.)
325 "Hail, Thou Once Despised Jesus" (1 Pet.)
61 "Come, Thou Almighty King" (1 Pet., Mark)
2247 "Wonder of Wonders" (1 Pet., Mark, Baptism)
2248 "Baptized in Water" (1 Pet., Mark, Baptism)
267 "O Love, How Deep" (Mark)
525 "We'll Understand It Better By and By" (Mark)
616 "Come, Sinners, to the Gospel Feast" (Mark, Communion)
2089 "Wild and Lone the Prophet's Voice" (Mark)
2105 "Jesus, Tempted in the Desert" (Mark)
2112 "Jesus Walked This Lonesome Valley" (Mark)
2122 "She Comes Sailing on the Wind" (Mark)

Contemporary Suggestions

S2161 "To Know You More" (Ps.)
S2167 "More Like You" (Ps.)
S2277 "Lord, Have Mercy" (Ps.)
M38 "I Want to Know You" ("In the Secret") (Ps.)
WO103; V-3 p. 36 (vocal solo)
M30 "Knowing You" (Ps., Mark)
MM63 "I Could Sing of Your Love Forever" (Ps.)
WY44; V-3 p. 22 (vocal solo)
MM107 "Show Me Your Ways" (Ps.)
MM108 "Lead Me, Lord" (Ps.)
MM113 "In the Presence of Jehovah" (Ps.)
S2250 "I've Just Come from the Fountain" (1 Pet., Mark)
S2272 "Holy Ground" (Mark, Lent)
SP86, WO57
S2071 "Jesus, Name Above All Names" (Mark)
R26, SP76

Vocal Solos

"Hungry" ("Falling On My Knees") (Ps.)
WY52, WO63
"God Will Make a Way" (Ps., Mark)
WO43, SP40
"Ah, Holy Jesus" (1 Pet.)
V-6 p. 24
"I Walked Today Where Jesus Walked" (Mark, Lent)
V-8 p. 14

Anthems

"A Lenten Prayer" (Gen., 1 Pet.)
David Ashley White; Paraclete Press PPM09208
Two-part with keyboard (opt. flute)

"A Lenten Walk" (Mark)
Arr. Hal H. Hopson; Augsburg 11-10568
Two-part mixed with organ

Other Suggestions

Visuals:
O Water, Noah's ark, animals, rainbow
P Praying hands, Ps. 25:1, 9*a*
E Baptism, cross, resurrection, open Bible, prison
G Rocks, sand, bones, Holy Spirit, no. 40, wild animals, angels
Introit: UM292, st. 1. "What Wondrous Love Is This"
Greeting: BOW326 (Ps.) or BOW329 (Mark)
Opening Prayer: BOW464 (Gen.)
Scripture Response: UM368, st. 3. "My Hope Is Built" (Gen.)
Prayer of Confession: BOW490 (Mark)
Response: S2275. "Kyrie" (Ps.)
Prayer: UM253 or BOW333 (Mark)
Prayer: BOW399. Week 3 (Gen.)
Prayer: UM493 or UM705 (Ps., Lent)
Song of Preparation: BOW193. "Prayer for Wisdom" (Ps.)
Great Thanksgiving for Early in Lent: BOW, p. 60
Blessing: BOW566 (Lent)

Genesis 17:1-7, 15-16

1 When Abram was ninety-nine years old, the LORD
appeared to Abram, and said to him, "I am God
Almighty; walk before me, and be blameless. 2 And I will
make my covenant between me and you, and will make
you exceedingly numerous." 3 Then Abram fell on his
face; and God said to him, 4 "As for me, this is my
covenant with you: You shall be the ancestor of a multi-
tude of nations. 5 No longer shall your name be Abram,
but your name shall be Abraham; for I have made you the
ancestor of a multitude of nations. 6 I will make you
exceedingly fruitful; and I will make nations of you, and
kings shall come from you. 7 I will establish my covenant
between me and you, and your offspring after you
throughout their generations, for an everlasting
covenant, to be God to you and to your offspring after
you."

15 God said to Abraham, "As for Sarai your wife, you
shall not call her Sarai, but Sarah shall be her name. 16 I
will bless her, and moreover I will give you a son by her. I
will bless her, and she shall give rise to nations; kings of
peoples shall come from her."

Psalm 22:23-31

23 You who fear the LORD, praise him! All you offspring
of Jacob, glorify him; stand in awe of him, all you off-
spring of Israel! 24 For he did not despise or abhor the
affliction of the afflicted; he did not hide his face from
me, but heard when I cried to him. 25 From you comes my
praise in the great congregation; my vows I will pay before
those who fear him. 26 The poor shall eat and be satisfied;
those who seek him shall praise the LORD. May your
hearts live forever! 27 All the ends of the earth shall
remember and turn to the LORD; and all the families of
the nations shall worship before him. 28 For dominion
belongs to the LORD, and he rules over the nations. 29 To
him, indeed, shall all who sleep in the earth bow down;
before him shall bow all who go down to the dust, and I
shall live for him. 30 Posterity will serve him; future gener-
ations will be told about the Lord, 31 and proclaim his
deliverance to a people yet unborn, saying that he has
done it.

Romans 4:13-25

13 For the promise that he would inherit the world did
not come to Abraham or to his descendants through the
law but through the righteousness of faith. 14 If it is the
adherents of the law who are to be the heirs, faith is null
and the promise is void. 15 For the law brings wrath; but
where there is no law, neither is there violation.

16 For this reason it depends on faith, in order that the
promise may rest on grace and be guaranteed to all his
descendants, not only to the adherents of the law but also
to those who share the faith of Abraham (for he is the
father of all of us, 17 as it is written, "I have made you the
father of many nations")—in the presence of the God in
whom he believed, who gives life to the dead and calls
into existence the things that do not exist. 18 Hoping
against hope, he believed that he would become "the
father of many nations," according to what was said, "So
numerous shall your descendants be." 19 He did not weak-
en in faith when he considered his own body, which was
already as good as dead (for he was about a hundred
years old), or when he considered the barrenness of
Sarah's womb. 20 No distrust made him waver concerning
the promise of God, but he grew strong in his faith as he
gave glory to God, 21 being fully convinced that God was
able to do what he had promised. 22 Therefore his faith
"was reckoned to him as righteousness." 23 Now the words,
"it was reckoned to him," were written not for his sake
alone, 24 but for ours also. It will be reckoned to us who
believe in him who raised Jesus our Lord from the dead,
25 who was handed over to death for our trespasses and
was raised for our justification.

Mark 8:31-38

31 Then he began to teach them that the Son of Man
must undergo great suffering, and be rejected by the
elders, the chief priests, and the scribes, and be killed,
and after three days rise again. 32 He said all this quite
openly. And Peter took him aside and began to rebuke
him. 33 But turning and looking at his disciples, he
rebuked Peter and said, "Get behind me, Satan! For you
are setting your mind not on divine things but on human
things."

34 He called the crowd with his disciples, and said to
them, "If any want to become my followers, let them deny
themselves and take up their cross and follow me. 35 For
those who want to save their life will lose it, and those
who lose their life for my sake, and for the sake of the
gospel, will save it. 36 For what will it profit them to gain
the whole world and forfeit their life? 37 Indeed, what can
they give in return for their life? 38 Those who are
ashamed of me and of my words in this adulterous and
sinful generation, of them the Son of Man will also be
ashamed when he comes in the glory of his Father with
the holy angels."

Notes:

Primary Hymns and Songs for the Day

116 "The God of Abraham Praise" (O) (Gen., Mark)
H-3 Handbell-62, 95; Choir-59; Organ-77
S-1 #211. Harmonization
415 "Take Up Thy Cross" (Mark)
424 "Must Jesus Bear the Cross Alone" (Mark)
2129 "I Have Decided to Follow Jesus" (Mark)
338 "Where He Leads Me" (Mark) (C)

Hymn Suggestions

100 "God, Whose Love Is Reigning O'er Us" (Gen.) (O)
451 "Be Thou My Vision" (Gen., Rom.)
508 "Faith, While Trees Are Still in Blossom" (Gen., Rom.)
589 "The Church of Christ, in Every Age" (Gen., Rom.)
2246 "Deep in the Shadows of the Past" (Gen.)
629 "You Satisfy the Hungry Heart" (Ps., Communion)
2180 "Why Stand So Far Away, My God?" (Ps.)
374 "Standing on the Promises" (Rom.)
385 "Let Us Plead for Faith Alone" (Rom.)
507 "Through It All" (Rom.)
541 "See How Great a Flame Aspires" (Rom.)
710 "Faith of Our Fathers" (Rom.)
2147 "There Are Some Things I May Not Know" (Rom.)
2196 "We Walk by Faith" (Rom.)
2211 "Faith Is Patience in the Night" (Rom.)
2255 "In the Singing" (Rom., Communion)
261 "Lord of the Dance" (Mark)
297 "Beneath the Cross of Jesus" (Mark)
442 "Weary of All Trumpeting" (Mark)
553 "And Are We Yet Alive" (Mark)
589 "The Church of Christ, in Every Age" (Mark)
2083 "My Song Is Love Unknown" (Mark, Lent)
2102 "Swiftly Pass the Clouds of Glory" (Mark)
2137 "Would I Have Answered When You Called" (Mark)
2149 "Living for Jesus" (Mark)
438 "Forth in Thy Name, O Lord" (Mark) (C)

Contemporary Suggestions

UM123 "El Shaddai" (Gen.)
S-2 #54 (verses for soloist)
S2036 "Give Thanks" (Ps.)
R266, SP170
UM99 "My Tribute" ("To God Be the Glory") (Rom.)
R68; V-8 p.5 (vocal solo)
S2108 "O How He Loves You and Me!" (Rom.)
R27, SP113
S2258 "Sing Alleluia to the Lord" (Rom.)
R202, SP93
S2266 "Here Is Bread, Here Is Wine" (Rom., Communion)
SP111 "There Is a Redeemer" (Rom., Lent)
R232
WG41 "Every Move I Make" (Mark)
WY76
M30 "Knowing You" ("All I Once Held Dear") (Mark, Lent)
M53 "Let It Be Said of Us" (Mark)
MM76 "The Wonderful Cross" (Mark, Lent)
WY190
MM79 "I Stand Amazed" (Mark, Lent)
WY211
MM98 "Take This Life" (Mark, Lent)
MM106 "I Come to the Cross" (Mark, Lent)

Vocal Solos

"Redeeming Grace" (Rom.)
V-4 p. 47
"Nothing . . . Everything" (Mark)
V-8 p. 162
"Lead Me to Calvary" (Mark)
V-8 p. 226

Anthems

"Be Thou My Vision" (Gen., Rom.)
Arr. Dan Forrest; Brookfield Press 08745013
SATB with piano

"A Covenant Prayer" (Mark)
Allen Pote; Hope AP645
SATB with piano

Other Suggestions

Visuals:
O Elderly man/woman, people of all nations, covenant
P Praising, hungry being fed, people of all nations, deliverance
E Elderly person holding a child, all nations, resurrection
G Wooden cross, crucifix, resurrection, sandals (follow)

Introit: 292, st. 1. "What Wondrous Love Is This"
Greeting: BOW343 (Mark)
Opening Prayer: BOW467 or BOW469 (Gen.)
Prayer of Confession: BOW476 (Mark) or BOW483 (Gen., Rom.)
Response: S2277. "Lord, Have Mercy" (Mark, Lent)
Prayer: UM268 or UM403 (Mark)
Prayer: BOW336 (Mark) or BOW511 (Ps.)
Prayer: BOW436 (Girl Scout Sunday)
Prayer of Thanksgiving: BOW551 (Gen., Mark)
Benediction: BOW189. "May This Mind Be in Us" (Rom.)

Exodus 20:1-17

1 Then God spoke all these words:
2 I am the LORD your God, who brought you out of the
land of Egypt, out of the house of slavery; 3 you shall have
no other gods before me.
4 You shall not make for yourself an idol, whether in the
form of anything that is in heaven above, or that is on the
earth beneath, or that is in the water under the earth.
5 You shall not bow down to them or worship them; for I
the LORD your God am a jealous God, punishing children
for the iniquity of parents, to the third and the fourth
generation of those who reject me, 6 but showing steadfast
love to the thousandth generation of those who love me
and keep my commandments.
7 You shall not make wrongful use of the name of the
LORD your God, for the LORD will not acquit anyone who
misuses his name.
8 Remember the sabbath day, and keep it holy. 9 Six
days you shall labor and do all your work. 10 But the sev-
enth day is a sabbath to the LORD your God; you shall not
do any work—you, your son or your daughter, your male
or female slave, your livestock, or the alien resident in
your towns. 11 For in six days the LORD made heaven and
earth, the sea, and all that is in them, but rested the sev-
enth day; therefore the LORD blessed the sabbath day and
consecrated it.
12 Honor your father and your mother, so that your days
may be long in the land that the LORD your God is giving
you.
13 You shall not murder.
14 You shall not commit adultery.
15 You shall not steal.
16 You shall not bear false witness against your neighbor.
17 You shall not covet your neighbor's house; you shall
not covet your neighbor's wife, or male or female slave, or
ox, or donkey, or anything that belongs to your neighbor.

Psalm 19

1 The heavens are telling the glory of God; and the fir-
mament proclaims his handiwork. 2 Day to day pours forth
speech, and night to night declares knowledge. 3 There is
no speech, nor are there words; their voice is not heard;
4 yet their voice goes out through all the earth, and their
words to the end of the world. In the heavens he has set a
tent for the sun, 5 which comes out like a bridegroom
from his wedding canopy, and like a strong man runs its
course with joy. 6 Its rising is from the end of the heavens,
and its circuit to the end of them; and nothing is hid from
its heat. 7 The law of the LORD is perfect, reviving the soul;
the decrees of the LORD are sure, making wise the simple;
8 the precepts of the LORD are right, rejoicing the heart;
the commandment of the LORD is clear, enlightening the
eyes; 9 the fear of the LORD is pure, enduring forever; the
ordinances of the LORD are true and righteous altogether.
10 More to be desired are they than gold, even much fine
gold; sweeter also than honey, and drippings of the hon-
eycomb. 11 Moreover by them is your servant warned; in
keeping them there is great reward. 12 But who can detect
their errors? Clear me from hidden faults. 13 Keep back
your servant also from the insolent; do not let them have
dominion over me. Then I shall be blameless, and inno-
cent of great transgression. 14 Let the words of my mouth
and the meditation of my heart be acceptable to you, O
LORD, my rock and my redeemer.

---

1 Corinthians 1:18-25

18 For the message about the cross is foolishness to those
who are perishing, but to us who are being saved it is the
power of God. 19 For it is written, "I will destroy the wis-
dom of the wise, and the discernment of the discerning I
will thwart." 20 Where is the one who is wise? Where is the
scribe? Where is the debater of this age? Has not God
made foolish the wisdom of the world? 21 For since, in the
wisdom of God, the world did not know God through wis-
dom, God decided, through the foolishness of our procla-
mation, to save those who believe. 22 For Jews demand
signs and Greeks desire wisdom, 23 but we proclaim Christ
crucified, a stumbling block to Jews and foolishness to
Gentiles, 24 but to those who are the called, both Jews and
Greeks, Christ the power of God and the wisdom of God.
25 For God's foolishness is wiser than human wisdom, and
God's weakness is stronger than human strength.

John 2:13-22

13 The Passover of the Jews was near, and Jesus went up
to Jerusalem. 14 In the temple he found people selling cat-
tle, sheep, and doves, and the money changers seated at
their tables. 15 Making a whip of cords, he drove all of
them out of the temple, both the sheep and the cattle. He
also poured out the coins of the money changers and
overturned their tables. 16 He told those who were selling
the doves, "Take these things out of here! Stop making
my Father's house a marketplace!" 17 His disciples remem-
bered that it was written, "Zeal for your house will con-
sume me." 18 The Jews then said to him, "What sign can
you show us for doing this?" 19 Jesus answered them,
"Destroy this temple, and in three days I will raise it up."
20 The Jews then said, "This temple has been under con-
struction for forty-six years, and will you raise it up in
three days?" 21 But he was speaking of the temple of his
body. 22 After he was raised from the dead, his disciples
remembered that he had said this; and they believed the
scripture and the word that Jesus had spoken.

Notes:

Primary Hymns and Songs for the Day

77 "How Great Thou Art" (Ps.) (O)
  H-3 Choir-103; Organ-105
  S-1 #163. Harmonization
295 "In the Cross of Christ I Glory" (1 Cor.)
  H-3 Handbell-72; Choir-113; Descant-89; Organ-119
  S-1 #276-77. Harmonization with descant
2112 "Jesus Walked This Lonesome Valley" (John)
504 "The Old Rugged Cross" (1 Cor.) (C)
  H-3 Choir-190; Organ-163

Hymn Suggestions

211 "O Come, O Come, Emmanuel" (Exod.) (See especially stanzas 2 and 3.)
395 "Take Time to Be Holy" (Exod., John)
410 "I Want a Principle Within" (Exod.)
417 "O For a Heart to Praise My God" (Exod.)
2077 "You Alone Are Holy" (Exod.)
2120 "Spirit, Spirit of Gentleness" (Exod.)
149 "Cantemos al Señor" ("Let's Sing Unto the Lord") (Ps.)
685 "Now On Land and Sea Descending" (Ps.)
425 "O Crucified Redeemer" (Ps., John)
2004 "Praise the Source of Faith and Learning" (Ps., 1 Cor.)
2012 "Let Us with a Joyful Mind" (Ps.)
132 "All My Hope Is Firmly Grounded" (1 Cor.)
160 "Rejoice, Ye Pure in Heart" (1 Cor.)
296 "Sing, My Tongue, the Glorious Battle" (1 Cor.)
265 "O Christ, the Healer" (1 Cor., John)
297 "Beneath the Cross of Jesus" (1 Cor., John)
552 "Here, O Lord, Your Servants Gather" (1 Cor., John)
577 "God of Grace and God of Glory" (1 Cor.)
627 "O the Depth of Love Divine" (1 Cor.)
2266 "Here Is Bread, Here Is Wine" (1 Cor.)
261 "Lord of the Dance" (John)
267 "O Love, How Deep" (John)
269 "Lord, Who Throughout These Forty Days" (John)
289 "Ah, Holy Jesus" (John)
427 "Where Cross the Crowded Ways of Life" (John)
433 "All Who Love and Serve Your City" (John)
2060 "God the Sculptor of the Mountains" (John)
2089 "Wild and Lone the Prophet's Voice" (John)

Contemporary Suggestions

UM404 "Every Time I Feel the Spirit" (Exod.)
S2018 "Honor and Praise" (Exod.)
S2002 "I Will Call Upon the Lord" (Ps.)
  R15, SP224
S2066 "Praise the Name of Jesus" (Ps.)
  R7, SP87
MM58 "All Heaven Declares" (Ps.)
MM80 "God of Wonders" (Ps.)
  WY14; V-3 p. 184 (vocal solo)
MM111 "The Heavens Shall Declare" (Ps.)
MM93 "Rock of Ages" (Ps., Matt.)
  WO125
MM99 "Shout to the North" (1 Cor.)
  WG114
MM76 "The Wonderful Cross" (1 Cor.)
  WY190
M53 "Let It Be Said of Us" (1 Cor.)
WG54 "Good To Me" (1 Cor.)
S2266 "Here Is Bread, Here Is Wine" (1 Cor.)
SP220 "You Are My All in All" (1 Cor., John)
  WY39
S2065 "More Precious than Silver" (John)
  SP99
S2164 "Sanctuary" (John)
  R185, M52

Vocal Solos

"Adonai" (Ps.)
V-10(90) p. 122
V-3 p. 63
"The Heavens Declare His Glory" (Ps.)
V-8 p. 248
"Ah, Holy Jesus" (John)
V-6 p. 24
"The Heart of Worship" (John)
MM71, WY184

Anthems

"Two Psalm Settings" ("Prayer of Dedication") (Ps.)
David Cherwien; Choristers Guild CGA1077
Unison/two-part (opt.) with keyboard (opt. handbells)

"Expectans expectavi" (John)
Charles Wood (free download at www.CPDL.org)
SATB with organ

Other Suggestions

Visuals:
  O Tablet/Ten Commandments, open manacles
  P Celestial images, tent, wedding canopy, bridegroom, runner
  E Wooden cross, clown or jester, (stumbling) block
  G Animals, whip, overturned table, spilled coins, cross
Introit: S2271. "Come! Come! Everybody Worship" (Exod.)
Act of Congregational Centering: BOW470 (1 Cor.)
Greeting: BOW330 (1 Cor.)
Opening Prayer: BOW460 (John)
Canticle: UM112. "Canticle of Wisdom" (1 Cor.)
Prayer of Confession: BOW479 (Exod.)
Litany: BOW496. The Ten Commandments (Exod.)
Prayer: UM268. Lent (Exod.)
Prayer: UM429. For Our Country (1 Cor., John)
Prayer: BOW335, BOW510, or BOW525 (1 Cor.)
Response: BOW193. "Prayer for Wisdom" (1 Cor.)
Prayer: BOW501 or BOW514 (John)
Response: BOW191. "May This Mind Be in Us" (John)

Numbers 21:4-9
[4]From Mount Hor they set out by the way to the Red
Sea, to go around the land of Edom; but the people
became impatient on the way. [5]The people spoke against
God and against Moses, "Why have you brought us up out
of Egypt to die in the wilderness? For there is no food and
no water, and we detest this miserable food." [6]Then the
LORD sent poisonous serpents among the people, and
they bit the people, so that many Israelites died. [7]The
people came to Moses and said, "We have sinned by
speaking against the LORD and against you; pray to the
LORD to take away the serpents from us." So Moses prayed
for the people. [8]And the LORD said to Moses, "Make a poi-
sonous serpent, and set it on a pole; and everyone who is
bitten shall look at it and live." [9]So Moses made a serpent
of bronze, and put it upon a pole; and whenever a serpent
bit someone, that person would look at the serpent of
bronze and live.

Psalm 107:1-3, 17-22
[1]O give thanks to the LORD, for he is good; for his stead-
fast love endures forever. [2]Let the redeemed of the LORD
say so, those he redeemed from trouble [3]and gathered in
from the lands, from the east and from the west, from the
north and from the south.
[17]Some were sick through their sinful ways, and because
of their iniquities endured affliction; [18]they loathed any
kind of food, and they drew near to the gates of death.
[19]Then they cried to the LORD in their trouble, and he
saved them from their distress; [20]he sent out his word and
healed them, and delivered them from destruction. [21]Let
them thank the LORD for his steadfast love, for his won-
derful works to humankind. [22]And let them offer thanks-
giving sacrifices, and tell of his deeds with songs of joy.

Ephesians 2:1-10
[1]You were dead through the trespasses and sins [2]in
which you once lived, following the course of this world,
following the ruler of the power of the air, the spirit that
is now at work among those who are disobedient. [3]All of
us once lived among them in the passions of our flesh, fol-
lowing the desires of flesh and senses, and we were by
nature children of wrath, like everyone else. [4]But God,
who is rich in mercy, out of the great love with which he
loved us [5]even when we were dead through our tres-
passes, made us alive together with Christ—by grace you
have been saved— [6]and raised us up with him and seated
us with him in the heavenly places in Christ Jesus, [7]so that
in the ages to come he might show the immeasurable
riches of his grace in kindness toward us in Christ Jesus.
[8]For by grace you have been saved through faith, and this
is not your own doing; it is the gift of God— [9]not the
result of works, so that no one may boast. [10]For we are
what he has made us, created in Christ Jesus for good
works, which God prepared beforehand to be our way of
life.

John 3:14-21
[14]"And just as Moses lifted up the serpent in the wilder-
ness, so must the Son of Man be lifted up, [15]that whoever
believes in him may have eternal life.
[16]"For God so loved the world that he gave his only Son,
so that everyone who believes in him may not perish but
may have eternal life.
[17]"Indeed, God did not send the Son into the world to
condemn the world, but in order that the world might be
saved through him. [18]Those who believe in him are not
condemned; but those who do not believe are con-
demned already, because they have not believed in the
name of the only Son of God. [19]And this is the judgment,
that the light has come into the world, and people loved
darkness rather than light because their deeds were evil.
[20]For all who do evil hate the light and do not come to
the light, so that their deeds may not be exposed. [21]But
those who do what is true come to the light, so that it may
be clearly seen that their deeds have been done in God."

Notes:

Primary Hymns and Songs for the Day

2031 "We Bring the Sacrifice of Praise" (Ps.) (O)
R3, SP1

378 "Amazing Grace" (Eph., Communion)
H-3 Handbell-14, 46; Choir-27; Descant-14; Organ-4
S-2 #5-7. Various treatments

2162 "Grace Alone" (Eph.)
MM100

206 "I Want to Walk as a Child of the Light" (John)

292 "What Wondrous Love Is This" (John) (C)
H-3 Handbell-102; Choir-212; Organ-185
S-1 #347. Harmonization

Hymn Suggestions

142 "If Thou But Suffer God to Guide Thee" (Num.)
108 "God Hath Spoken by the Prophets" (Num., John)
102 "Now Thank We All Our God" (Ps.)
2009 "O God Beyond All Praising" (Ps.)
2172 "We Are Called" (Ps., John)
121 "There's a Wideness in God's Mercy" (Eph.)
355 "Depth of Mercy" (Eph.)
357 "Just as I Am, Without One Plea" (Eph.)
361 "Rock of Ages, Cleft for Me" (Eph.)
363 "And Can It Be That I Should Gain" (Eph.)
365 "Grace Greater Than Our Sin" (Eph., John)
381 "Savior, Like a Shepherd Lead Us" (Eph.)
385 "Let Us Plead for Faith Alone" (Eph.)
579 "Lord God, Your Love Has Called Us Here" (Eph.)
2196 "We Walk by Faith" (Eph.)
2211 "Faith Is Patience in the Night" (Eph.)
2255 "In the Singing" (Eph., Communion)
98 "To God Be the Glory" (John)
184 "Of the Father's Love Begotten" (John)
185 "When Morning Gilds the Skies" (John)
188 "Christ Is the World's Light" (John)
194 "Morning Glory, Starlit Sky" (John)
267 "O Love, How Deep" (John)
287 "O Love Divine, What Hast Thou Done" (John)
364 "Because He Lives" (John)
2084 "Come, Let Us with Our Lord Arise" (John)
2085 "He Came Down" (John)
2121 "O Holy Spirit, Root of Life" (John)
2149 "Living for Jesus" (John)
2259 "Victim Divine" (John, Lent)
434 "Cuando El Pobre" (One Great Hour)

Contemporary Suggestions

MM103 "How Great are You, Lord" (Num., Eph.)
S2036 "Give Thanks" (Num., Ps.)
MM68 "Forever" (Ps.)
WY57
MM79 "I Stand Amazed" (Ps.)
WY211
MM66 "We Fall Down" (Eph.)
WG169
UM176 "Majesty" (Eph.)
WG63 "Hallelujah" ("Your Love Is Amazing") (Eph., John)
S2073 "Celebrate Love" (Eph., John)
S2258 "Sing Alleluia to the Lord" (Eph., John)
S2108 "O How He Loves You and Me!" (John)
SP111 "There Is a Redeemer" (John)
R232
M7 "I Believe in Jesus" (John)
WO68
M25 "No Greater Love" (John)
MM77 "Above All" (John)
WO2; V-3 p. 17 or V-10(03) p. 18 (vocal solo)
MM82 "You Are My King" ("Amazing Love") (John)
WY65
MM94 "That's Why We Praise Him" (John)
WG122
MM106 "I Come to the Cross" (John, Lent)
WG142 "This Is Love" (John)

Vocal Solos

"And Can It Be That I Should Gain" (Eph.)
V-1 p. 29
"Redeeming Grace" (Eph.)
V-4 p. 47
"God So Loved" (John)
V-10 (90) p. 165

Anthems

"What Wondrous Love Is This" (John)
Arr. Drew Collins; Kjos 6319
Two-part mixed with keyboard

"As Moses Lifted Up" (John)
Ralph M. Johnson; Choristers Guild CGA550
Unison with organ and flute

Other Suggestions

Visuals:
O Bronze serpent on a pole, wilderness, empty bowl/cup
P Map or globe, praying hands, thanksgiving, singing, Ps. 107:2
E Death (black), resurrection, gift, life preserver (salvation)
G Light/darkness, wooden cross, crucifix, John 3:16, life preserver

Greeting: BOW326 (Eph.) or BOW424 (One Great Hour)
Opening Prayer: BOW251 (John)
Prayer of Confession: BOW480 (Num., Eph.)
Response: S2275. "Kyrie" (Eph.)
Song of Assurance: S2141. "There's a Song" (Eph.)
Prayer: UM456. For Courage to Do Justice (One Great Hour)
Prayer: BOW334 (Num., Ps., Eph.) or BOW336 (John)
Prayer: BOW500. For Blessing, Mercy, and Courage (Ps.)
Poem: UM58 or UM342 (Eph.)
Prayer of Thanksgiving: BOW551 (Ps., Eph.)
Blessing: BOW563 (Eph., John)

Jeremiah 31:31-34
31 The days are surely coming, says the LORD, when I will
make a new covenant with the house of Israel and the
house of Judah. 32 It will not be like the covenant that I
made with their ancestors when I took them by the hand
to bring them out of the land of Egypt—a covenant that
they broke, though I was their husband, says the LORD.
33 But this is the covenant that I will make with the house
of Israel after those days, says the LORD: I will put my law
within them, and I will write it on their hearts; and I will
be their God, and they shall be my people. 34 No longer
shall they teach one another, or say to each other, "Know
the LORD," for they shall all know me, from the least of
them to the greatest, says the LORD; for I will forgive their
iniquity, and remember their sin no more.

Psalm 51:1-12
1 Have mercy on me, O God, according to your steadfast
love; according to your abundant mercy blot out my trans-
gressions. 2 Wash me thoroughly from my iniquity, and
cleanse me from my sin. 3 For I know my transgressions,
and my sin is ever before me. 4 Against you, you alone,
have I sinned, and done what is evil in your sight, so that
you are justified in your sentence and blameless when you
pass judgment. 5 Indeed, I was born guilty, a sinner when
my mother conceived me. 6 You desire truth in the inward
being; therefore teach me wisdom in my secret heart.
7 Purge me with hyssop, and I shall be clean; wash me, and
I shall be whiter than snow. 8 Let me hear joy and glad-
ness; let the bones that you have crushed rejoice. 9 Hide
your face from my sins, and blot out all my iniquities.
10 Create in me a clean heart, O God, and put a new and
right spirit within me. 11 Do not cast me away from your
presence, and do not take your holy spirit from me.
12 Restore to me the joy of your salvation, and sustain in
me a willing spirit.

Hebrews 5:5-10
5 So also Christ did not glorify himself in becoming a
high priest, but was appointed by the one who said to
him, "You are my Son, today I have begotten you"; 6 as he
says also in another place, "You are a priest forever,
according to the order of Melchizedek."
7 In the days of his flesh, Jesus offered up prayers and
supplications, with loud cries and tears, to the one who
was able to save him from death, and he was heard
because of his reverent submission. 8 Although he was a
Son, he learned obedience through what he suffered;
9 and having been made perfect, he became the source of
eternal salvation for all who obey him, 10 having been des-
ignated by God a high priest according to the order of
Melchizedek.

John 12:20-33
20 Now among those who went up to worship at the festi-
val were some Greeks. 21 They came to Philip, who was
from Bethsaida in Galilee, and said to him, "Sir, we wish
to see Jesus." 22 Philip went and told Andrew; then Andrew
and Philip went and told Jesus. 23 Jesus answered them,
"The hour has come for the Son of Man to be glorified.
24 Very truly, I tell you, unless a grain of wheat falls into
the earth and dies, it remains just a single grain; but if it
dies, it bears much fruit. 25 Those who love their life lose
it, and those who hate their life in this world will keep it
for eternal life. 26 Whoever serves me must follow me, and
where I am, there will my servant be also. Whoever serves
me, the Father will honor.
27 "Now my soul is troubled. And what should I say—
'Father, save me from this hour'? No, it is for this reason
that I have come to this hour. 28 Father, glorify your
name." Then a voice came from heaven, "I have glorified
it, and I will glorify it again." 29 The crowd standing there
heard it and said that it was thunder. Others said, "An
angel has spoken to him." 30 Jesus answered, "This voice
has come for your sake, not for mine. 31 Now is the judg-
ment of this world; now the ruler of this world will be dri-
ven out. 32 And I, when I am lifted up from the earth, will
draw all people to myself." 33 He said this to indicate the
kind of death he was to die.

Notes:

Primary Hymns and Songs for the Day

157 "Jesus Shall Reign" (Heb., John) (O)
H-3 Handbell-29, 57; Choir-117; Descant-31; Organ-31
S-1 #100-103. Various treatments
383 "This Is a Day of New Beginnings" (Jer., John)
2133 "Give Me a Clean Heart" (Jer., Ps.)
2152 "Change My Heart, O God" (Jer., Ps.)
R143, SP195
2083 "My Song Is Love Unknown" (Heb.)
2129 "I Have Decided to Follow Jesus" (John) (C)

Hymn Suggestions

553 "And Are We Yet Alive" (John) (O)
420 "Breathe on Me, Breath of God" (Jer.)
480 "O Love That Wilt Not Let Me Go" (Jer.)
593 "Here I Am, Lord" (Jer.)
606 "Come, Let Us Use the Grace Divine" (Jer.)
2140 "Since Jesus Came Into My Heart" (Jer., Ps.)
2060 "God the Sculptor of the Mountains" (Jer., Communion)
2247 "Wonder of Wonders" (Jer., Baptism)
410 "I Want a Principle Within" (Jer., Ps.)
417 "O For a Heart to Praise My God"(Ps.)
168 "At the Name of Jesus" (Heb., John)
282 " 'Tis Finished! The Messiah Dies" (Heb.)
287 "O Love Divine, What Hast Thou Done" (Heb., John)
289 "Ah, Holy Jesus" (Heb.)
300 "O The Lamb" (Heb.)
325 "Hail, Thou Once Despised Jesus" (Heb.)
2149 "Living for Jesus" (Heb.)
2259 "Victim Divine" (Heb., Communion, Lent)
159 "Lift High the Cross" (John)
165 "Hallelujah! What a Savior" (John)
256 "We Would See Jesus" (John)
290 "Go to Dark Gethsemane" (John)
297 "Beneath the Cross of Jesus" (John)
338 "Where He Leads Me" (John)
396 "O Jesus, I Have Promised" (John)
398 "Jesus Calls Us" (John)
413 "A Charge to Keep I Have" (John)
424 "Must Jesus Bear the Cross Alone" (John)
2137 "Would I Have Answered When You Called" (John)
2213 "Healer of Our Every Ill" (John)
415 "Take Up Thy Cross" (John) (C)

Contemporary Suggestions

S2154 "Please Enter My Heart, Hosanna" (Jer., Ps., John)
S2157 "Come and Fill Our Hearts" (Jer., John)
M49 "Refresh My Heart" (Jer., Ps.)
MM65 "Before the Throne of God Above" (Jer., Heb.)
MM85 "The Potter's Hand" (Jer.)
MM112 "Jesus, Lover of My Soul" (Jer., Lent)
WO111
MM89 "Purified" (Jer., Ps.)
MM97 "I Give You My Heart" (Jer., Ps.)
WY71
M26 "The Power of Your Love" (Ps.)
WG133
M35 "White as Snow"
M50 "Refiner's Fire" (Ps.)
MM90 "Purify My Heart" (Ps.)
R187
MM91 "Take My Life" (Ps., John)
H49, R150
MM94 "That's Why We Praise Him" (Heb.)
WG122
S2016 "Glorify Thy Name" (John)
S2086 "Open Our Eyes, Lord" (Ps., John)
SP199, R91
S2222 "The Servant Song" (John)
R148, SP193
MM67 "We Want to See Jesus Lifted High" (John)
WO149

Vocal Solos

"A Contrite Heart" (Ps.)
V-4 p. 10
"Clean Before My Lord" (Ps.)
V-8 p. 233
"Nothing . . . Everything" (John)
V-8 p. 162

Anthems

"Lord, I Call to You" (Ps.)
Mozart/arr. Hal Hopson; Hinshaw HMC-1145
SATB with keyboard

"Beneath the Cross of Jesus" (John)
Arr. Bradley Ellingboe; Kjos 9043
SATB and clarinet (or C instrument) with piano

Other Suggestions

Visuals:
O Heart, Exodus, open Bible, love at work
P Water, bones, rejoicing, Ps. 51:7*b*
E Miter/chasuble, praying hands, crucifix, cross
G Clock or hourglass, crucifixion, bowl/pitcher/towel (service)
Introit: UM292, st. 1. "What Wondrous Love Is This"
Greeting: BOW329 (Heb.) or BOW343 (John)
Opening Prayer: BOW447. The Collect (Ps.)
Prayer: UM353. Ash Wednesday (Jer., Ps.)
Prayer of Confession: BOW475 (Ps.) or BOW488 (Jer.)
Response: S2277. "Lord, Have Mercy" (Jer., Lent)
Prayer: BOW337 (Heb., John) or BOW514 (Heb.)
Prayer: BOW518, BOW522, or BOW530 (Jer., Ps.)
Scripture Response: UM479, st. 4. "Jesus, Lover of My Soul" (Jer.)
Prayer of Thanksgiving: BOW550 (Jer., Ps.)
Blessing: BOW566. Sarum Blessing (Jer.)

Mark 11:1-11 (Palms)

[1] When they were approaching Jerusalem, at Bethphage and Bethany, near the Mount of Olives, he sent two of his disciples [2] and said to them, "Go into the village ahead of you, and immediately as you enter it, you will find tied there a colt that has never been ridden; untie it and bring it. [3] If anyone says to you, 'Why are you doing this?' just say this, 'The Lord needs it and will send it back here immediately.' " [4] They went away and found a colt tied near a door, outside in the street. As they were untying it, [5] some of the bystanders said to them, "What are you doing, untying the colt?" [6] They told them what Jesus had said; and they allowed them to take it. [7] Then they brought the colt to Jesus and threw their cloaks on it; and he sat on it. [8] Many people spread their cloaks on the road, and others spread leafy branches that they had cut in the fields. [9] Then those who went ahead and those who followed were shouting, Hosanna! Blessed is the one who comes in the name of the Lord! [10] Blessed is the coming kingdom of our ancestor David! Hosanna in the highest heaven!"

[11] Then he entered Jerusalem and went into the temple; and when he had looked around at everything, as it was already late, he went out to Bethany with the twelve.

Psalm 118:1-2, 19-29 (Palms)

[1] O give thanks to the LORD, for he is good; his steadfast love endures forever! [2] Let Israel say, "His steadfast love endures forever."

[19] Open to me the gates of righteousness, that I may enter through them and give thanks to the LORD. [20] This is the gate of the LORD; the righteous shall enter through it. [21] I thank you that you have answered me and have become my salvation. [22] The stone that the builders rejected has become the chief cornerstone. [23] This is the LORD's doing; it is marvelous in our eyes. [24] This is the day that the LORD has made; let us rejoice and be glad in it. [25] Save us, we beseech you, O LORD! O LORD, we beseech you, give us success! [26] Blessed is the one who comes in the name of the LORD. We bless you from the house of the LORD. [27] The LORD is God, and he has given us light. Bind the festal procession with branches, up to the horns of the altar. [28] You are my God, and I will give thanks to you; you are my God, I will extol you. [29] O give thanks to the LORD, for he is good, for his steadfast love endures forever.

Isaiah 50:4-9*a*

[4] The Lord GOD has given me the tongue of a teacher, that I may know how to sustain the weary with a word. Morning by morning he wakens—wakens my ear to listen as those who are taught. [5] The Lord GOD has opened my ear, and I was not rebellious, I did not turn backward. [6] I gave my back to those who struck me, and my cheeks to those who pulled out the beard; I did not hide my face from insult and spitting. [7] The Lord GOD helps me; therefore I have not been disgraced; therefore I have set my face like flint, and I know that I shall not be put to shame; [8] he who vindicates me is near. Who will contend with me? Let us stand up together. Who are my adversaries? Let them confront me. [9a] It is the Lord GOD who helps me.

Psalm 31:9-16

[9] Be gracious to me, O LORD, for I am in distress; my eye wastes away from grief, my soul and body also. [10] For my life is spent with sorrow, and my years with sighing; my strength fails because of my misery, and my bones waste away. [11] I am the scorn of all my adversaries, a horror to my neighbors, an object of dread to my acquaintances; those who see me in the street flee from me. [12] I have passed out of mind like one who is dead; I have become like a broken vessel. [13] For I hear the whispering of many—terror all around!—as they scheme together against me, as they plot to take my life. [14] But I trust in you, O LORD; I say, "You are my God." [15] My times are in your hand; deliver me from the hand of my enemies and persecutors. [16] Let your face shine upon your servant; save me in your steadfast love.

Philippians 2:5-11

[5] Let the same mind be in you that was in Christ Jesus, [6] who, though he was in the form of God, did not regard equality with God as something to be exploited, [7] but emptied himself, taking the form of a slave, being born in human likeness. And being found in human form, [8] he humbled himself and became obedient to the point of death—even death on a cross. [9] Therefore God also highly exalted him and gave him the name that is above every name, [10] so that at the name of Jesus every knee should bend, in heaven and on earth and under the earth, [11] and every tongue should confess that Jesus Christ is Lord, to the glory of God the Father.

Mark 14:1–15:47 or Mark 15:1-39 (40-47)

[1] It was two days before the Passover and the festival of Unleavened Bread. The chief priests and the scribes were looking for a way to arrest Jesus by stealth and kill him; [2] for they said, "Not during the festival, or there may be a riot among the people."

[3] While he was at Bethany in the house of Simon the leper, as he sat at the table, a woman came with an alabaster jar of very costly ointment of nard, and she broke open the jar and poured the ointment on his head. [4] But some were there who said to one another in anger, "Why was the ointment wasted in this way? [5] For this ointment could have been sold for more than three hundred denarii, and the money given to the poor." And they scolded her. [6] But Jesus said, "Let her alone; why do you trouble her? She has performed a good service for me. [7] For you always have the poor with you, and you can show kindness to them whenever you wish; but you will not always have me.
[8] She has done what she could; she has anointed my body beforehand for its burial. [9] Truly I tell you, wherever the

good news is proclaimed in the whole world, what she has
done will be told in remembrance of her."
10 Then Judas Iscariot, who was one of the twelve, went to
the chief priests in order to betray him to them. 11 When
they heard it, they were greatly pleased, and promised to
give him money. So he began to look for an opportunity to
betray him.
12 On the first day of Unleavened Bread, when the
Passover lamb is sacrificed, his disciples said to him,
"Where do you want us to go and make the preparations
for you to eat the Passover?" 13 So he sent two of his disci-
ples, saying to them, "Go into the city, and a man carrying
a jar of water will meet you; follow him, 14 and wherever he
enters, say to the owner of the house, 'The Teacher asks,
Where is my guest room where I may eat the Passover with
my disciples?' 15 He will show you a large room upstairs,
furnished and ready. Make preparations for us there." 16 So
the disciples set out and went to the city, and found every-
thing as he had told them; and they prepared the Passover
meal.
17 When it was evening, he came with the twelve. 18 And
when they had taken their places and were eating, Jesus
said, "Truly I tell you, one of you will betray me, one who is
eating with me." 19 They began to be distressed and to say
to him one after another, "Surely, not I?" 20 He said to
them, "It is one of the twelve, one who is dipping bread
into the bowl with me. 21 For the Son of Man goes as it is
written of him, but woe to that one by whom the Son of
Man is betrayed! It would have been better for that one
not to have been born."
22 While they were eating, he took a loaf of bread, and
after blessing it he broke it, gave it to them, and said,
"Take; this is my body." 23 Then he took a cup, and after
giving thanks he gave it to them, and all of them drank
from it. 24 He said to them, "This is my blood of the
covenant, which is poured out for many. 25 Truly I tell you,
I will never again drink of the fruit of the vine until that
day when I drink it new in the kingdom of God."
26 When they had sung the hymn, they went out to the
Mount of Olives. 27 And Jesus said to them, "You will all
become deserters; for it is written, 'I will strike the shep-
herd, and the sheep will be scattered.' 28 But after I am
raised up, I will go before you to Galilee." 29 Peter said to
him, "Even though all become deserters, I will not."
30 Jesus said to him, "Truly I tell you, this day, this very
night, before the cock crows twice, you will deny me three
times." 31 But he said vehemently, "Even though I must die
with you, I will not deny you." And all of them said the
same.
32 They went to a place called Gethsemane; and he said
to his disciples, "Sit here while I pray." 33 He took with him
Peter and James and John, and began to be distressed and
agitated. 34 And he said to them, "I am deeply grieved, even
to death; remain here, and keep awake." 35 And going a lit-
tle farther, he threw himself on the ground and prayed
that, if it were possible, the hour might pass from him.
36 He said, "Abba, Father, for you all things are possible;
remove this cup from me; yet, not what I want, but what
you want." 37 He came and found them sleeping; and he
said to Peter, "Simon, are you asleep? Could you not keep
awake one hour? 38 Keep awake and pray that you may not
come into the time of trial; the spirit indeed is willing, but
the flesh is weak." 39 And again he went away and prayed,
saying the same words. 40 And once more he came and
found them sleeping, for their eyes were very heavy; and
they did not know what to say to him. 41 He came a third
time and said to them, "Are you still sleeping and taking
your rest? Enough! The hour has come; the Son of Man is
betrayed into the hands of sinners. 42 Get up, let us be
going. See, my betrayer is at hand."
43 Immediately, while he was still speaking, Judas, one of
the twelve, arrived; and with him there was a crowd with
swords and clubs, from the chief priests, the scribes, and
the elders. 44 Now the betrayer had given them a sign, say-
ing, "The one I will kiss is the man; arrest him and lead
him away under guard." 45 So when he came, he went up to
him at once and said, "Rabbi!" and kissed him. 46 Then
they laid hands on him and arrested him. 47 But one of
those who stood near drew his sword and struck the slave
of the high priest, cutting off his ear. 48 Then Jesus said to
them, "Have you come out with swords and clubs to arrest
me as though I were a bandit? 49 Day after day I was with
you in the temple teaching, and you did not arrest me. But
let the scriptures be fulfilled." 50 All of them deserted him
and fled.
51 A certain young man was following him, wearing noth-
ing but a linen cloth. They caught hold of him, 52 but he
left the linen cloth and ran off naked.
53 They took Jesus to the high priest; and all the chief
priests, the elders, and the scribes were assembled.
54 Peter had followed him at a distance, right into the
courtyard of the high priest; and he was sitting with the
guards, warming himself at the fire. 55 Now the chief
priests and the whole council were looking for testimony
against Jesus to put him to death; but they found none.
56 For many gave false testimony against him, and their
testimony did not agree. 57 Some stood up and gave false
testimony against him, saying, 58 "We heard him say, 'I will
destroy this temple that is made with hands, and in three
days I will build another, not made with hands.' " 59 But
even on this point their testimony did not agree. 60 Then
the high priest stood up before them and asked Jesus,
"Have you no answer? What is it that they testify against
you? 61 But he was silent and did not answer. Again the
high priest asked him, "Are you the Messiah, the Son of
the Blessed One?" 62 Jesus said, "I am; and 'you will see the
Son of Man seated at the right hand of the Power,' and
'coming with the clouds of heaven.' " 63 Then the high
priest tore his clothes and said, "Why do we still need wit-
nesses? 64 You have heard his blasphemy! What is your

decision?" All of them condemned him as deserving
death. 65 Some began to spit on him, to blindfold him,
and to strike him, saying to him, "Prophesy!" The guards
also took him over and beat him.
66 While Peter was below in the courtyard, one of the ser-
vant-girls of the high priest came by. 67 When she saw Peter
warming himself, she stared at him and said, "You also
were with Jesus, the man from Nazareth." 68 But he denied
it, saying, "I do not know or understand what you are talk-
ing about." And he went out into the forecourt. Then the
cock crowed. 69 And the servant-girl, on seeing him, began
again to say to the bystanders, "This man is one of them."
70 But again he denied it. Then after a little while the
bystanders again said to Peter, "Certainly you are one of
them; for you are a Galilean." 71 But he began to curse, and
he swore an oath, "I do not know this man you are talking
about." 72 At that moment the cock crowed for the second
time. Then Peter remembered that Jesus had said to him,
"Before the cock crows twice, you will deny me three
times." And he broke down and wept.
1 As soon as it was morning, the chief priests held a con-
sultation with the elders and scribes and the whole coun-
cil. They bound Jesus, led him away, and handed him over
to Pilate. 2 Pilate asked him, "Are you the King of the
Jews?" He answered him, "You say so." 3 Then the chief
priests accused him of many things. 4 Pilate asked him
again, "Have you no answer? See how many charges they
bring against you." 5 But Jesus made no further reply, so
that Pilate was amazed.
6 Now at the festival he used to release a prisoner for
them, anyone for whom they asked. 7 Now a man called
Barabbas was in prison with the rebels who had com-
mitted murder during the insurrection. 8 So the crowd
came and began to ask Pilate to do for them according to
his custom. 9 Then he answered them, "Do you want me
to release for you the King of the Jews?" 10 For he realized
that it was out of jealousy that the chief priests had
handed him over. 11 But the chief priests stirred up the
crowd to have him release Barabbas for them instead.
12 Pilate spoke to them again, "Then what do you wish me
to do with the man you call the King of the Jews?" 13 They
shouted back, "Crucify him!" 14 Pilate asked them, "Why,
what evil has he done?" But they shouted all the more,
"Crucify him!" 15 So Pilate, wishing to satisfy the crowd,
released Barabbas for them; and after flogging Jesus, he
handed him over to be crucified.
16 Then the soldiers led him into the courtyard of the
palace (that is, the governor's headquarters); and they
called together the whole cohort. 17 And they clothed him in
a purple cloak; and after twisting some thorns into a crown,
they put it on him. 18 And they began saluting him, "Hail,
King of the Jews!" 19 They struck his head with a reed, spat
upon him, and knelt down in homage to him. 20 After mock-
ing him, they stripped him of the purple cloak and put his
own clothes on him. Then they led him out to crucify him.
21 They compelled a passer-by, who was coming in from
the country, to carry his cross; it was Simon of Cyrene, the
father of Alexander and Rufus. 22 Then they brought Jesus
to the place called Golgotha (which means the place of a
skull). 23 And they offered him wine mixed with myrrh; but
he did not take it. 24 And they crucified him, and divided
his clothes among them, casting lots to decide what each
should take.
25 It was nine o'clock in the morning when they crucified
him. 26 The inscription of the charge against him read,
"The King of the Jews." 27 And with him they crucified two
bandits, one on his right and one on his left. 29 Those who
passed by derided him, shaking their heads and saying,
"Aha! You who would destroy the temple and build it in
three days, 30 save yourself, and come down from the
cross!" 31 In the same way the chief priests, along with the
scribes, were also mocking him among themselves and say-
ing, "He saved others; he cannot save himself. 32 Let the
Messiah, the King of Israel, come down from the cross
now, so that we may see and believe." Those who were cru-
cified with him also taunted him.
33 When it was noon, darkness came over the whole land
until three in the afternoon. 34 At three o'clock Jesus cried
out with a loud voice, "Eloi, Eloi, lema sabachthani?"
which means, "My God, my God, why have you forsaken
me?" 35 When some of the bystanders heard it, they said,
"Listen, he is calling for Elijah." 36 And someone ran, filled
a sponge with sour wine, put it on a stick, and gave it to
him to drink, saying, "Wait, let us see whether Elijah will
come to take him down." 37 Then Jesus gave a loud cry and
breathed his last. 38 And the curtain of the temple was torn
in two, from top to bottom. 39 Now when the centurion,
who stood facing him, saw that in this way he breathed his
last, he said, "Truly this man was God's Son!"
40 There were also women looking on from a distance;
among them were Mary Magdalene, and Mary the mother
of James the younger and of Joses, and Salome. 41 These
used to follow him and provided for him when he was in
Galilee; and there were many other women who had come
up with him to Jerusalem.
42 When evening had come, and since it was the day of
Preparation, that is, the day before the sabbath, 43 Joseph
of Arimathea, a respected member of the council, who was
also himself waiting expectantly for the kingdom of God,
went boldly to Pilate and asked for the body of Jesus.
44 Then Pilate wondered if he were already dead; and sum-
moning the centurion, he asked him whether he had been
dead for some time. 45 When he learned from the centuri-
on that he was dead, he granted the body to Joseph.
46 Then Joseph bought a linen cloth, and taking down the
body, wrapped it in the linen cloth, and laid it in a tomb
that had been hewn out of the rock. He then rolled a
stone against the door of the tomb. 47 Mary Magdelene
and Mary the mother of Joses saw where the body was laid.

Primary Hymns and Songs for the Day

278 "Hosanna, Loud Hosanna" (Palms Gospel) (O)
    H-3 Handbell-16, 22, 68; Choir-101; Descant-37
    S-1 #115. Harmonization
280 "All Glory, Laud, and Honor" (Palms Gospel)
    H-3 Handbell-45; Choir-22; Descant-96; Organ-144
    S-1 #309-10. Harmonization with descant
2109 "Hosanna! Hosanna!" (Palms Gospel)
296 "Sing, My Tongue, the Glorious Battle" (Passion)
298 "When I Survey the Wondrous Cross" (Passion) (C)
    H-3 Handbell-6, 102; Choir-213; Descant-49; Organ-49
    S-1 #155. Descant

Hymn Suggestions

277 "Tell Me the Stories of Jesus" (Palms Gospel)
279 "Mantos y Palmas" ("Filled with Excitement") (Palms Gospel)
638 "This Is the Feast of Victory" (Palms, Communion)
2083 "My Song Is Love Unknown" (Palm Sunday)
2256 "Holy, Holy, Holy Lord" (Palms Gospel)
166 "All Praise to Thee, for Thou, O King Divine" (Phil., Passion Gospel)
168 "At the Name of Jesus" (Phil.)
193 "Jesus! the Name High Over All" (Phil.)
536 "Precious Name" (Phil.)
561 "Jesus, United by Thy Grace" (Phil.)
2100 "Thou Didst Leave Thy Throne" (Phil.)
2111 "We Sang Our Glad Hosannas" (Palms and Passion)
267 "O Love, How Deep" (Passion Gospel)
285 "To Mock Your Reign, O Dearest Lord" (Passion)
286 "O Sacred Head, Now Wounded" (Passion Gospel)
287 "O Love Divine, What Hast Thou Done" (Passion)
288 "Were You There" (Passion Gospel)
291 "He Never Said a Mumbalin' Word" (Isa., Passion)
581 "Lord, Whose Love Through Humble Service" (Passion)
633 "The Bread of Life for All Is Broken" (Passion, Communion)
2104 "An Outcast among Outcasts" (Passion Gospel)
2110 "Why Has God Forsaken Me?" (Passion Gospel)
2263 "Broken for Me" (Passion, Communion)
159 "Lift High the Cross" (Passion Gospel) (C)

Contemporary Suggestions

UM657 "This Is the Day" (Ps. 118)
S2270 "I Will Enter His Gates" (Ps. 118)
S2069 "All Hail King Jesus" (Palms Gospel)
S2075 "King of Kings" (Palm Sunday)
S2091 "The King of Glory Comes" (Palm Sunday)
S2154 "Please Enter My Heart, Hosanna" (Palms Gospel)
SP82 "Hosanna" (Palms Gospel)
    R71, WG80
MM68 "Forever" (Ps. 118)
    WY57
MM57 "Open the Eyes of My Heart" (Isa., Phil.)
    V-3 p. 162 (vocal solo)
S2070 "He Is Exalted" (Phil.)
S2071 "Jesus, Name Above All Names" (Phil.)
UM177 "He Is Lord" (Phil.)
SP234 "At the Name of Jesus" (Phil.)
    R133
MM56 "Come, Now Is the Time to Worship" (Phil.)
    WY178; V-3 p. 114 (vocal solo)
MM111 "The Heavens Shall Declare" (Phil., Palm Sunday)
MM77 "Above All" (Passion Gospel)
    WO2; V-3 p. 17 or V-10(03) p. 18 (vocal solo)
UM261 "Lord of the Dance" (Passion Gospel)
S2198 "Stay with Me" ("Nohu pû") (Passion Gospel)
WO120 "Redeemer, Savior, Friend" (Passion Gospel)

Vocal Solos

"Ride On, Jesus" (Palm Sunday)
V-7 p. 8
"The Palms" (Palm/Passion Sunday)
V-8 p. 206
"The Holy City" (Palm/Passion Sunday)
V-8 p. 195
"These Thousand Hills" (Passion Gospel)
V-3 p. 30

Anthems

"This Is the Day" (Ps. 118)
Ken and Rhonda Beard; Abingdon Press 9780687644728
SATB with piano

"Surely He Has Borne Our Griefs" (Passion Gospel)
Allen Pote; Hope C5391
SATB with piano

Other Suggestions

Visuals:

Palms Gospel	Colt, palms, cloaks, "Hosanna!"
Psalm 118	Gates, cornerstone, Ps. 118:24, 26*a*, 29
O	Jesus teaching, Christ's passion, flint
Psalm 13	Praying hands, grief, broken pottery
E	Manacles, wooden cross, crucifix, resurrection, Phil. 2:9, 10
Passion Gospel	Perfume bottle, water jar, cup/bread/wine, cock crowing, sword, bowl of water, wooden cross, placard, purple cloak, sponge/vinegar, torn curtain, shroud, hourglass

Introit: UM658. "This Is the Day" (Ps. 118)
Greeting: BOW245 (Palms) or BOW450 (Ps. 118)
Opening Prayer: BOW468 (Passion Sunday)
Canticle: UM167. "Canticle of Christ's Obedience" (Phil.) (see S-1, p. 381)
Prayer: UM281. Passion/Palm Sunday
Prayer: BOW336 or BOW348 (Passion Gospel)
Prayer of Confession: BOW482 (Mark)
Response: BOW189. "May This Mind Be in Us" (Phil.)
Responses: S2257. "Communion Setting"

Exodus 12:1-4 (5-10), 11-14

1 The LORD said to Moses and Aaron in the land of
Egypt: 2 This month shall mark for you the beginning of
months; it shall be the first month of the year for you.
3 Tell the whole congregation of Israel that on the tenth
of this month they are to take a lamb for each family, a
lamb for each household. 4 If a household is too small for
a whole lamb, it shall join its closest neighbor in obtain-
ing one; the lamb shall be divided in proportion to the
number of people who eat of it. 5 Your lamb shall be with-
out blemish, a year-old male; you may take it from the
sheep or from the goats. 6 You shall keep it until the four-
teenth day of this month; then the whole assembled con-
gregation of Israel shall slaughter it at twilight. 7 They
shall take some of the blood and put it on the two door-
posts and the lintel of the houses in which they eat it.
8 They shall eat the lamb that same night; they shall eat it
roasted over the fire with unleavened bread and bitter
herbs. 9 Do not eat any of it raw or boiled in water, but
roasted over the fire, with its head, legs, and inner
organs. 10 You shall let none of it remain until the morn-
ing; anything that remains until the morning you shall
burn. 11 This is how you shall eat it: your loins girded,
your sandals on your feet, and your staff in your hand;
and you shall eat it hurriedly. It is the passover of the
LORD. 12 For I will pass through the land of Egypt that
night, and I will strike down every firstborn in the land of
Egypt, both human beings and animals; on all the gods
of Egypt I will execute judgments: I am the LORD.
13 The blood shall be a sign for you on the houses where
you live: when I see the blood, I will pass over you, and
no plague shall destroy you when I strike the land of
Egypt.

14 This day shall be a day of remembrance for you. You
shall celebrate it as a festival to the LORD; throughout your
generations you shall observe it as a perpetual ordinance.

Psalm 116:1-4, 12-19

1 I love the LORD, because he has heard my voice and my
supplications. 2 Because he inclined his ear to me, there-
fore I will call on him as long as I live. 3 The snares of
death encompassed me; the pangs of Sheol laid hold on
me; I suffered distress and anguish. 4 Then I called on the
name of the LORD: "O LORD, I pray, save my life!"

12 What shall I return to the LORD for all his bounty to
me? 13 I will lift up the cup of salvation and call on the
name of the LORD, 14 I will pay my vows to the LORD in the
presence of all his people. 15 Precious in the sight of the
LORD is the death of his faithful ones. 16 O LORD, I am your
servant; I am your servant, the child of your serving girl.
You have loosed my bonds. 17 I will offer to you a thanksgiv-
ing sacrifice and call on the name of the LORD. 18 I will pay
my vows to the LORD in the presence of all his people, 19 in
the courts of the house of the LORD, in your midst, O
Jerusalem. Praise the LORD!

1 Corinthians 11:23-26

23 For I received from the Lord what I also handed on to
you, that the Lord Jesus on the night when he was
betrayed took a loaf of bread, 24 and when he had given
thanks, he broke it and said, "This is my body that is for
you. Do this in remembrance of me." 25 In the same way he
took the cup also, after supper, saying, "This cup is the
new covenant in my blood. Do this, as often as you drink
it, in remembrance of me." 26 For as often as you eat this
bread and drink the cup, you proclaim the Lord's death
until he comes.

John 13:1-17, 31*b*-35

1 Now before the festival of the Passover, Jesus knew that
his hour had come to depart from this world and go to the
Father. Having loved his own who were in the world, he
loved them to the end. 2 The devil had already put it into
the heart of Judas son of Simon Iscariot to betray him.
And during supper 3 Jesus, knowing that the Father had
given all things into his hands, and that he had come from
God and was going to God, 4 got up from the table, took
off his outer robe, and tied a towel around himself. 5 Then
he poured water into a basin and began to wash the disci-
ples' feet and to wipe them with the towel that was tied
around him. 6 He came to Simon Peter, who said to him,
"Lord, are you going to wash my feet?" 7 Jesus answered,
"You do not know now what I am doing, but later you will
understand." 8 Peter said to him, "You will never wash my
feet." Jesus answered, "Unless I wash you, you have no
share with me." 9 Simon Peter said to him, "Lord, not my
feet only but also my hands and my head!" 10 Jesus said to
him, "One who has bathed does not need to wash, except
for the feet, but is entirely clean. And you are clean,
though not all of you." 11 For he knew who was to betray
him; for this reason he said, "Not all of you are clean."

12 After he had washed their feet, had put on his robe, and
had returned to the table, he said to them, "Do you know
what I have done to you? 13 You call me Teacher and Lord—
and you are right, for that is what I am. 14 So if I, your Lord
and Teacher, have washed your feet, you also ought to wash
one another's feet. 15 For I have set you an example, that you
also should do as I have done to you. 16 Very truly, I tell you,
servants are not greater than their master, nor are messen-
gers greater than the one who sent them. 17 If you know
these things, you are blessed if you do them.

31b "Now the Son of Man has been glorified, and God has
been glorified in him. 32 If God has been glorified in him,
God will also glorify him in himself and will glorify him at
once. 33 Little children, I am with you only a little longer.
You will look for me; and as I said to the Jews so now I say
to you, 'Where I am going, you cannot come.' 34 I give you
a new commandment, that you love one another. Just as I
have loved you, you also should love one another. 35 By this
everyone will know that you are my disciples, if you have
love for one another."

Primary Hymns and Songs for the Day

616 "Come, Sinners, to the Gospel Feast" (O) (Ps., 1 Cor., Communion)
H-3 Choir-68; Descant-52; Organ-55
S-1 #164-66. Various treatments
614 "For the Bread Which You Have Broken" (1 Cor.)
H-3 Choir-67
S-2 #63-64. Descant/harmonization
2254 "In Remembrance of Me" (1 Cor., Communion)
2263 "Broken for Me" (1 Cor., Communion)
432 "Jesu, Jesu" (John) (C)
R289; S-1 #63 (vocal part)

Hymn Suggestions

448 "Go Down, Moses" (Exod.)
523 "Saranam, Saranam" ("Refuge") (Exod., Ps.)
586 "Let My People Seek Their Freedom" (Exod.)
2060 "God the Sculptor of the Mountains" (Exod., Communion)
2246 "Deep in the Shadows of the Past" (Exod.)
615 "For the Bread Which You Have Broken" (1 Cor.)
618 "Let Us Break Bread Together" (1 Cor., Comm.)
2050 "Mothering God, You Gave Me Birth" (1 Cor., Communion)
2261 "Life-giving Bread" (1 Cor., Communion)
637 "Una Espiga" ("Sheaves of Summer") (1 Cor., John, Communion)
624 "Bread of the World" (John, Communion)
267 "O Love, How Deep" (John)
286 "O Sacred Head, Now Wounded" (John)
287 "O Love Divine, What Hast Thou Done" (John)
292 "What Wondrous Love Is This" (John)
396 "O Jesus, I Have Promised" (John)
430 "O Master, Let Me Walk with Thee" (John)
549 "Where Charity and Love Prevail" (John)
579 "Lord God, Your Love Has Called Us Here" (John)
581 "Lord, Whose Love Through Humble Service" (John)
2111 "We Sang Our Glad Hosannas" (Holy Thursday)
2175 "Together We Serve" (John)
2177 "Wounded World that Cries for Healing" (John)
2213 "Healer of Our Every Ill" (John)
2268 "As We Gather at Your Table" (John, Communion)

Contemporary Suggestions

UM123 "El Shaddai" (Exod.)
S-2 #54 (verses for soloist)
S2002 "I Will Call Upon the Lord" (Ps.)
R15, SP224
S2031 "We Bring the Sacrifice of Praise" (Ps.)
R3, SP1
S2068 "I Love You, Lord" (Ps.)
R36, SP72
MM79 "I Stand Amazed" (Ps., Lent)
WY211
WO89 "I Will Not Forget You" (Ps.)
UM640 "Take Our Bread" (1 Cor., Communion)
S2176 "Make Me a Servant" (John)
SP193
S2179 "Live in Charity" ("Ubi Caritas") (John)
R226
S2222 "The Servant Song" (John)
R148, SP193
S2223 "They'll Know We Are Christians by Our Love" (John)
S2198 "Stay With Me" ("Nohu pū") (Holy Thursday)
UM620 "One Bread, One Body" (Communion)

Vocal Solos

"Wondrous Love" (John)
V-6 p. 47
"O the Deep, Deep Love of Jesus" (John, Communion)
V-8 p. 247

Anthems

"Jesus So Lowly" (John)
Harold Friedell; H.W. Gray CMR 2018
SATB *a cappella*

"Seek to Serve" (John)
Lloyd Pfautsch; Hope APM 003
Two-part mixed with keyboard

Other Suggestions

Visuals:
O Lamb, sandals, staff, Passover meal
P Cup or goblet, open manacles
E Bread/wine/pottery chalice, Passover meal
G Passover meal, outer garment, towel/basin/water/pitcher, twelve disciples, Last Supper, stripping of the altar, darkness

Suggested Service of Worship: BOW351 (Holy Thursday)
Greeting: BOW344 or BOW455 (1 Cor., John)
Opening Prayer: BOW460 (John)
Prayer of Confession: BOW491 (John)
Prayer: BOW349 or BOW511 (John)
Prayer: UM283. Holy Thursday (John, 1 Cor.)
Prayer: UM639. Bread and Justice (John)
Response: BOW187. "Jesus, We Are Here" (John)
Great Thanksgiving for Holy Thursday: BOW, p. 64
Blessing: BOW563 (John)

Isaiah 52:13–53:12

[13] See, my servant shall prosper; he shall be exalted and lifted up, and shall be very high. [14] Just as there were many who were astonished at him—so marred was his appearance, beyond human semblance, and his form beyond that of mortals— [15] so he shall startle many nations; kings shall shut their mouths because of him; for that which had not been told them they shall see, and that which they had not heard they shall contemplate.

[1] Who has believed what we have heard? And to whom has the arm of the LORD been revealed? [2] For he grew up before him like a young plant, and like a root out of dry ground; he had no form or majesty that we should look at him, nothing in his appearance that we should desire him. [3] He was despised and rejected by others; a man of suffering and acquainted with infirmity; and as one from whom others hide their faces he was despised, and we held him of no account. [4] Surely he has borne our infirmities and carried our diseases; yet we accounted him stricken, struck down by God, and afflicted. [5] But he was wounded for our transgressions, crushed for our iniquities; upon him was the punishment that made us whole, and by his bruises we are healed. [6] All we like sheep have gone astray; we have all turned to our own way, and the LORD has laid on him the iniquity of us all. [7] He was oppressed, and he was afflicted, yet he did not open his mouth; like a lamb that is led to the slaughter, and like a sheep that before its shearers is silent, so he did not open his mouth. [8] By a perversion of justice he was taken away. Who could have imagined his future? For he was cut off from the land of the living, stricken for the transgression of my people. [9] They made his grave with the wicked and his tomb with the rich, although he had done no violence, and there was no deceit in his mouth. [10] Yet it was the will of the LORD to crush him with pain. When you make his life an offering for sin, he shall see his offspring, and shall prolong his days; through him the will of the LORD shall prosper. [11] Out of his anguish he shall see light; he shall find satisfaction through his knowledge. The righteous one, my servant, shall make many righteous, and he shall bear their iniquities. [12] Therefore I will allot him a portion with the great, and he shall divide the spoil with the strong; because he poured out himself to death, and was numbered with the transgressors; yet he bore the sin of many, and made intercession for the transgressors.

Psalm 22

[1] My God, my God, why have you forsaken me? Why are you so far from helping me, from the words of my groaning? [2] O my God, I cry by day, but you do not answer; and by night, but find no rest. [3] Yet you are holy, enthroned on the praises of Israel. [4] In you our ancestors trusted; they trusted, and you delivered them. [5] To you they cried, and were saved; in you they trusted, and were not put to shame. [6] But I am a worm, and not human; scorned by others, and despised by the people. [7] All who see me mock at me; they make mouths at me, they shake their heads; [8] "Commit your cause to the LORD; let him deliver—let him rescue the one in whom he delights!" [9] Yet it was you who took me from the womb; you kept me safe on my mother's breast. [10] On you I was cast from my birth, and since my mother bore me you have been my God. [11] Do not be far from me, for trouble is near and there is no one to help. [12] Many bulls encircle me, strong bulls of Bashan surround me; [13] they open wide their mouths at me, like a ravening and roaring lion. [14] I am poured out like water, and all my bones are out of joint; my heart is like wax; it is melted within my breast; [15] my mouth is dried up like a potsherd, and my tongue sticks to my jaws; you lay me in the dust of death. [16] For dogs are all around me; a company of evildoers encircles me. My hands and feet have shriveled; [17] I can count all my bones. They stare and gloat over me; [18] they divide my clothes among themselves, and for my clothing they cast lots. [19] But you, O LORD, do not be far away! O my help, come quickly to my aid! [20] Deliver my soul from the sword, my life from the power of the dog! [21] Save me from the mouth of the lion! From the horns of the wild oxen you have rescued me. [22] I will tell of your name to my brothers and sisters; in the midst of the congregation I will praise you: [23] You who fear the LORD, praise him! All you offspring of Jacob, glorify him; stand in awe of him, all you offspring of Israel! [24] For he did not despise or abhor the affliction of the afflicted; he did not hide his face from me, but heard when I cried to him. [25] From you comes my praise in the great congregation; my vows I will pay before those who fear him. [26] The poor shall eat and be satisfied; those who seek him shall praise the LORD. May your hearts live forever! [27] All the ends of the earth shall remember and turn to the LORD; and all the families of the nations shall worship before him. [28] For dominion belongs to the LORD, and he rules over the nations. [29] To him, indeed, shall all who sleep in the earth bow down; before him shall bow all who go down to the dust, and I shall live for him. [30] Posterity will serve him; future generations will be told about the Lord, [31] and proclaim his deliverance to a people yet unborn, saying that he has done it.

Hebrews 10:16-25

[16] "This is the covenant that I will make with them after those days, says the Lord: I will put my laws in their hearts, and I will write them on their minds," [17] he also adds, "I will remember their sins and their lawless deeds no more." [18] Where there is forgiveness of these, there is no longer any offering for sin.

[19] Therefore, my friends, since we have confidence to enter the sanctuary by the blood of Jesus, [20] by the new and living way that he opened for us through the curtain (that is, through his flesh), [21] and since we have a great

priest over the house of God, 22 let us approach with a true
heart in full assurance of faith, with our hearts sprinkled
clean from an evil conscience and our bodies washed with
pure water. 23 Let us hold fast to the confession of our hope
without wavering, for he who has promised is faithful. 24 And
let us consider how to provoke one another to love and
good deeds, 25 not neglecting to meet together, as is the
habit of some, but encouraging one another, and all the
more as you see the Day approaching.

John 18:1–19:42

1 After Jesus had spoken these words, he went out with
his disciples across the Kidron valley to a place where there
was a garden, which he and his disciples entered. 2 Now
Judas, who betrayed him, also knew the place, because
Jesus often met there with his disciples. 3 So Judas brought
a detachment of soldiers together with police from the
chief priests and the Pharisees, and they came there with
lanterns and torches and weapons. 4 Then Jesus, knowing
all that was to happen to him, came forward and asked
them, "Whom are you looking for?" 5 They answered,
"Jesus of Nazareth." Jesus replied, "I am he." Judas, who
betrayed him, was standing with them. 6 When Jesus said to
them, "I am he," they stepped back and fell to the ground.
7 Again he asked them, "Whom are you looking for?" And
they said, "Jesus of Nazareth." 8 Jesus answered, "I told you
that I am he. So if you are looking for me, let these men
go." 9 This was to fulfill the word that he had spoken, "I did
not lose a single one of those whom you gave me." 10 Then
Simon Peter, who had a sword, drew it, struck the high
priest's slave, and cut off his right ear. The slave's name
was Malchus. 11 Jesus said to Peter, "Put your sword back
into its sheath. Am I not to drink the cup that the Father
has given me?"

12 So the soldiers, their officer, and the Jewish police
arrested Jesus and bound him. 13 First they took him to
Annas, who was the father-in-law of Caiaphas, the high
priest that year. 14 Caiaphas was the one who had advised
the Jews that it was better to have one person die for the
people.

15 Simon Peter and another disciple followed Jesus. Since
that disciple was known to the high priest, he went with
Jesus into the courtyard of the high priest, 16 but Peter was
standing outside at the gate. So the other disciple, who was
known to the high priest, went out, spoke to the woman
who guarded the gate, and brought Peter in. 17 The woman
said to Peter, "You are not also one of this man's disciples,
are you?" He said, "I am not." 18 Now the slaves and the
police had made a charcoal fire because it was cold, and
they were standing around it and warming themselves.
Peter also was standing with them and warming himself.

19 Then the high priest questioned Jesus about his disci-
ples and about his teaching. 20 Jesus answered, "I have spo-
ken openly to the world; I have always taught in syna-
gogues and in the temple, where all the Jews come togeth-
er. I have said nothing in secret. 21 Why do you ask me? Ask
those who heard what I said to them; they know what I
said." 22 When he had said this, one of the police standing
nearby struck Jesus on the face, saying, "Is that how you
answer the high priest?" 23 Jesus answered, "If I have spo-
ken wrongly, testify to the wrong. But if I have spoken
rightly, why do you strike me?" 24 Then Annas sent him
bound to Caiaphas the high priest.

25 Now Simon Peter was standing and warming himself.
They asked him, "You are not also one of his disciples, are
you?" He denied it and said, "I am not." 26 One of the
slaves of the high priest, a relative of the man whose ear
Peter had cut off, asked, "Did I not see you in the garden
with him?" 27 Again Peter denied it, and at that moment the
cock crowed.

28 Then they took Jesus from Caiaphas to Pilate's head-
quarters. It was early in the morning. They themselves did
not enter the headquarters, so as to avoid ritual defilement
and to be able to eat the Passover. 29 So Pilate went out to
them and said, "What accusation do you bring against this
man?" 30 They answered, "If this man were not a criminal,
we would not have handed him over to you." 31 Pilate said
to them, "Take him yourselves and judge him according to
your law." The Jews replied, "We are not permitted to put
anyone to death." 32 (This was to fulfill what Jesus had said
when he indicated the kind of death he was to die.)

33 Then Pilate entered the headquarters again, sum-
moned Jesus, and asked him, "Are you the King of the
Jews?" 34 Jesus answered, "Do you ask this on your own, or
did others tell you about me?" 35 Pilate replied, "I am not a
Jew, am I? Your own nation and the chief priests have
handed you over to me. What have you done?" 36 Jesus
answered, "My kingdom is not from this world. If my king-
dom were from this world, my followers would be fighting
to keep me from being handed over to the Jews. But as it
is, my kingdom is not from here." 37 Pilate asked him, "So
you are a king?" Jesus answered, "You say that I am a king.
For this I was born, and for this I came into the world, to
testify to the truth. Everyone who belongs to the truth lis-
tens to my voice." 38 Pilate asked him, "What is truth?"

After he had said this, he went out to the Jews again and
told them, "I find no case against him. 39 But you have a
custom that I release someone for you at the Passover. Do
you want me to release for you the King of the Jews?"
40 They shouted in reply, "Not this man, but Barabbas!"
Now Barabbas was a bandit.

1 Then Pilate took Jesus and had him flogged. 2 And the
soldiers wove a crown of thorns and put it on his head, and
they dressed him in a purple robe. 3 They kept coming up
to him, saying, "Hail, King of the Jews!" and striking him
on the face. 4 Pilate went out again and said to them,
"Look, I am bringing him out to you to let you know that I
find no case against him." 5 So Jesus came out, wearing the
crown of thorns and the purple robe. Pilate said to them,

"Here is the man!" 6 When the chief priest and the police
saw him, they shouted, "Crucify him! Crucify him!" Pilate
said to them, "Take him yourselves and crucify him; I find
no case against him." 7 The Jews answered him, "We have a
law, and according to that law he ought to die because he
has claimed to be the Son of God."
8 Now when Pilate heard this, he was more afraid than
ever. 9 He entered his headquarters again and asked Jesus,
"Where are you from?" But Jesus gave him no answer.
10 Pilate therefore said to him, "Do you refuse to speak to
me? Do you not know that I have power to release you,
and power to crucify you?" 11 Jesus answered him, "You
would have no power over me unless it had been given
you from above; therefore the one who handed me over
to you is guilty of a greater sin." 12 From then on Pilate
tried to release him, but the Jews cried out, "If you release
this man, you are no friend of the emperor. Everyone who
claims to be a king sets himself against the emperor."
13 When Pilate heard these words, he brought Jesus out-
side and sat on the judge's bench at a place called The
Stone Pavement, or in Hebrew Gabbatha. 14 Now it was the
day of Preparation for the Passover; and it was about
noon. He said to the Jews, "Here is your King!" 15 They
cried out, "Away with him! Away with him! Crucify him!"
Pilate asked them, "Shall I crucify your King?" The chief
priests answered, "We have no king but the emperor."
16 Then he handed him over to them to be crucified.
So they took Jesus; 17 and carrying the cross by himself,
he went out to what is called The Place of the Skull, which
in Hebrew is called Golgotha. 18 There they crucified him,
and with him two others, one on either side, with Jesus
between them. 19 Pilate also had an inscription written and
put on the cross. It read, "Jesus of Nazareth, the King of
the Jews." 20 Many of the Jews read this inscription,
because the place where Jesus was crucified was near the
city; and it was written in Hebrew, in Latin, and in Greek.
21 Then the chief priests of the Jews said to Pilate, "Do not
write, 'The King of the Jews,' but, 'This man said, I am
King of the Jews.' " 22 Pilate answered, "What I have writ-
ten I have written." 23 When the soldiers had crucified
Jesus, they took his clothes and divided them into four
parts, one for each soldier. They also took his tunic; now
the tunic was seamless, woven in one piece from the top.
24 So they said to one another, "Let us not tear it, but cast
lots for it to see who will get it." This was to fulfill what the
scripture says, "They divided my clothes among them-
selves, and for my clothing they cast lots." 25 And that is
what the soldiers did.
Meanwhile, standing near the cross of Jesus were his
mother, and his mother's sister, Mary the wife of Clopas,
and Mary Magdalene. 26 When Jesus saw his mother and
the disciple whom he loved standing beside her, he said to
his mother, "Woman, here is your son." 27 Then he said to
the disciple, "Here is your mother." And from that hour
the disciple took her into his own home.
28 After this, when Jesus knew that all was now finished,
he said (in order to fulfill the scripture), "I am thirsty."
29 A jar full of sour wine was standing there. So they put a
sponge full of the wine on a branch of hyssop and held it
to his mouth. 30 When Jesus had received the wine, he
said, "It is finished." Then he bowed his head and gave up
his spirit.
31 Since it was the day of Preparation, the Jews did not
want the bodies left on the cross during the sabbath, espe-
cially because that sabbath was a day of great solemnity. So
they asked Pilate to have the legs of the crucified men bro-
ken and the bodies removed. 32 Then the soldiers came
and broke the legs of the first and of the other who had
been crucified with him. 33 But when they came to Jesus
and saw that he was already dead, they did not break his
legs. 34 Instead, one of the soldiers pierced his side with a
spear, and at once blood and water came out. 35 (He who
saw this has testified so that you also may believe. His testi-
mony is true, and he knows that he tells the truth.) 36
These things occurred so that the scripture might be ful-
filled, "None of his bones shall be broken."
37 And again another passage of scripture says, "They will
look on the one whom they have pierced."
38 After these things, Joseph of Arimathea, who was a dis-
ciple of Jesus, though a secret one because of his fear of
the Jews, asked Pilate to let him take away the body of
Jesus. Pilate gave him permission; so he came and
removed his body. 39 Nicodemus, who had at first come to
Jesus by night, also came, bringing a mixture of myrrh
and aloes, weighing about a hundred pounds. 40 They took
the body of Jesus and wrapped it with the spices in linen
cloths, according to the burial custom of the Jews.
41 Now there was a garden in the place where he was cruci-
fied, and in the garden there was a new tomb in which no
one had ever been laid. 42 And so, because it was the
Jewish day of Preparation, and the tomb was nearby, they
laid Jesus there.

Notes:

Primary Hymns and Songs for the Day

288 "Were You There" (John) (O)
  H-3 Handbell-101; Choir-209
  S-2 #195-96. Descant/harmonization
165 "Hallelujah! What a Savior" (Isa.)
  H-3 Choir-134
286 "O Sacred Head, Now Wounded" (John)
  H-3 Handbell-82; Choir-148; Descant-86; Organ-111
298 "When I Survey the Wondrous Cross" (John) (C)
  H-3 Handbell-6, 102; Choir-213; Descant-49; Organ-49
  S-1 #155. Descant

Hymn Suggestions

359 "Alas! and Did My Savior Bleed" (John) (O)
294 "Alas! and Did My Savior Bleed" (John) (O)
291 "He Never Said a Mumbalin' Word" (Isa., John)
2180 "Why Stand So Far Away, My God?" (Ps., John)
289 "Ah, Holy Jesus" (Heb.)
419 "I Am Thine, O Lord" (Heb.)
472 "Near to the Heart of God" (Heb.)
640 "Take Our Bread" (Heb., Communion)
2140 "Since Jesus Came Into My Heart" (Heb.)
2259 "Victim Divine" (Heb., Communion)
274 "Woman in the Night" (John)
282 " 'Tis Finished! The Messiah Dies" (John)
285 "To Mock Your Reign, O Dearest Lord" (John)
287 "O Love Divine, What Hast Thou Done" (John)
290 "Go to Dark Gethsemane" (John)
470 "My God, I Love Thee" (John)
633 "The Bread of Life for All Is Broken" (John, Communion)
2100 "Thou Didst Leave Thy Throne" (John)
2106 "When Jesus Wept" (John)
2110 "Why Has God Forsaken Me?" (John)
2111 "We Sang Our Glad Hosannas" (John)
2219 "Goodness Is Stronger than Evil" (Good Friday)
295 "In the Cross of Christ I Glory" (John) (C)

Contemporary Suggestions

SP64 "Our God Reigns" (Isa.)
M35 "White as Snow"
MM65 "Before the Throne of God Above" (Heb.)
MM81 "Amazing Love" (Heb., John)
  R272
MM82 "You Are My King" ("Amazing Love") (Heb., John)
  WY65
MM106 "I Come to the Cross" (Heb., John)
WG142 "This Is Love" (Heb., Good Friday)
S2108 "O How He Loves You and Me!" (John)
  R27, SP113
UM261 "Lord of the Dance" (John)
UM488 "Jesus, Remember Me" (John)
  R227
M24 "Jesus, We Crown You with Praise" (John)
MM77 "Above All" (John)
  WO2; V-3 p. 17 or V-10(03) p. 18 (vocal solo)
WO120 "Redeemer, Savior, Friend" (John)
WO173 "You Are God" (John)

Vocal Solos

"He Was Despised" from Messiah (Isa.)
"He Was Cut Off Out of the Land of the Living" (recitative)
"But Thou Didst Not Leave His Soul in Hell" (aria)
V-2
"Ah, Holy Jesus" (Isa., John)
V-6 p. 24
"Look What You've Done" (Heb.)
V-3 p. 122
" 'Tis Finished! The Messiah Dies" (John)
V-1 p. 63
"Were You There?" (John)
V-7 p. 60

Anthems

"Lamb of God" (John, Good Friday)
Matthew Everett; Kjos 9037
SAATB, soprano solo, with piano

"Agnus Dei" (John, Good Friday)
Paul Basler; Walton Music HL08501577
SATB with piano

Other Suggestions

Visuals:
Black draping the cross, black paraments, or none
  O Plant, root, suffering, crucifix, lamb, darkness/light,
  P Exodus, mother breastfeeding, water, bones, sword, dog
  E Heb. 10:16*b*, crucifix
  G Sword, charcoal fire, cock crowing, whip, purple robe, rugged cross, tunic, crucifix, nails, crown of thorns, ladder, sponge on branch, spear, shroud
Introit: S2199. "Stay with Us" (John)
Greeting: BOW329 (Heb.)
Prayer of Confession: BOW491 (John)
Response: S2113. "Lamb of God" (John)
Prayer: UM284 or BOW335 or BOW337 (John)
Reading of Seven Last Words: BOW365
Suggestions for Way of the Cross: BOW366
Reading: UM293. "Behold the Savior of Mankind" (John)
Scripture Response: UM290. "Go to Dark Gethsemane." Use this hymn to supplement the reading from John. Sing stanza 1 before beginning 18:1. Sing stanza 2 after 19:3. Sing stanza 3 after 19:30. Sing UM288, stanza 5 at the conclusion of the reading.
Dismissal: BOW559 (John)

Acts 10:34-43

34 Then Peter began to speak to them: "I truly under-
stand that God shows no partiality, 35 but in every nation
anyone who fears him and does what is right is acceptable
to him. 36 You know the message he sent to the people of
Israel, preaching peace by Jesus Christ—he is Lord of all.
37 That message spread throughout Judea, beginning in
Galilee after the baptism that John announced: 38 how
God anointed Jesus of Nazareth with the Holy Spirit and
with power; how he went about doing good and healing
all who were oppressed by the devil, for God was with him.
39 We are witnesses to all that he did both in Judea and in
Jerusalem. They put him to death by hanging him on a
tree; 40 but God raised him on the third day and allowed
him to appear, 41 not to all the people but to us who were
chosen by God as witnesses, and who ate and drank with
him after he rose from the dead. 42 He commanded us to
preach to the people and to testify that he is the one
ordained by God as judge of the living and the dead. 43 All
the prophets testify about him that everyone who believes
in him receives forgiveness of sins through his name."

Psalm 118:1-2, 14-24

1 O give thanks to the LORD, for he is good; his steadfast
love endures forever! 2 Let Israel say, "His steadfast love
endures forever."

14 The LORD is my strength and my might; he has
become my salvation. 15 There are glad songs of victory in
the tents of the righteous: "The right hand of the LORD
does valiantly; 16 the right hand of the LORD is exalted; the
right hand of the LORD does valiantly." 17 I shall not die,
but I shall live, and recount the deeds of the LORD. 18 The
LORD has punished me severely, but he did not give me
over to death. 19 Open to me the gates of righteousness,
that I may enter through them and give thanks to the
LORD. 20 This is the gate of the LORD; the righteous shall
enter through it. 21 I thank you that you have answered me
and have become my salvation. 22 The stone that the
builders rejected has become the chief cornerstone.
23 This is the LORD's doing; it is marvelous in our eyes.
24 This is the day that the LORD has made; let us rejoice
and be glad in it.

1 Corinthians 15:1-11

1 Now I would remind you, brothers and sisters, of the
good news that I proclaimed to you, which you in turn
received, in which also you stand, 2 through which also you
are being saved, if you hold firmly to the message that I
proclaimed to you—unless you have come to believe in
vain.

3 For I handed on to you as of first importance what I in
turn had received: that Christ died for our sins in accor-
dance with the scriptures, 4 and that he was buried, and
that he was raised on the third day in accordance with the
scriptures, 5 and that he appeared to Cephas, then to the
twelve. 6 Then he appeared to more than five hundred
brothers and sisters at one time, most of whom are still
alive, though some have died. 7 Then he appeared to
James, then to all the apostles. 8 Last of all, as to one
untimely born, he appeared also to me. 9 For I am the
least of the apostles, unfit to be called an apostle, because
I persecuted the church of God. 10 But by the grace of
God I am what I am, and his grace toward me has not
been in vain. On the contrary, I worked harder than any
of them—though it was not I, but the grace of God that is
with me. 11 Whether then it was I or they, so we proclaim
and so you have come to believe.

John 20:1-18 (or Mark 16:1-8)

1 Early on the first day of the week, while it was still dark,
Mary Magdalene came to the tomb and saw that the stone
had been removed from the tomb. 2 So she ran and went
to Simon Peter and the other disciple, the one whom
Jesus loved, and said to them, "They have taken the Lord
out of the tomb, and we do not know where they have laid
him." 3 Then Peter and the other disciple set out and went
toward the tomb. 4 The two were running together, but
the other disciple outran Peter and reached the tomb
first. 5 He bent down to look in and saw the linen wrap-
pings lying there, but he did not go in. 6 Then Simon
Peter came, following him, and went into the tomb. He
saw the linen wrappings lying there, 7 and the cloth that
had been on Jesus' head, not lying with the linen wrap-
pings but rolled up in a place by itself. 8 Then the other
disciple, who reached the tomb first, also went in, and he
saw and believed; 9 for as yet they did not understand the
scripture, that he must rise from the dead. 10 Then the dis-
ciples returned to their homes.

11 But Mary stood weeping outside the tomb. As she
wept, she bent over to look into the tomb; 12 and she saw
two angels in white, sitting where the body of Jesus had
been lying, one at the head and the other at the feet.
13 They said to her, "Woman, why are you weeping?" She
said to them, "They have taken away my Lord, and I do
not know where they have laid him." 14 When she had said
this, she turned around and saw Jesus standing there, but
she did not know that it was Jesus. 15 Jesus said to her,
"Woman, why are you weeping? Whom are you looking
for?" Supposing him to be the gardener, she said to him,
"Sir, if you have carried him away, tell me where you have
laid him, and I will take him away." 16 Jesus said to her,
"Mary!" She turned and said to him in Hebrew,
"Rabbouni!" (which means Teacher). 17 Jesus said to her,
"Do not hold on to me, because I have not yet ascended
to the Father. But go to my brothers and say to them, 'I
am ascending to my Father and your Father, to my God
and your God.' " 18 Mary Magdalene went and announced
to the disciples, "I have seen the Lord"; and she told them
that he had said these things to her.

Primary Hymns and Songs for the Day

302 "Christ the Lord Is Risen Today" (1 Cor., John) (O)
  H-3 Handbell-8, 51; Choir-49; Descant-31; Organ-32
  S-1 #104-8. Various treatments
2115 "Christ Has Risen" (1 Cor., John)
327 "Crown Him with Many Crowns" (John) (C)
  H-3 Handbell-55; Choir-60; Descant-30; Organ-27
  S-1 #86-88. Various treatments

Hymn Suggestions

304 "Easter People, Raise Your Voices" (1 Cor., John)
610 "We Know That Christ Is Raised" (Acts, Baptism)
2043 "Alleluia" (Ps.)
2084 "Come, Let Us with Our Lord Arise" (Ps., John)
2267 "Taste and See" (Ps., Communion)
257 "We Meet You, O Christ" (Acts)
303 "The Day of Resurrection" (1 Cor., John)
306 "The Strife Is O'er, the Battle Done" (1 Cor.)
307 "Christ Is Risen" (1 Cor., John, Communion)
310 "He Lives" (1 Cor., John)
313 "Cristo Vive" ("Christ Is Risen") (1 Cor., John)
394 "Something Beautiful" (1 Cor.)
2116 "Christ the Lord Is Risen" (John)
134 "O Mary, Don't You Weep" (John)
274 "Woman in the Night" (John, Mark)
308 "Thine Be the Glory" (John)
309 "On the Day of Resurrection" (John, Communion)
314 "In the Garden" (John)
317 "O Sons and Daughters, Let Us Sing" (John, Mark)
318 "Christ Is Alive" (Mark)
319 "Christ Jesus Lay in Death's Strong Bands" (Mark)
322 "Up from the Grave He Arose" (Mark)
364 "Because He Lives" (Mark)
2111 "We Sang Our Glad Hosannas" (John)
2242 "Walk with Me" (John, Mark)
702 "Sing with All the Saints in Glory" (1 Cor.) (C)

Contemporary Suggestions

WO53 "Holy and Anointed One" (Acts)
  M32
MM68 "Forever" (Ps.)
  WY57
UM84 "Thank You, Lord" (Ps.)
S2270 "I Will Enter His Gates" (Ps.)
S2162 "Grace Alone" (1 Cor.)
S2088 "Lord, I Lift Your Name on High" (1 Cor., John)
S2077 "You Alone Are Holy" (John)
S2116 "Christ the Lord Is Risen" (John, Mark)
S2219 "Goodness Is Stronger than Evil" (Easter)
S2258 "Sing Alleluia to the Lord" (John, Mark, Easter)
SP64 "Our God Reigns" (John)
WO19 "Celebrate Jesus" (John)
WO108 "Jesus Is Alive" (John)
WY25 "I Can Only Imagine" (John)
  V-3 p. 8 (vocal solo)
UM186 "Alleluia" (Easter)
  S2078 (alternate text and tune)
M20 "Jesus Is Alive" (Easter)
M21 "Blessing, Honor and Glory" (Easter)
  R81
MM94 "That's Why We Praise Him" (Easter)
  WG122
MM73 "My Redeemer Lives" (Easter)
  WG98
WY90 "Redeemer" (Easter)

Vocal Solos

"Jesus Christ Is Risen Today" (John)
V-1 p. 50
"I Know That My Redeemer Liveth" (Easter)
V-2
"Ten Thousand Angels" (Easter)
V-8 p. 218
"The First Day of My Life" (Easter)
V-9 p. 22

Anthems

"Alleluia" (John)
Doug Andrews; Brookfield Press 08745352
SATB with keyboard

"Easter Alleluia!" (John)
Mark A. Miller; Abingdon Press 9780687644209
SATB with piano (opt. children's choir)

Other Suggestions

Visuals:
  O (Acts) Crucifixion/Resurrection, Acts 10:39*a*
  P Cornerstone
  E Butterfly, empty tomb, open Bible, empty cross in shroud
  G Basket of spices, stone, angels, shroud, risen Christ
Introit: S2026. "Halle, Halle, Halleluja" (Easter)
Introit: UM324. "Hail Thee, Festival Day" (Mark)
Greeting: BOW386 (John)
Opening Prayer: BOW394 (1 Cor.)
Affirmation of Faith: UM888 (1 Cor.)
Response: S2039, st. 5. "Holy, Holy" (Easter)
Prayer of Intercession: BOW399, Week 1 (Easter)
Prayer of Thanksgiving and Intercession: BOW395 (John)
Great Thanksgiving for Easter Day: BOW66
Response: S2081, BOW203. "Thank You, Jesus" (Ps.)
Dismissal With Blessing: BOW376 (John)
Hymns Appropriate for Sunrise Service with Guitar:
  "Morning Has Broken" (UM145) (Easter)
  "Lord of the Dance" (UM261) (Acts)
  "The First One Ever" (UM276) (John)
  "This Is the Day" (UM657, SP236) (Ps.)
  "Spirit Song" (UM347, R248, SP134) (Acts, John)
Benediction: S2072. "Amen, Amen" (Easter)

Happylujah!

Simple musical fun for your smallest singers

Written specifically for pre-readers, this collection offers your tiny, yet enthusiastic singers a wide variety of musical styles including: traditional, praise and global worship and movement songs, hymns, and spirituals.

Happylujah! also offers ease for you—with loads of practical helps, created by specialists who teach songs to young children every week in choirs and Sunday schools.

- The Happylujah! Leader & Accompanist Book
  - —Teaching tips
  - —Full piano and vocal scores
  - —Guitar chords
  - —Rhythm and singing games
  - —Guidance for rehearsals
  - —A handy index
  - —Suggestions for how to use each song in a worship or educational setting
- The *Happylujah!* Listening & Accompaniment 2-CD Set
  Split-tracks of all songs, recorded with children's voices and piano accompaniment to encourage the children to add rhythm instruments, clapping, and movement.

Book & CD Set. CA8-9780687651948. $75.00
Leader & Accompanist Book. CA8-9780687643127. $35.00
Listening & Accompaniment 2-CD Set. CA8-9780687643226. $40.00

Songs and Activities for Children Ages 4–6

Double-Take!

A Christmas Pageant as Told by Matthew and Luke

Dennis Hartin

The Story of the birth of Christ told with humor, mystery, and awe. Did you know that the Bible actually tells the story from two different perspectives? Matthew's version has no shepherds and no choir of angels, and Herod is a major character. Luke's version has no wise men and no Herod, and Joseph (the protagonist in Matthew's version) is mute. Other differences abound.

In *Double Take,* we are presented with both versions: Matthew's in Act 1 and Luke's in Acts 2 and 3. Most Christmas musicals contain characters from both versions.

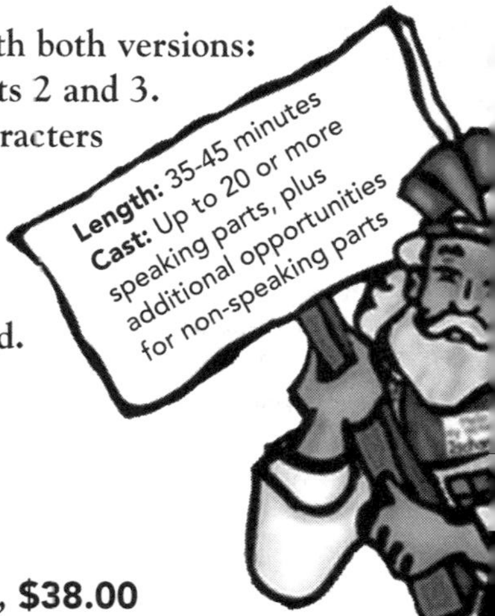

- Reproducible script & song texts
- Audio CD in split-track format.
- Only two full cast rehearsals needed.
- Flexible staging.
- Vocal/piano scores included.
- Appropriate for all ages!

Abingdon Press.
CA8-9780687651887. Spiral-bound, **$38.00**

Acts 4:32-35

32 Now the whole group of those who believed were of one heart and soul, and no one claimed private ownership of any possessions, but everything they owned was held in common. 33 With great power the apostles gave their testimony to the resurrection of the Lord Jesus, and great grace was upon them all. 34 There was not a needy person among them, for as many as owned lands or houses sold them and brought the proceeds of what was sold. 35 They laid it at the apostles' feet, and it was distributed to each as any had need.

Psalm 133

1 How very good and pleasant it is when kindred live together in unity! 2 It is like the precious oil on the head, running down upon the beard, on the beard of Aaron, running down over the collar of his robes. 3 It is like the dew of Hermon, which falls on the mountains of Zion. For there the LORD ordained his blessing, life forevermore.

---

1 John 1:1–2:2

1 We declare to you what was from the beginning, what we have heard, what we have seen with our eyes, what we have looked at and touched with our hands, concerning the word of life— 2 this life was revealed, and we have seen it and testify to it, and declare to you the eternal life that was with the Father and was revealed to us— 3 we declare to you what we have seen and heard so that you also may have fellowship with us; and truly our fellowship is with the Father and with his Son Jesus Christ. 4 We are writing these things so that our joy may be complete.

5 This is the message we have heard from him and proclaim to you, that God is light and in him there is no darkness at all. 6 If we say that we have fellowship with him while we are walking in darkness, we lie and do not do what is true; 7 but if we walk in the light as he himself is in the light, we have fellowship with one another, and the blood of Jesus his Son cleanses us from all sin. 8 If we say that we have no sin, we deceive ourselves, and the truth is not in us. 9 If we confess our sins, he who is faithful and just will forgive us our sins and cleanse us from all unrighteousness. 10 If we say that we have not sinned, we make him a liar, and his word is not in us.

1 My little children, I am writing these things to you so that you may not sin. But if anyone does sin, we have an advocate with the Father, Jesus Christ the righteous; 2 and he is the atoning sacrifice for our sins, and not for ours only but also for the sins of the whole world.

John 20:19-31

19 When it was evening on that day, the first day of the week, and the doors of the house where the disciples had met were locked for fear of the Jews, Jesus came and stood among them and said, "Peace be with you." 20 After he said this, he showed them his hands and his side. Then the disciples rejoiced when they saw the Lord. 21 Jesus said to them again, "Peace be with you. As the Father has sent me, so I send you." 22 When he had said this, he breathed on them and said to them, "Receive the Holy Spirit. 23 If you forgive the sins of any, they are forgiven them; if you retain the sins of any, they are retained."

24 But Thomas (who was called the Twin), one of the twelve, was not with them when Jesus came. 25 So the other disciples told him, "We have seen the Lord." But he said to them, "Unless I see the mark of the nails in his hands, and put my finger in the mark of the nails and my hand in his side, I will not believe."

26 A week later his disciples were again in the house, and Thomas was with them. Although the doors were shut, Jesus came and stood among them and said, "Peace be with you." 27 Then he said to Thomas, "Put your finger here and see my hands. Reach out your hand and put it in my side. Do not doubt but believe." 28 Thomas answered him, "My Lord and my God!" 29 Jesus said to him, "Have you believed because you have seen me? Blessed are those who have not seen and yet have come to believe."

30 Now Jesus did many other signs in the presence of his disciples, which are not written in this book. 31 But these are written so that you may come to believe that Jesus is the Messiah, the Son of God, and that through believing you may have life in his name.

Notes:

Primary Hymns and Songs for the Day

307 "Christ Is Risen" (John) (O)
H-3 Choir-113; Descant-102; Organ-171
S-1 #345. Handbell/keyboard arrangement
2231 "O Look and Wonder" ("Miren Que Bueno!") (Ps.)
420 "Breathe on Me, Breath of God" (John)
H-3 Handbell-49; Choir-45; Descant-101; Organ-166
2196 "We Walk by Faith" (John)
H-3 Choir-21
2206 "Without Seeing You" (John)
206 "I Want to Walk as a Child of the Light" (1 John) (C)
S-2 #91. Descant

Hymn Suggestions

547 "O Church of God, United" (Acts)
552 "Here, O Lord, Your Servants Gather" (Acts)
554 "All Praise to Our Redeeming Lord" (Acts)
555 "Forward Through the Ages" (Acts)
560 "Help Us Accept Each Other" (Acts)
561 "Jesus, United by Thy Grace" (Acts)
562 "Jesus, Lord, We Look to Thee" (Acts)
566 "Blest Be the Dear Uniting Love" (Acts)
407 "Close to Thee" (1 John)
467 "Trust and Obey" (1 John)
605 "Wash, O God, Our Sons and Daughters" (1 John)
608 "This Is the Spirit's Entry Now" (1 John, Baptism)
632 "Draw Us in the Spirit's Tether" (1 John, Comm.)
2149 "Living for Jesus" (1 John)
2158 "Just a Closer Walk with Thee" (1 John)
2172 "We Are Called" (1 John)
2214 "Lead Me, Guide Me" (1 John)
2242 "Walk with Me" (1 John, John)
2259 "Victim Divine" (1 John, Communion)
336 "Of All the Spirit's Gifts to Me" (John)
355 "Depth of Mercy" (John)
384 "Love Divine, All Loves Excelling" (John)
420 "Breathe on Me, Breath of God" (John)
462 " 'Tis So Sweet to Trust in Jesus" (John)
465 "Holy Spirit, Truth Divine" (John)
475 "Come Down, O Love Divine" (John)
503 "Let It Breathe on Me" (John)
543 "O Breath of Life" (John)
623 "Here, O My Lord, I See Thee" (John, Communion)
636 "Christian People, Raise Your Song" (John, Communion)
2046 "Womb of Life" (John)
2114 "At the Font We Start Our Journey" (John, Baptism)
2117 "Spirit of God" (John)
2187 "Now It Is Evening" (John)
2211 "Faith Is Patience in the Night" (John)
557 "Blest Be the Tie That Binds" (Acts) (C)

Contemporary Suggestions

UM558 "We Are the Church" (Acts)
S2161 "Grace Alone" (Acts)
S2204 "Light of the World" (1 John)
S2235 "We Are Marching" ("Siyahamba") (1 John)
WY139 "Here I Am to Worship" (1 John)
S2039 "Holy, Holy" (1 John)
S2073 "Celebrate Love" (1 John, Easter)
MM82 "You Are My King" ("Amazing Love") (1 John)
WY65
S2086 "Open Our Eyes, Lord" (John)
S2119 "Where the Spirit of the Lord Is" (John)
M26 "The Power of Your Love" (John)
WG133
WG142 "This Is Love" (John)
WO68 "I Believe In Jesus" (John)
WO68
WO78 "I Walk By Faith" (John)
UM328 "Surely the Presence of the Lord" (John)
R167, SP243; S-2, #200 (stanzas for soloist)
UM376 "Dona Nobis Pacem" (John)

Vocal Solos

"Just a Closer Walk with Thee" (1 John)
V-8 p. 323
"I Know That My Redeemer Liveth" (John, Easter)
V-2

Anthems

"Hallelujah to the Risen Lamb!" (Acts, John)
Arr. Lloyd Larson; Choristers Guild CGA1056
SAT (opt. B) with piano

"Dona Nobis Pacem" (John)
Arr. Hal Hopson; Hope c5181
Two-part with keyboard

Other Suggestions

Visuals:
O (Acts) Offering plates filled with money
P Oil, clasped hands, dew
E Light/darkness, water (cleansing), briefcase (advocate), 1 John 2:1*b*
G Lock, wind (breath/Holy Spirit), risen Christ, question mark, dove, peace

Greeting: BOW390 (Acts)
Opening Prayer: BOW392 (1 John)
Litany: UM556 or BOW495 (Acts, Ps.)
Canticle: UM205. "Canticle of Light and Darkness" (1 John) (see S-1, p. 383)
Call to Prayer: UM330. "Daw-Kee, Aim Daw-Tsi-Taw" ("Great Spirit, Now I Pray") (John)
Prayer: UM639. Bread and Justice (Acts, Ps.)
Prayer: BOW503 or BOW518 (Acts, John)
Response: UM503. "Let It Breathe on Me" (John)
Prayer of Intercession: BOW399, Week 2 (Easter)
Prayer of Thanksgiving and Intercession: BOW396 (John)
Blessing: BOW560 (John)

Acts 3:12-19

12 When Peter saw it, he addressed the people,"You Israelites, why do you wonder at this, or why do you stare at us, as though by our own power or piety we had made him walk? 13 The God of Abraham, the God of Isaac, and the God of Jacob, the God of our ancestors has glorified his servant Jesus, whom you handed over and rejected in the presence of Pilate, though he had decided to release him. 14 But you rejected the Holy and Righteous One and asked to have a murderer given to you, 15 and you killed the Author of life, whom God raised from the dead. To this we are witnesses. 16 And by faith in his name, his name itself has made this man strong, whom you see and know; and the faith that is through Jesus has given him this perfect health in the presence of all of you.

17 "And now, friends, I know that you acted in ignorance, as did also your rulers. 18 In this way God fulfilled what he had foretold through all the prophets, that his Messiah would suffer. 19 Repent therefore, and turn to God so that your sins may be wiped out."

Psalm 4

1 Answer me when I call, O God of my right! You gave me room when I was in distress. Be gracious to me, and hear my prayer. 2 How long, you people, shall my honor suffer shame? How long will you love vain words, and seek after lies? 3 But know that the LORD has set apart the faithful for himself; the LORD hears when I call to him. 4 When you are disturbed, do not sin; ponder it on your beds, and be silent. 5 Offer right sacrifices, and put your trust in the LORD. 6 There are many who say, "O that we might see some good! Let the light of your face shine on us, O LORD!" 7 You have put gladness in my heart more than when their grain and wine abound. 8 I will both lie down and sleep in peace; for you alone, O LORD, make me lie down in safety.

1 John 3:1-7

1 See what love the Father has given us, that we should be called children of God; and that is what we are. The reason the world does not know us is that it did not know him. 2 Beloved, we are God's children now; what we will be has not yet been revealed. What we do know is this: when he is revealed, we will be like him, for we will see him as he is. 3 And all who have this hope in him purify themselves, just as he is pure.

4 Everyone who commits sin is guilty of lawlessness; sin is lawlessness. 5 You know that he was revealed to take away sins, and in him there is no sin. 6 No one who abides in him sins; no one who sins has either seen him or known him. 7 Little children, let no one deceive you. Everyone who does what is right is righteous, just as he is righteous.

Luke 24:36*b*-48

36b Jesus himself stood among them and said to them, "Peace be with you." 37 They were startled and terrified, and thought that they were seeing a ghost. 38 He said to them, "Why are you frightened, and why do doubts arise in your hearts? 39 Look at my hands and my feet; see that it is I myself. Touch me and see; for a ghost does not have flesh and bones as you see that I have." 40 And when he had said this, he showed them his hands and his feet. 41 While in their joy they were disbelieving and still wondering, he said to them, "Have you anything here to eat?" 42 They gave him a piece of broiled fish, 43 and he took it and ate in their presence.

44 Then he said to them, "These are my words that I spoke to you while I was still with you—that everything written about me in the law of Moses, the prophets, and the psalms must be fulfilled." 45 Then he opened their minds to understand the scriptures, 46 and he said to them, "Thus it is written, that the Messiah is to suffer and to rise from the dead on the third day, 47 and that repentance and forgiveness of sins is to be proclaimed in his name to all nations, beginning from Jerusalem. 48 You are witnesses of these things."

Notes:

Primary Hymns and Songs for the Day

308 "Thine Be the Glory" (Luke) (O)
- H-3 Handbell-98; Choir-195; Descant-59
- S-1 #190. Arrangement for choir, handbells, trumpets, organ
- S-2 #95. Various treatments

473 "Lead Me, Lord" (Ps.)

2108 "O How He Loves You and Me!" (1 John)
R27, SP113

2115 "Christ Has Risen" (Luke)
- H-3 Choir-80; Descant-52
- S-1 #160-62. Various treatments
- S-2 #87-88. Brass/timpani introduction/arrangement

318 "Christ Is Alive" (Acts, Luke) (C)
- H-3 Handbell-50; Choir-47; Descant-101; Organ-167
- S-1 #334-35. Descant/harmonization

Hymn Suggestions

304 "Easter People, Raise Your Voices" (Luke) (O)
339 "Come, Sinners, to the Gospel Feast" (Acts) (O)
616 "Come, Sinners, to the Gospel Feast" (Acts)
340 "Come, Ye Sinners, Poor and Needy" (Acts)
363 "And Can It Be That I Should Gain" (Acts, Heritage)
310 "He Lives" (Acts, Luke)
577 "God of Grace and God of Glory" (Acts, Heritage)
2214 "Lead Me, Guide Me" (Ps.)
175 "Jesus, the Very Thought of Thee" (1 John, Luke)
267 "O Love, How Deep" (1 John, Luke)
306 "The Strife Is O'er, the Battle Done" (1 John)
2085 "He Came Down" (1 John)
2147 "There Are Some Things I May Not Know" (1 John)
2248 "Baptized in Water" (1 John, Baptism)
78 "Heleluyan" (Luke, Native American)
148 "Many and Great, O God" (Luke, Native American)
257 "We Meet You, O Christ" (Luke)
309 "On the Day of Resurrection" (Luke)
315 "Come, Ye Faithful, Raise the Strain" (Luke)
367 "He Touched Me" (Luke)
462 " 'Tis So Sweet to Trust in Jesus" (Luke)
596 "Blessed Jesus, at Thy Word" (Luke)
623 "Here, O My Lord, I See Thee" (Luke, Communion)
635 "Because Thou Hast Said" (Luke, Communion)
2184 "Sent Out in Jesus' Name" (Luke)
2199 "Stay with Us" (Luke)
2213 "Healer of Our Every Ill" (Luke)
2059 "I Am Your Mother" (Native American)
546 "The Church's One Foundation" (Heritage)
2269 "Come, Share the Lord" (Luke, Communion)

Contemporary Suggestions

S2031 "We Bring the Sacrifice of Praise" (Ps.)
S2154 "Please Enter My Heart, Hosanna" (Ps.)
M49 "Refresh My Heart" (Ps.)
MM108 "Lead Me, Lord" (Ps.)
S2039 "Holy, Holy" (1 John)
S2073 "Celebrate Love" (1 John)
SP48 "Behold, What Manner of Love" (1 John)
MM77 "Above All" (1 John, Luke, Easter)
WO2; V-3 p. 17 or V-10(03) p. 18 (vocal solo)
MM57 "Open the Eyes of My Heart" (Luke)
V-3 p. 162 (vocal solo)
WO19 "Celebrate Jesus" (Luke, Easter)
WO108 "Jesus Is Alive" (Luke, Easter)
S2006 "Lord God, Almighty" (Luke)
S2086 "Open Our Eyes, Lord" (Luke)
S2273 "Jesus, We Are Here" (Luke)
UM349 "Turn Your Eyes upon Jesus" (Luke)
UM666 "Shalom to You" (Luke)

Vocal Solos

"Author of Life Divine" (Acts)
V-1 p. 39
"I Walked Today Where Jesus Walked" (Luke, Easter)
V-8 p. 14

Anthems

"As Tenderly As a Father" (1 John)
John Shepherd; Hinshaw HMC-472
Two-part with keyboard

"O Sacrum Convivium" (Luke)
James Biery; Morningstar MSM60-8311
SATB *a cappella*

Other Suggestions

Visuals:
- **O (Acts)** Portrait of Christ crucified, risen, names given to Jesus, eraser (forgiveness)
- **P** Praying hands, person pondering, light, rejoicing
- **E** Children, risen Christ, 1 John 3:1
- **G** Risen Christ, fear, broiled fish, open Bible, Luke 24:36*c*, 48, witnessing

Introit: S2273, BOW187. "Jesus, We Are Here" (Luke)
Act of Centering: BOW470 (Native American)
Response: BOW197. Shawnee Traveling Song (Native American)
Greeting: BOW379 or BOW425 or BOW458 (Easter, Native American)
Opening Prayer: BOW455 (Native American)
Canticle: UM646. "Canticle of Love" (Ps., 1 John)
Call to Prayer: S2193. "Lord, Listen to Your Children" (Ps.)
Prayer of Confession: BOW487 (Native American)
Prayer: UM329. Prayer to the Holy Spirit (Luke, Native American)
Prayer: BOW512. For Guidance (1 John)
Prayers: S2201. "Prayers of the People" (Ps.)
Prayer of Intercession: BOW399, Week 3 (Easter)
Prayer: BOW426 or BOW439 (Heritage Sunday)
Response: S2200. "O Lord, Hear My Prayer" (Ps.)
Prayer of Thanksgiving: UM553 (Acts) or BOW396 (Luke)
Blessing: BOW560 (Ps.)

Acts 4:5-12

5 The next day their rulers, elders, and scribes assembled in Jerusalem, 6 with Annas the high priest, Caiaphas, John, and Alexander, and all who were of the high-priestly family. 7 When they had made the prisoners stand in their midst, they inquired, "By what power or by what name did you do this?" 8 Then Peter, filled with the Holy Spirit, said to them, "Rulers of the people and elders, 9 if we are questioned today because of a good deed done to someone who was sick and are asked how this man has been healed, 10 let it be known to all of you, and to all the people of Israel, that this man is standing before you in good health by the name of Jesus Christ of Nazareth, whom you crucified, whom God raised from the dead. 11 This Jesus is 'the stone that was rejected by you, the builders; it has become the cornerstone.' 12 There is salvation in no one else, for there is no other name under heaven given among mortals by which we must be saved."

Psalm 23

1 The LORD is my shepherd, I shall not want. 2 He makes me lie down in green pastures; he leads me beside still waters; 3 he restores my soul. He leads me in right paths for his name's sake. 4 Even though I walk through the darkest valley, I fear no evil; for you are with me; your rod and your staff—they comfort me. 5 You prepare a table before me in the presence of my enemies; you anoint my head with oil; my cup overflows. 6 Surely goodness and mercy shall follow me all the days of my life, and I shall dwell in the house of the LORD my whole life long.

1 John 3:16-24

16 We know love by this, that he laid down his life for us—and we ought to lay down our lives for one another. 17 How does God's love abide in anyone who has the world's goods and sees a brother or sister in need and yet refuses help?

18 Little children, let us love, not in word or speech, but in truth and action. 19 And by this we will know that we are from the truth and will reassure our hearts before him 20 whenever our hearts condemn us; for God is greater than our hearts, and he knows everything. 21 Beloved, if our hearts do not condemn us, we have boldness before God; 22 and we receive from him whatever we ask, because we obey his commandments and do what pleases him.

23 And this is his commandment, that we should believe in the name of his Son Jesus Christ and love one another, just as he has commanded us. 24 All who obey his commandments abide in him, and he abides in them. And by this we know that he abides in us, by the Spirit that he has given us.

John 10:11-18

11 "I am the good shepherd. The good shepherd lays down his life for the sheep. 12 The hired hand, who is not the shepherd and does not own the sheep, sees the wolf coming and leaves the sheep and runs away—and the wolf snatches them and scatters them. 13 The hired hand runs away because a hired hand does not care for the sheep. 14 I am the good shepherd. I know my own and my own know me, 15 just as the Father knows me and I know the Father. And I lay down my life for the sheep. 16 I have other sheep that do not belong to this fold. I must bring them also, and they will listen to my voice. So there will be one flock, one shepherd. 17 For this reason the Father loves me, because I lay down my life in order to take it up again. 18 No one takes it from me, but I lay it down of my own accord. I have power to lay it down, and I have power to take it up again. I have received this command from my Father."

Notes:

Primary Hymns and Songs for the Day

546 "The Church's One Foundation" (Acts) (O)
  H-3 Handbell-94; Choir-180; Descant-16; Organ-9
  S-1 #25-26. Descant/harmonization
138 "The King of Love My Shepherd Is" (Ps., 1 John, John)
  H-3 Handbell-96; Choir-188, 221; Descant-93; Organ-135
  S-1 #298-99. Harmonizations
381 "Savior, Like a Shepherd Lead Us" (Ps., John)
  H-3 Choir-167; Organ-15
  S-2 #29. Harmonization
2214 "Lead Me, Guide Me" (Ps.)
2058 "Shepherd Me, O God" (Ps., John)
559 "Christ Is Made the Sure Foundation" (Acts) (C)
  H-3 Choir-49; Descant-103; Organ-180
  S-1 #346. Descant

Hymn Suggestions

128 "He Leadeth Me: O Blessed Thought" (Ps.) (O)
168 "At the Name of Jesus" (Acts)
2220 "We Are God's People" (Acts)
136 "The Lord's My Shepherd, I'll Not Want" (Ps.)
407 "Close to Thee" (Ps.)
474 "Precious Lord, Take My Hand" (Ps.)
497 "Send Me, Lord" (Ps.)
518 "O Thou, in Whose Presence" (Ps., John)
2112 "Jesus Walked This Lonesome Valley" (Ps.)
2206 "Without Seeing You" (Ps.)
408 "The Gift of Love" (1 John)
434 "Cuando El Pobre" ("When the Poor Ones") (1 John)
549 "Where Charity and Love Prevail" (1 John)
566 "Blest Be the Dear Uniting Love" (1 John)
2083 "My Song Is Love Unknown" (1 John)
2178 "Here Am I" (1 John)
2223 "They'll Know We Are Christians by Our Love" (1 John)
2260 "Let Us Be Bread" (1 John, Communion)
2245 "Within the Day-to-Day" (1 John)
115 "How Like a Gentle Spirit" (John)
289 "Ah, Holy Jesus" (John)
419 "I Am Thine, O Lord" (John)
650 "Give Me the Faith Which Can Remove" (John)
700 "Abide with Me" (Ps., 1 John., John) (C)

Contemporary Suggestions

S2162 "Grace Alone" (Acts)
  MM100
WY145 "In Christ Alone" (Acts, Easter)
S2054 "Nothing Can Trouble" ("Nada Te Turbe") (Ps.)
S2113 "Lamb of God" (Ps.)
M45 "God Is Good All the Time" (Ps.)
  WO35
WO43 "God Will Make a Way" (Ps.)
  SP40
S2038 "Father, I Adore You" (1 John)
  SP194
S2159 "Jesus, Draw Me Close" (1 John)
S2224 "Make Us One" (1 John)
  SP137
S2226 "Bind Us Together" (1 John)
  R292, SP140
MM63 "I Could Sing of Your Love Forever" (1 John)
  WY44; V-3 p. 22 (vocal solo)
S2244 "People Need the Lord" (1 John, John)
UM174 "His Name Is Wonderful" (1 John)
  R30, SP90

Vocal Solos

"How Firm a Foundation" (Acts)
V-6 p. 31
"God, Our Ever Faithful Shepherd" (Ps.)
V-4 p. 15
"Come, Praise the Lord!" (Ps.)
V-8 p. 304
"Adore" (John)
V-3 p. 49

Anthems

"My Shepherd Knows" (Ps.)
Arr. John Purifoy; Brookfield Press 08745073
SATB with piano

"My Shepherd Will Supply My Need" (Ps.)
Mack Wilburg; Hinshaw HMC1424
SATB with flute, oboe, harp (keyboard)

Other Suggestions

Visuals:
  O (Acts) Stone, cornerstone
  P Shepherd, Christ as shepherd, sheep, water, path
  E Cross, people sacrificing for others, pitcher/bowl/towel
  G Christ the Shepherd, sheep, wolf, crucifix, John 10:11
Greeting: BOW381 (John) or BOW456 (Acts)
Opening Prayer: BOW393 or BOW460 (Acts, Ps., John)
Canticle: UM646. "Canticle of Love" (1 John.) (see S-1, p. 387)
Psalter: UM137. Psalm 23
Prayer: UM457 (Acts) or UM460 (Ps.)
Prayer: BOW506. For the Church (Acts)
Prayer: BOW518. For Others (1 John)
Prayer: BOW529. A Prayer of Saint Patrick (Ps., John)
Prayer of Intercession: BOW399 Week 4 or BOW398 (Ps., John)
Dismissal with a Blessing: BOW376 (Acts, Easter)
Response: S2179, R226. "Live in Charity" (1 John)
Great Thanksgiving for Easter Season: BOW66

Acts 8:26-40

26 Then an angel of the Lord said to Philip, "Get up and go toward the south to the road that goes down from Jerusalem to Gaza." (This is a wilderness road.) 27 So he got up and went. Now there was an Ethiopian eunuch, a court official of the Candace, queen of the Ethiopians, in charge of her entire treasury. He had come to Jerusalem to worship 28 and was returning home; seated in his chariot, he was reading the prophet Isaiah. 29 Then the Spirit said to Philip, "Go over to this chariot and join it." 30 So Philip ran up to it and heard him reading the prophet Isaiah. He asked, "Do you understand what you are reading?" 31 He replied, "How can I, unless someone guides me?" And he invited Philip to get in and sit beside him. 32 Now the passage of the scripture that he was reading was this: "Like a sheep he was led to the slaughter, and like a lamb silent before its shearer, so he does not open his mouth. 33 In his humiliation justice was denied him. Who can describe his generation? For his life is taken away from the earth." 34 The eunuch asked Philip, "About whom, may I ask you, does the prophet say this, about himself or about someone else?" 35 Then Philip began to speak, and starting with this scripture, he proclaimed to him the good news about Jesus. 36 As they were going along the road, they came to some water; and the eunuch said, "Look, here is water! What is to prevent me from being baptized?" 38 He commanded the chariot to stop, and both of them, Philip and the eunuch, went down into the water, and Philip baptized him. 39 When they came up out of the water, the Spirit of the Lord snatched Philip away; the eunuch saw him no more, and went on his way rejoicing. 40 But Philip found himself at Azotus, and as he was passing through the region, he proclaimed the good news to all the towns until he came to Caesarea.

Psalm 22:25-31

25 From you comes my praise in the great congregation; my vows I will pay before those who fear him. 26 The poor shall eat and be satisfied; those who seek him shall praise the LORD. May your hearts live forever! 27 All the ends of the earth shall remember and turn to the LORD; and all the families of the nations shall worship before him. 28 For dominion belongs to the LORD, and he rules over the nations. 29 To him, indeed, shall all who sleep in the earth bow down; before him shall bow all who go down to the dust, and I shall live for him. 30 Posterity will serve him; future generations will be told about the Lord, 31 and proclaim his deliverance to a people yet unborn, saying that he has done it.

---

1 John 4:7-21

7 Beloved, let us love one another, because love is from God; everyone who loves is born of God and knows God. 8 Whoever does not love does not know God, for God is love. 9 God's love was revealed among us in this way: God sent his only Son into the world so that we might live through him. 10 In this is love, not that we loved God but that he loved us and sent his Son to be the atoning sacrifice for our sins. 11 Beloved, since God loved us so much, we also ought to love one another. 12 No one has ever seen God; if we love one another, God lives in us, and his love is perfected in us.

13 By this we know that we abide in him and he in us, because he has given us of his Spirit. 14 And we have seen and do testify that the Father has sent his Son as the Savior of the world. 15 God abides in those who confess that Jesus is the Son of God, and they abide in God. 16 So we have known and believe the love that God has for us.

God is love, and those who abide in love abide in God, and God abides in them. 17 Love has been perfected among us in this: that we may have boldness on the day of judgment, because as he is, so are we in this world. 18 There is no fear in love, but perfect love casts out fear; for fear has to do with punishment, and whoever fears has not reached perfection in love. 19 We love because he first loved us. 20 Those who say, "I love God," and hate their brothers or sisters, are liars; for those who do not love a brother or sister whom they have seen, cannot love God whom they have not seen. 21 The commandment we have from him is this: those who love God must love their brothers and sisters also.

John 15:1-8

1 "I am the true vine, and my Father is the vinegrower. 2 He removes every branch in me that bears no fruit. Every branch that bears fruit he prunes to make it bear more fruit. 3 You have already been cleansed by the word that I have spoken to you. 4 Abide in me as I abide in you. Just as the branch cannot bear fruit by itself unless it abides in the vine, neither can you unless you abide in me. 5 I am the vine, you are the branches. Those who abide in me and I in them bear much fruit, because apart from me you can do nothing. 6 Whoever does not abide in me is thrown away like a branch and withers; such branches are gathered, thrown into the fire, and burned. 7 If you abide in me, and my words abide in you, ask for whatever you wish, and it will be done for you. 8 My Father is glorified by this, that you bear much fruit and become my disciples."

Notes:

Primary Hymns and Songs for the Day

610 "We Know That Christ Is Raised" (Acts, Baptism) (O)
- H-3 Handbell-100; Choir-214; Organ-37
- S-1 #118-27. Various treatments

549 "Where Charity and Love Prevail" (1 John)
- H-3 Handbell-104; Choir-219; Descant-95; Organ-143
- S-2 #162. Harmonization

397 "I Need Thee Every Hour" (John)
- H-3 Choir-107

2076 "O Blessed Spring" (John)

571 "Go, Make of All Disciples" (Acts) (C)
- H-3 Handbell-74; Choir-123; Descant-64; Organ-71
- S-1 #195-97. Various treatments

Hymn Suggestions

111 "How Can We Name a Love" (1 John, John)
165 "Hallelujah! What a Savior" (Acts)
287 "O Love Divine, What Hast Thou Done" (Acts)
289 "Ah, Holy Jesus" (Acts)
2246 "Deep in the Shadows of the Past" (Acts)
2247 "Wonder of Wonders" (Acts, Baptism)
2248 "Baptized in Water" (Acts, Baptism)
2251 "We Were Baptized in Christ Jesus" (Acts, Baptism)
2123 "Loving Spirit" (Acts, Mother's Day)
662 "Stand Up, and Bless the Lord" (Ps., 1 John)
92 "For the Beauty of the Earth" (1 John)
98 "To God Be the Glory" (1 John)
121 "There's a Wideness in God's Mercy" (1 John)
172 "My Jesus, I Love Thee" (1 John)
183 "Jesu, Thy Boundless Love to Me" (1 John)
184 "Of the Father's Love Begotten" (1 John)
292 "What Wondrous Love Is This" (1 John)
305 "Camina, Pueblo de Dios" ("Walk On, O People of God") (1 John, Easter)
332 "Spirit of Faith, Come Down" (1 John)
645 "O Perfect Love" (1 John)
647 "Your Love, O God, Has Called Us Here" (1 John)
2110 "Why Has God Forsaken Me?" (1 John)
2135 "When Cain Killed Abel" (1 John, Christian Home)
2213 "Healer of Our Every Ill" (1 John)
2259 "Victim Divine" (1 John)
113 "Source and Sovereign, Rock and Cloud" (1 John, John)
124 "Seek the Lord" (1 John, John)
529 "How Firm a Foundation" (John)
544 "Like the Murmur of the Dove's Song" (John)
2050 "Mothering God, You Gave Me Birth" (John, Mother's Day)
2060 "God the Sculptor of the Mountains" (John)
2261 "Life-giving Bread" (John, Communion)
445 "Happy the Home When God Is There" (Christian Home)
2189 "A Mother Lined a Basket" (Mother's Day)

Contemporary Suggestions

S2250 "I've Just Come from the Fountain" (Acts, Baptism)
M1 "Ancient of Days" (Ps.)
MM56 "Come, Now Is the Time to Worship" (Ps.)
WY178; V-3 p. 114 (vocal solo)
S2022 "Great Is the Lord" (1 John)
S2073 "Celebrate Love" (1 John)
S2179 "Live in Charity" ("Ubi Caritas") (1 John)
S2223 "They'll Know We Are Christians by Our Love" (1 John)
S2224 "Make Us One" (1 John)
S2226 "Bind Us Together" (1 John)
S2260 "Let Us Be Bread" (1 John, Communion)
M25 "No Greater Love" (1 John)
MM63 "I Could Sing of Your Love Forever" (1 John)
WY44; V-3 p. 22 (vocal solo)
MM82 "You Are My King" ("Amazing Love") (1 John)
WY65
M13 "Be Glorified" (John)
S2150 "Lord, Be Glorified" (John)
S2188 "The Family Prayer Song" (Christian Home)

Vocal Solos

"Wondrous Love" (1 John)
V-6 p. 47
"I Am the Vine" (John)
V-8 p. 280

Anthems

"Of the Father's Love Begotten" (1 John)
Arr. John Helgen; Kjos 8963
SATB with piano (opt. solo)

"I Am the Vine" (John)
Carlton R. Young; Abingdon Press 0687493811
SATB with keyboard (opt. flute and clarinet)

Other Suggestions

Visuals:
- **O (Acts)** Open scroll/Bible open to Isaiah, water (baptism)
- **P** Poor being fed, globe, flags of nations, earth from space
- **E** Cross, sacrificial love, Christ, 1 John 4:16*b*, 18*a*
- **G** Grapevine, grapes, pruned branches, fire, John 15:5

Greeting: BOW381 (John), BOW411 (1 John) or BOW451 (Ps.)
Opening Prayer: BOW392 (Acts)
Opening Prayer: BOW463 or BOW466 (Mother's Day)
Prayer: UM401. For Holiness of Heart (1 John)
Prayer of Intercession: BOW399, Week 5 (Easter)
Call to Baptism: BOW173. "Come Be Baptized" (Acts)
Baptism Response: BOW174 or BOW175 (Acts)
Prayer: BOW437 (Festival of the Christian Home)
Prayer of Intercession: BOW438 (Mother's Day)
Prayer of Thanksgiving: BOW553 (John)

Acts 10:44-48

44 While Peter was still speaking, the Holy Spirit fell upon all who heard the word. 45 The circumcised believers who had come with Peter were astounded that the gift of the Holy Spirit had been poured out even on the Gentiles, 46 for they heard them speaking in tongues and extolling God. Then Peter said, 47 "Can anyone withhold the water for baptizing these people who have received the Holy Spirit just as we have?" 48 So he ordered them to be baptized in the name of Jesus Christ. Then they invited him to stay for several days.

Psalm 98

1 O sing to the LORD a new song, for he has done marvelous things. His right hand and his holy arm have gotten him victory. 2 The LORD has made known his victory; he has revealed his vindication in the sight of the nations. 3 He has remembered his steadfast love and faithfulness to the house of Israel. All the ends of the earth have seen the victory of our God. 4 Make a joyful noise to the LORD, all the earth; break forth into joyous song and sing praises. 5 Sing praises to the LORD with the lyre, with the lyre and the sound of melody. 6 With trumpets and the sound of the horn make a joyful noise before the King, the LORD. 7 Let the sea roar, and all that fills it; the world and those who live in it. 8 Let the floods clap their hands; let the hills sing together for joy 9 at the presence of the LORD, for he is coming to judge the earth. He will judge the world with righteousness, and the peoples with equity.

1 John 5:1-6

1 Everyone who believes that Jesus is the Christ has been born of God, and everyone who loves the parent loves the child. 2 By this we know that we love the children of God, when we love God and obey his commandments. 3 For the love of God is this, that we obey his commandments. And his commandments are not burdensome, 4 for whatever is born of God conquers the world. And this is the victory that conquers the world, our faith. 5 Who is it that conquers the world but the one who believes that Jesus is the Son of God?

6 This is the one who came by water and blood, Jesus Christ, not with the water only but with the water and the blood. And the Spirit is the one that testifies, for the Spirit is the truth.

John 15:9-17

9 "As the Father has loved me, so I have loved you; abide in my love. 10 If you keep my commandments, you will abide in my love, just as I have kept my Father's commandments and abide in his love. 11 I have said these things to you so that my joy may be in you, and that your joy may be complete.

12 "This is my commandment, that you love one another as I have loved you. 13 No one has greater love than this, to lay down one's life for one's friends. 14 You are my friends if you do what I command you. 15 I do not call you servants any longer, because the servant does not know what the master is doing; but I have called you friends, because I have made known to you everything that I have heard from my Father. 16 You did not choose me but I chose you. And I appointed you to go and bear fruit, fruit that will last, so that the Father will give you whatever you ask him in my name. 17 I am giving you these commands so that you may love one another."

Notes:

Primary Hymns and Songs for the Day

139 "Praise to the Lord, the Almighty" (Ps.) (O)
 H-3 Handbell-89; Choir-163; Descant-69; Organ-79
 S-1 #218-22. Various treatments
393 "Spirit of the Living God" (Acts)
 H-3 Choir-176
 S-1 #212. Vocal descant idea
548 "In Christ There Is No East or West" (Acts, John)
 H-3 Choir-111; Descant-74; Organ-88
 S-1 #231-33. Various treatments
2045 "Sing a New Song to the Lord" (Ps.)
560 "Help Us Accept Each Other" (Acts, John) (C)
 H-3 Choir-97
 S-2 #1. Descant

Hymn Suggestions

96 "Praise the Lord Who Reigns Above" (Ps.)
246 "Joy to the World" (Ps.)
2114 "At the Font We Start Our Journey" (Acts)
2247 "Wonder of Wonders" (Acts, Baptism)
2248 "Baptized in Water" (Acts, Baptism)
2251 "We Were Baptized in Christ Jesus" (Acts, Baptism)
332 "Spirit of Faith, Come Down" (Acts)
544 "Like the Murmur of the Dove's Song" (Acts)
475 "Come Down, O Love Divine" (Acts, John)
537 "Filled with the Spirit's Power" (Acts, John)
552 "Here, O Lord, Your Servants Gather" (Acts, John)
557 "Blest Be the Tie That Binds" (Acts, John)
369 "Blessed Assurance" (1 John)
370 "Victory in Jesus" (Ps., 1 John)
372 "How Can We Sinners Know" (1 John)
428 "For the Healing of the Nations" (1 John)
442 "Weary of All Trumpeting" (1 John)
447 "Our Parent, by Whose Name" (1 John)
2111 "We Sang Our Glad Hosannas" (1 John)
617 "I Come with Joy" (John, Communion)
659 "Jesus Our Friend and Brother" (John)
2142 "Blessed Quietness" (John)
2213 "Healer of Our Every Ill" (John)
2260 "Let Us Be Bread" (John, Communion)

Contemporary Suggestions

S2250 "I've Just Come from the Fountain" (Acts, Baptism)
S2028 "Clap Your Hands" (Ps.)
S2074 "Shout to the Lord" (Ps.)
 M16, WY126; V-3 p. 56 (vocal solo)
S2144 "Why We Sing" (Ps.)
SP23 "Sing Unto the Lord a New Song" (Ps.)
SP147 "I Will Celebrate" (Ps.)
 R77, M46, WO83
S2159 "Jesus, Draw Me Close" (1 John)
S2204 "Light of the World" (1 John)
S2219 "Goodness Is Stronger than Evil" (1 John)
S2223 "They'll Know We Are Christians by Our Love" (John)
S2226 "Bind Us Together" (John)
 R292, SP140
S2224 "Make Us One" (John)
 SP137
S2179 "Live in Charity" ("Ubi Caritas") (John)
 R226
M25 "No Greater Love" (John)
MM63 "I Could Sing of Your Love Forever" (John)
 WY44; V-3 p. 22 (vocal solo)

Vocal Solos

"Praise to the Lord, the Almighty" (Ps.)
V-6 p. 18
"I Will Sing of Thy Great Mercies" (John)
V-4 p. 43
"This Is My Commandment" (John)
V-8 p. 284

Anthems

"The Earth Is the Lord's" (Ps.)
Kenney Potter; Hinshaw Music HMC2091
Unison treble with piano

"Welcome" (Acts, John)
Mark A. Miller; Abingdon Press 9780687644407
SATB with solo (opt.) with piano

Other Suggestions

Visuals:

O (Acts)	Dove/ flames (Holy Spirit), water (baptism)
P	Lyre, sheet music, trumpet, sea, floods, hills, scales of justice
E	Water, wine, symbols of the Holy Spirit
G	Sacrificial love, cross, friendship, fruit (love enacted), John 15:9*c*

Introit: BOW181. "Sing to the Lord a New Song" (Ps.)
Greeting: BOW303 (Ps.) or BOW382 (John)
Greeting: Psalm 98:1. Sing to the Lord.
Opening Prayer: UM335 (Acts) or BOW394 (1 John)
Prayer of Intercession: BOW399, Week 6 (Easter)
Prayer of Thanksgiving/Intercession: BOW397 (1 John)
Prayer: UM481 or BOW518 (1 John, John)
Canticle: UM646. "Canticle of Love" (John) (see S-1, p. 387)

Acts 1:1-11

1 In the first book, Theophilus, I wrote about all that
Jesus did and taught from the beginning 2 until the day
when he was taken up to heaven, after giving instructions
through the Holy Spirit to the apostles whom he had cho-
sen. 3 After his suffering he presented himself alive to
them by many convincing proofs, appearing to them dur-
ing forty days and speaking about the kingdom of God.
4 While staying with them, he ordered them not to leave
Jerusalem, but to wait there for the promise of the Father.
"This," he said, "is what you have heard from me; 5 for
John baptized with water, but you will be baptized with
the Holy Spirit not many days from now."

6 So when they had come together, they asked him,
"Lord, is this the time when you will restore the kingdom
to Israel?" 7 He replied, "It is not for you to know the
times or periods that the Father has set by his own author-
ity. 8 But you will receive power when the Holy Spirit has
come upon you; and you will be my witnesses in
Jerusalem, in all Judea and Samaria, and to the ends of
the earth." 9 When he had said this, as they were watching,
he was lifted up, and a cloud took him out of their sight.
10 While he was going and they were gazing up toward
heaven, suddenly two men in white robes stood by them.
11 They said, "Men of Galilee, why do you stand looking
up toward heaven? This Jesus, who has been taken up
from you into heaven, will come in the same way as you
saw him go into heaven."

Psalm 47

1 Clap your hands, all you peoples; shout to God with
loud songs of joy. 2 For the LORD, the Most High, is awe-
some, a great king over all the earth. 3 He subdued peo-
ples under us, and nations under our feet. 4 He chose our
heritage for us, the pride of Jacob whom he loves. 5 God
has gone up with a shout, the LORD with the sound of a
trumpet. 6 Sing praises to God, sing praises; sing praises to
our King, sing praises. 7 For God is the king of all the
earth; sing praises with a psalm. 8 God is king over the
nations; God sits on his holy throne. 9 The princes of the
peoples gather as the people of the God of Abraham. For
the shields of the earth belong to God; he is highly
exalted.

Ephesians 1:15-23

15 I have heard of your faith in the Lord Jesus and your
love toward all the saints, and for this reason 16 I do not
cease to give thanks for you as I remember you in my
prayers. 17 I pray that the God of our Lord Jesus Christ,
the Father of glory, may give you a spirit of wisdom and
revelation as you come to know him, 18 so that, with the
eyes of your heart enlightened, you may know what is the
hope to which he has called you, what are the riches of
his glorious inheritance among the saints, 19 and what is
the immeasurable greatness of his power for us who
believe, according to the working of his great power.
20 God put this power to work in Christ when he raised
him from the dead and seated him at his right hand in
the heavenly places, 21 far above all rule and authority and
power and dominion, and above every name that is
named, not only in this age but also in the age to come.
22 And he has put all things under his feet and has made
him the head over all things for the church, 23 which is his
body, the fullness of him who fills all in all.

Luke 24:44-53

44 Then he said to them, "These are my words that I
spoke to you while I was still with you—that everything
written about me in the law of Moses, the prophets, and
the psalms must be fulfilled." 45 Then he opened their
minds to understand the scriptures, 46 and he said to
them, "Thus it is written, that the Messiah is to suffer and
to rise from the dead on the third day, 47 and that repen-
tance and forgiveness of sins is to be proclaimed in his
name to all nations, beginning from Jerusalem. 48 You are
witnesses of these things. 49 And see, I am sending upon
you what my Father promised; so stay here in the city
until you have been clothed with power from on high."

50 Then he led them out as far as Bethany, and, lifting
up his hands, he blessed them. 51 While he was blessing
them, he withdrew from them and was carried up into
heaven. 52 And they worshiped him, and returned to
Jerusalem with great joy; 53 and they were continually in
the temple blessing God.

Notes:

Primary Hymns and Songs for the Day

312 "Hail the Day that Sees Him Rise" (Acts, Luke) (O)
H-3 Handbell-72; Choir-50; Descant-69; Organ-78
S-1 #213. Descant

327 "Crown Him with Many Crowns" (Ps., Eph., Luke)
H-3 Handbell-55; Choir-60; Descant-30; Organ-27
S-1 #86-88. Various treatments

2074 "Shout to the Lord" (Ps.)
M16, WY126; V-3 p. 56 (vocal solo)

157 "Jesus Shall Reign" (Ps., Eph.) (C)
H-3 Handbell-29, 57; Choir-117; Descant-31; Organ-31
S-1 #100-103. Various treatments

Hymn Suggestions

2247 "Wonder of Wonders" (Acts, Baptism)
163 "Ask Ye What Great Thing I Know" (Acts, Luke)
173 "Christ, Whose Glory Fills the Skies" (Acts, Luke)
302 "Christ the Lord Is Risen Today" (Acts, Luke)
304 "Easter People, Raise Your Voices" (Acts, Luke)
307 "Christ Is Risen" (Acts, Luke)
308 "Thine Be the Glory" (Acts, Luke)
310 "He Lives" (Acts, Luke)
318 "Christ Is Alive" (Acts, Luke)
319 "Christ Jesus Lay in Death's Strong Bands" (Acts, Luke)
322 "Up from the Grave He Arose" (Acts, Luke)
324 "Hail Thee, Festival Day" (Acts, Luke)
541 "See How Great a Flame Aspires" (Acts)
703 "Swing Low, Sweet Chariot" (Acts)
711 "For All the Saints" (Acts, Eph.)
175 "Jesus, the Very Thought of Thee" (Eph.)
178 "Hope of the World" (Eph.)
368 "My Hope Is Built" (Eph.)
2147 "There Are Some Things I May Not Know" (Eph.)
2220 "We Are God's People" (Eph.)
2261 "Life-giving Bread" (Eph., Communion)
2269 "Come, Share the Lord" (Eph., Communion)
2276 "Glory to God in the Highest" (Ps., Eph.)
2279 "The Trees of the Field" (Ps.)
R302, SP128
2077 "You Alone Are Holy" (Luke)
2114 "At the Font We Start Our Journey" (Luke, Baptism)
2115 "Christ Has Risen" (Luke)
2117 "Spirit of God" (Luke)
2184 "Sent Out in Jesus' Name" (Luke)
2199 "Stay with Us" (Luke)
2239 "Go Ye, Go Ye into the World" (Luke)
2268 "As We Gather at Your Table" (Luke, Communion)
2282 "I'll Fly Away" (Luke, Ascension)

Contemporary Suggestions

S2118 "Holy Spirit, Come to Us" (Acts)
UM494 "Kum Ba Yah" ("Come By Here") (Acts)
MM88 "Holy Spirit, Rain Down" (Acts)
S2028 "Clap Your Hands" (Ps.)
S2070 "He Is Exalted" (Ps., Ascension)
R238, SP66, WY198, WG71
WY218 "Our Love Is Loud" (Ps.)
MM68 "Forever" (Eph.)
WY57
MM77 "Above All" (Eph., Ascension)
WO2; V-3 p. 17 or V-10(03) p. 18 (vocal solo)
S2006 "Lord God, Almighty" (Luke)
R40
S2078 "Alleluia" (Luke)
S2078
S2088 "Lord, I Lift Your Name on High" (Ascension)
R4, M2
S2116 "Christ the Lord Is Risen" (Luke, Ascension)
MM78 "Once Again" (Ascension)
WY145 "In Christ Alone" (Ascension)

Vocal Solos

"Jesus Christ Is Risen Today" (Acts, Luke)
V-1 p. 50
"If God Be For Us" (Acts, Luke)
V-2
"Praise Forevermore" (Ps., Luke)
V-3 p. 68
"Ride On, Jesus" (Ascension)
V-7 p. 8

Anthems

"Gaelic Benediction" (Acts, Luke)
Jerry Ulrich; Abingdon Press 9780687114845
SAB with piano (opt. C instrument)

"Go Ye, Go Ye into the World" (Luke)
Natalie Sleeth; Choristers Guild CGA209
Three-part with keyboard

Other Suggestions

Visuals:
O (Acts) Water, dove, flames, shell (baptism)
P Clapping hands, feet, trumpet, singing, shield
E Witnessing, Ascension, risen Christ, saints
G Bible, risen Christ, map or globe, Ascension, Luke 24:48

Introit: S2273, BOW187. "Jesus, We Are Here" (Acts)
Greeting: BOW387, BOW389, or BOW402 (Acts, Luke, Eph.)
Prayer: BOW393 and BOW403 (Acts, Luke, Eph.)
Prayer: UM323. The Ascension (Acts, Luke, Eph.)
Prayer: UM542. Day of Pentecost (Acts)
Prayer: BOW440 or BOW542 (Memorial Day)
Prayer of Intercession: BOW399, Week 7 (Easter)
Great Thanksgiving for Easter Season: BOW66
Benediction: BOW218. "Benediction for Pentecost" (Acts, Luke)
Alternate lessons for the Seventh Sunday of Easter: Acts 1:15-17, 21-26; Ps. 1; 1 John 5:9-13; John 17:6-19

MAY 31, 2009

Acts 2:1-21
1 When the day of Pentecost had come, they were all
together in one place. 2 And suddenly from heaven there
came a sound like the rush of a violent wind, and it filled
the entire house where they were sitting. 3 Divided
tongues, as of fire, appeared among them, and a tongue
rested on each of them. 4 All of them were filled with the
Holy Spirit and began to speak in other languages, as the
Spirit gave them ability.
5 Now there were dgvout Jews from every nation under
heaven living in Jerusalem. 6 And at this sound the crowd
gathered and was bewildered, because each one heard
them speaking in the native language of each. 7 Amazed
and astonished, they asked, "Are not all these who are
speaking Galileans? 8 And how is it that we hear, each of
us, in our own native language? 9 Parthians, Medes,
Elamites, and residents of Mesopotamia, Judea and
Cappadocia, Pontus and Asia, 10 Phrygia and Pamphylia,
Egypt and the parts of Libya belonging to Cyrene, and vis-
itors from Rome, both Jews and proselytes, 11 Cretans and
Arabs—in our own languages we hear them speaking
about God's deeds of power." 12 All were amazed and per-
plexed, saying to one another, "What does this mean?"
13 But others sneered and said, "They are filled with new
wine."
14 But Peter, standing with the eleven, raised his voice
and addressed them, "Men of Judea and all who live in
Jerusalem, let this be known to you, and listen to what I
say. 15 Indeed, these are not drunk, as you suppose, for it
is only nine o'clock in the morning. 16 No, this is what was
spoken through the prophet Joel: 17 'In the last days it will
be, God declares, that I will pour out my Spirit upon all
flesh, and your sons and your daughters shall prophesy,
and your young men shall see visions, and your old men
shall dream dreams. 18 Even upon my slaves, both men
and women, in those days I will pour out my Spirit; and
they shall prophesy. 19 And I will show portents in the
heaven above and signs on the earth below, blood, and
fire, and smoky mist. 20 The sun shall be turned to dark-
ness and the moon to blood, before the coming of the
Lord's great and glorious day. 21 Then everyone who calls
on the name of the Lord shall be saved.' "

Psalm 104:24-34, 35*b*
24 O LORD, how manifold are your works! In wisdom
you have made them all; the earth is full of your crea-
tures. 25 Yonder is the sea, great and wide, creeping things
innumerable are there, living things both small and great.
26 There go the ships, and Leviathan that you formed to
sport in it. 27 These all look to you to give them their food
in due season; 28 when you give to them, they gather it up;
when you open your hand, they are filled with good
things. 29 When you hide your face, they are dismayed;
when you take away their breath, they die and return to
their dust. 30 When you send forth your spirit, they are cre-
ated; and you renew the face of the ground. 31 May the
glory of the LORD endure forever; may the LORD rejoice in
his works— 32 who looks on the earth and it trembles, who
touches the mountains and they smoke. 33 I will sing to the
LORD as long as I live; I will sing praise to my God while I
have being. 34 May my meditation be pleasing to him, for I
rejoice in the LORD.
35b Bless the LORD, O my soul. Praise the LORD!

Romans 8:22-27
22 We know that the whole creation has been groaning
in labor pains until now; 23 and not only the creation, but
we ourselves, who have the first fruits of the Spirit, groan
inwardly while we wait for adoption, the redemption of
our bodies. 24 For in hope we were saved. Now hope that is
seen is not hope. For who hopes for what is seen? 25 But if
we hope for what we do not see, we wait for it with
patience.
26 Likewise the Spirit helps us in our weakness; for we
do not know how to pray as we ought, but that very Spirit
intercedes with sighs too deep for words. 27 And God, who
searches the heart, knows what is the mind of the Spirit,
because the Spirit intercedes for the saints according to
the will of God.

John 15:26-27; 16:4*b*-15
26 "When the Advocate comes, whom I will send to you
from the Father, the Spirit of truth who comes from the
Father, he will testify on my behalf. 27 You also are to testify
because you have been with me from the beginning.
4b "I did not say these things to you from the begin-
ning, because I was with you. 5 But now I am going to him
who sent me; yet none of you asks me, 'Where are you
going?' 6 But because I have said these things to you, sor-
row has filled your hearts. 7 Nevertheless I tell you the
truth: it is to your advantage that I go away, for if I do not
go away, the Advocate will not come to you; but if I go, I
will send him to you. 8 And when he comes, he will prove
the world wrong about sin and righteousness and judg-
ment: 9 about sin, because they do not believe in me;
10 about righteousness, because I am going to the Father
and you will see me no longer; 11 about judgment, because
the ruler of this world has been condemned.
12 "I still have many things to say to you, but you cannot
bear them now. 13 When the Spirit of truth comes, he will
guide you into all the truth; for he will not speak on his
own, but will speak whatever he hears, and he will declare
to you the things that are to come. 14 He will glorify me,
because he will take what is mine and declare it to you.
15 All that the Father has is mine. For this reason I said
that he will take what is mine and declare it to you."

Primary Hymns and Songs for the Day

332 "Spirit of Faith, Come Down" (Acts) (O)
347 "Spirit Song" (Acts, John)
R248, SP134
393 "Spirit of the Living God" (Acts, John)
H-3 Choir-176
S-1 #212. Vocal descant idea
539 "O Spirit of the Living God" (Acts) (C)
H-3 Handbell-44; Choir-21; Descant-40; Organ-40
S-1 #131-32. Introduction/descant

Hymn Suggestions

2236 "Gather Us In" (Acts, Communion) (O)
324 "Hail Thee, Festival Day" (Acts)
334 "Sweet, Sweet Spirit" (Acts)
420 "Breathe on Me, Breath of God" (Acts)
422 "Jesus, Thine All-Victorious Love" (Acts)
590 "Christ Loves the Church" (Acts)
537 "Filled with the Spirit's Power" (Acts)
538 "Wind Who Makes All Winds that Blow" (Acts)
541 "See How Great a Flame Aspires" (Acts)
543 "O Breath of Life" (Acts)
544 "Like the Murmur of the Dove's Song" (Acts)
547 "O Church of God, United" (Acts)
2027 "Now Praise the Hidden God of Love" (Acts)
2117 "Spirit of God" (Acts)
2120 "Spirit, Spirit of Gentleness" (Acts, Rom.)
2122 "She Comes Sailing on the Wind" (Acts)
2123 "Loving Spirit" (Acts, Pentecost)
2237 "As a Fire Is Meant for Burning" (Acts)
2238 "In the Midst of New Dimensions" (Acts, Pentecost)
2246 "Deep in the Shadows of the Past" (Acts)
2269 "Come, Share the Lord" (Acts, Communion)
368 "My Hope Is Built" (Acts, Rom.)
500 "Spirit of God, Descend Upon My Heart" (Acts, Rom.)
475 "Come Down, O Love Divine" (Acts, John)
651 "Come, Holy Ghost, Our Souls Inspire" (Acts, John)
2213 "Healer of Our Every Ill" (Acts, John)
73 "O Worship the King" (Ps.)
148 "Many and Great, O God" (Ps.)
404 "Every Time I Feel the Spirit" (Rom.)
2121 "O Holy Spirit, Root of Life" (Rom.)
454 "Open My Eyes, That I May See" (John)
640 "Take Our Bread" (Acts, Communion)
2077 "You Alone Are Holy" (Acts)

Contemporary Suggestions

S2039 "Holy, Holy" (Acts)
SP141, R206
S2049 "God Is Here Today" ("Dios Está Aquí) (Acts)
S2119 "Where the Spirit of the Lord Is" (Acts)
S2272 "Holy Ground" (Acts)
SP86, WO57
SP240 "As We Gather" (Acts)
R6
MM57 "Open the Eyes of My Heart" (Acts)
V-3 p. 162 (vocal solo)
MM99 "Shout to the North" (Acts, Rom.)
WG114
MM88 "Holy Spirit, Rain Down" (Acts, John)
UM328 "Surely the Presence of the Lord" (Acts, John)
R167, SP243; S-2, #200 (stanzas for soloist)
UM333 "I'm Goin'a Sing When the Spirit Says Sing" (Acts, John)
M4 "Let It Rise" (Ps.)
SP32 "Bless the Lord, O My Soul" (Ps.)
S2165 "Cry of My Heart" (Rom.)
M39, WG32

Vocal Solos

"Spirit of Faith Come Down" (Acts, Pentecost)
V-1 p. 43
"Consume Me" (Acts)
V-3 p. 148
"Ev'ry Time I Feel De Spirit" (Acts, Pentecost)
V-7 p. 78
"New Wind Blowin' "(Acts, Pentecost)
V-8 p. 192

Anthems

"There's a Spirit of Love in This Place" (Acts)
Mark A. Miller; Abingdon Press 9780687644629
SATB with piano (opt. solo)

"If Ye Love Me" (John)
Philip Stopford; Hal Leonard 08745638
SSATBB *a cappella*

Other Suggestions

Visuals:
O (Acts) Wind, tongues of fire, praising, all races of people
P Sea/ships, whales, dove, volcano, singing, Ps. 104:35*b*
E Praying hands, Holy Spirit (flames, dove descending)
G Briefcase (Advocate), Trinity (triangle, trefoil, others)

Introit: S2125. "Come, Holy Spirit" (Acts)
Greeting: BOW390 or BOW406 (Acts) or BOW382 (Rom.)
Opening Prayer: BOW464 (Rom.)
Canticle: UM406. "Canticle of Prayer" (Rom.)
Call to Prayer: BOW214. "Spirit of God" (Acts)
Prayer of Confession: BOW482 or BOW489 (Acts)
Prayer: UM329, UM542, or UM574 (Acts, Pentecost)
Prayer: BOW404, BOW407, or BOW408 (Acts, John)
Hymn: BOW223. "O Holy Spirit" (Acts)
Great Thanksgiving for Pentecost: BOW68
Benediction Response: S2241. "The Spirit Sends Us Forth to Serve" (Acts, Pentecost)

Isaiah 6:1-8

[1] In the year that King Uzziah died, I saw the Lord sitting on a throne, high and lofty; and the hem of his robe filled the temple. [2] Seraphs were in attendance above him; each had six wings: with two they covered their faces, and with two they covered their feet, and with two they flew. [3] And one called to another and said: "Holy, holy, holy is the LORD of hosts; the whole earth is full of his glory." [4] The pivots on the thresholds shook at the voices of those who called, and the house filled with smoke. [5] And I said: "Woe is me! I am lost, for I am a man of unclean lips, and I live among a people of unclean lips; yet my eyes have seen the King, the LORD of hosts!"

[6] Then one of the seraphs flew to me, holding a live coal that had been taken from the altar with a pair of tongs. [7] The seraph touched my mouth with it and said: "Now that this has touched your lips, your guilt has departed and your sin is blotted out." [8] Then I heard the voice of the Lord saying, "Whom shall I send, and who will go for us?" And I said, "Here am I; send me!"

Psalm 29

[1]Ascribe to the LORD, O heavenly beings, ascribe to the LORD glory and strength. [2]Ascribe to the LORD the glory of his name; worship the LORD in holy splendor. [3]The voice of the LORD is over the waters; the God of glory thunders, the LORD, over mighty waters. [4]The voice of the LORD is powerful; the voice of the LORD is full of majesty. [5]The voice of the LORD breaks the cedars; the LORD breaks the cedars of Lebanon. [6]He makes Lebanon skip like a calf, and Sirion like a young wild ox. [7]The voice of the LORD flashes forth flames of fire. [8] The voice of the LORD shakes the wilderness; the LORD shakes the wilderness of Kadesh. [9] The voice of the LORD causes the oaks to whirl, and strips the forest bare; and in his temple all say, "Glory!" [10]The LORD sits enthroned over the flood; the LORD sits enthroned as king forever. [11]May the LORD give strength to his people! May the LORD bless his people with peace!

Romans 8:12-17

[12] So then, brothers and sisters, we are debtors, not to the flesh, to live according to the flesh— [13] for if you live according to the flesh, you will die; but if by the Spirit you put to death the deeds of the body, you will live. [14] For all who are led by the Spirit of God are children of God. [15] For you did not receive a spirit of slavery to fall back into fear, but you have received a spirit of adoption. When we cry, "Abba! Father!" [16] it is that very Spirit bearing witness with our spirit that we are children of God, [17] and if children, then heirs, heirs of God and joint heirs with Christ—if, in fact, we suffer with him so that we may also be glorified with him.

John 3:1-17

[1] Now there was a Pharisee named Nicodemus, a leader of the Jews. [2] He came to Jesus by night and said to him, "Rabbi, we know that you are a teacher who has come from God; for no one can do these signs that you do apart from the presence of God." [3] Jesus answered him, "Very truly, I tell you, no one can see the kingdom of God without being born from above." [4] Nicodemus said to him, "How can anyone be born after having grown old? Can one enter a second time into the mother's womb and be born?" [5] Jesus answered, "Very truly, I tell you, no one can enter the kingdom of God without being born of water and Spirit. [6] What is born of the flesh is flesh, and what is born of the Spirit is spirit. [7] Do not be astonished that I said to you, 'You must be born from above.' [8] The wind blows where it chooses, and you hear the sound of it, but you do not know where it comes from or where it goes. So it is with everyone who is born of the Spirit." [9] Nicodemus said to him, "How can these things be?" [10]Jesus answered him, "Are you a teacher of Israel, and yet you do not understand these things?

[11] "Very truly, I tell you, we speak of what we know and testify to what we have seen; yet you do not receive our testimony. [12] If I have told you about earthly things and you do not believe, how can you believe if I tell you about heavenly things? [13] No one has ascended into heaven except the one who descended from heaven, the Son of Man. [14] And just as Moses lifted up the serpent in the wilderness, so must the Son of Man be lifted up, [15] that whoever believes in him may have eternal life.

[16] "For God so loved the world that he gave his only Son, so that everyone who believes in him may not perish but may have eternal life.

[17] "Indeed, God did not send the Son into the world to condemn the world, but in order that the world might be saved through him."

Notes:

Primary Hymns and Songs for the Day

64 "Holy, Holy, Holy!" (O) (Isa., Trinity)
  H-3 Handbell-68; Choir-99; Descant-80; Organ-97
  S-1 #245-48. Various treatments
2256 "Holy, Holy, Holy Lord" (Isa., Communion)
159 "Lift High the Cross" (John)
331 "Holy Spirit, Come, Confirm Us" (Trinity) (C)
  H-3 Choir-67
  S-2 #63-64. Descant/harmonization
662 "Stand Up and Bless the Lord" (Isa.) (C)

Hymn Suggestions

65 "Santo! Santo! Santo!" (Isa., Trinity) (O)
85 "We Believe in One True God" (Isa., Trinity)
88 "Maker, in Whom We Live" (Isa., Trinity)
90 "Ye Watchers and Ye Holy Ones" (Isa., Trinity)
436 "The Voice of God Is Calling" (Isa.)
497 "Send Me, Lord" (Isa.)
508 "Faith, While Trees Are Still in Blossom" (Isa.)
582 "Whom Shall I Send" (Isa.)
593 "Here I Am, Lord" (Isa.)
626 "Let All Mortal Flesh Keep Silence" (Isa.)
638 "This Is the Feast of Victory" (Isa., Communion)
2019 "Holy" ("Santo") (Isa.)
332 "Spirit of Faith, Come Down" (Rom.)
404 "Every Time I Feel the Spirit" (Rom.)
414 "Thou Hidden Love of God" (Rom.)
2052 "The Lone, Wild Bird" (Rom.)
109 "Creating God, Your Fingers Trace" (Rom., Trinity)
372 "How Can We Sinners Know" (Rom., John)
2050 "Mothering God, You Gave Me Birth" (Rom., John)
2248 "Baptized in Water" (Rom., Baptism)
98 "To God Be the Glory" (John)
184 "Of the Father's Love Begotten" (John, Trinity)
267 "O Love, How Deep" (John, Trinity)
605 "Wash, O God, Our Sons and Daughters" (John, Baptism)
610 "We Know That Christ Is Raised" (John, Baptism)
2046 "Womb of Life" (John, Trinity)
2084 "Come, Let Us with Our Lord Arise" (John)
  R18
2085 "He Came Down" (John)
2220 "We Are God's People" (John)
2236 "Gather Us In" (John)
2174 "What Does the Lord Require of You" (Peace with Justice)

Contemporary Suggestions

MM77 "Above All" (Isa., John)
  WO2; V-3 p. 17 or V-10(03) p. 18 (vocal solo)
S2007 "Santo, Santo, Santo" ("Holy, Holy, Holy")
S2039 "Holy, Holy" (Isa., Rom.)
M6 "Because We Believe" (Isa.)
SP37 "Holy, Holy, Holy" (Isa.)
  R208, MM95, H2
SP91 "Holy Is the Lord" (Isa.)
  R203
SP220 "You Are My All in All" (Isa., John)
UM393 "Spirit of the Living God" (Rom.)
  R90, SP131, S-1 #212 (vocal descant)
MM82 "You Are My King" ("Amazing Love") (Rom., John)
  WY65
S2223 "They'll Know We Are Christians by Our Love" (Rom., Trinity)
S2108 "O How He Loves You and Me!" (John)
S2073 "Celebrate Love" (John)
M7 "I Believe in Jesus" (John, Trinity)
  WO68
SP111 "There Is a Redeemer" (John, Trinity)
  R232
S2006 "Lord God, Almighty" (Trinity)
S2171 "Make Me a Channel of Your Peace" (Peace with Justice)

Vocal Solos

"Alleluia" (Isa., Trinity)
V-8 p. 358
"Abba Father" (Rom.)
V-3 p. 109
"Serve the Lord" (John, Trinity)
V-10(90) p. 127

Anthems

"Ev'ry Time I Feel the Spirit" (Rom.)
Arr. Moses Hogan; Hal Leonard 08745536
Two-part with piano

"We Believe" (The Apostles' Creed) (Trinity)
John Purifoy; Brookfield Press 08744797
SATB with keyboard

Other Suggestions

Visuals:
  O Seraphs, incense, glowing coals
  P Storm, flames, lightning, wind, skipping calf
  E Crown (heirs), open manacles (handcuffs)
  G Wind, white garment, water, flame/dove (Holy Spirit)
Call to Worship: UM234, sts. 2, 3. "O Come, All Ye Faithful" (John, Trinity)
Greeting: BOW391 or BOW411 (Trinity) or BOW300 (Ps.)
Opening Prayer: BOW392 (John)
Prayer of Confession: BOW428 (Peace with Justice)
Prayer: BOW412 (Trinity Sunday)
Prayer: BOW513. For Justice (Peace with Justice)
Canticle: UM80. "Canticle of the Holy Trinity"
Affirmation of Faith: UM880. The Nicene Creed (Trinity)
Communion Responses: S2257. "Communion Setting" (Isa.)
Offering Response: BOW182. "Doxology" (John)
Blessing: BOW563 (Trinity) or BOW521 (Peace/Justice)

1 Samuel 15:34–16:13

[34]Then Samuel went to Ramah; and Saul went up to his house in Gibeah of Saul. [35]Samuel did not see Saul again until the day of his death, but Samuel grieved over Saul. And the LORD was sorry that he had made Saul king over Israel.

[1]The LORD said to Samuel, "How long will you grieve over Saul? I have rejected him from being king over Israel. Fill your horn with oil and set out; I will send you to Jesse the Bethlehemite, for I have provided for myself a king among his sons." [2]Samuel said, "How can I go? If Saul hears of it, he will kill me." And the LORD said, "Take a heifer with you, and say, 'I have come to sacrifice to the LORD.' [3]Invite Jesse to the sacrifice, and I will show you what you shall do; and you shall anoint for me the one whom I name to you." [4]Samuel did what the LORD commanded, and came to Bethlehem. The elders of the city came to meet him trembling, and said, "Do you come peaceably?" [5]He said, "Peaceably; I have come to sacrifice to the LORD; sanctify yourselves and come with me to the sacrifice." And he sanctified Jesse and his sons and invited them to the sacrifice.

[6]When they came, he looked on Eliab and thought, "Surely the LORD's anointed is now before the LORD." [7]But the LORD said to Samuel, "Do not look on his appearance or on the height of his stature, because I have rejected him; for the LORD does not see as mortals see; they look on the outward appearance, but the LORD looks on the heart." [8]Then Jesse called Abinadab, and made him pass before Samuel. He said, "Neither has the LORD chosen this one." [9]Then Jesse made Shammah pass by. And he said, "Neither has the LORD chosen this one." [10]Jesse made seven of his sons pass before Samuel, and Samuel said to Jesse, "The LORD has not chosen any of these." [11]Samuel said to Jesse, "Are all your sons here?" And he said, "There remains yet the youngest, but he is keeping the sheep." And Samuel said to Jesse, "Send and bring him; for we will not sit down until he comes here." [12]He sent and brought him in. Now he was ruddy, and had beautiful eyes, and was handsome. The LORD said, "Rise and anoint him; for this is the one." [13]Then Samuel took the horn of oil, and anointed him in the presence of his brothers; and the spirit of the LORD came mightily upon David from that day forward. Samuel then set out and went to Ramah.

Psalm 20

[1]The LORD answer you in the day of trouble! The name of the God of Jacob protect you! [2]May he send you help from the sanctuary, and give you support from Zion. [3]May he remember all your offerings, and regard with favor your burnt sacrifices. [4]May he grant you your heart's desire, and fulfill all your plans. [5]May we shout for joy over your victory, and in the name of our God set up our banners. May the LORD fulfill all your petitions. [6]Now I know that the LORD will help his anointed; he will answer him from his holy heaven with mighty victories by his right hand. [7]Some take pride in chariots, and some in horses, but our pride is in the name of the LORD our God. [8]They will collapse and fall, but we shall rise and stand upright. [9]Give victory to the king, O LORD; answer us when we call.

---

2 Corinthians 5:6-10 (11-13), 14-17

[6]So we are always confident; even though we know that while we are at home in the body we are away from the Lord— [7]for we walk by faith, not by sight. [8]Yes, we do have confidence, and we would rather be away from the body and at home with the Lord. [9]So whether we are at home or away, we make it our aim to please him. [10]For all of us must appear before the judgment seat of Christ, so that each may receive recompense for what has been done in the body, whether good or evil.

[11]Therefore, knowing the fear of the Lord, we try to persuade others; but we ourselves are well known to God, and I hope that we are also well known to your consciences. [12]We are not commending ourselves to you again, but giving you an opportunity to boast about us, so that you may be able to answer those who boast in outward appearance and not in the heart. [13]For if we are beside ourselves, it is for God; if we are in our right mind, it is for you. [14]For the love of Christ urges us on, because we are convinced that one has died for all; therefore all have died. [15]And he died for all, so that those who live might live no longer for themselves, but for him who died and was raised for them.

[16]From now on, therefore, we regard no one from a human point of view; even though we once knew Christ from a human point of view, we know him no longer in that way. [17]So if anyone is in Christ, there is a new creation: everything old has passed away; see, everything has become new!

Mark 4:26-34

[26]He also said, "The kingdom of God is as if someone would scatter seed on the ground, [27]and would sleep and rise night and day, and the seed would sprout and grow, he does not know how. [28]The earth produces of itself, first the stalk, then the head, then the full grain in the head. [29]But when the grain is ripe, at once he goes in with his sickle, because the harvest has come."

[30]He also said, "With what can we compare the kingdom of God, or what parable will we use for it? [31]It is like a mustard seed, which, when sown upon the ground, is the smallest of all the seeds on earth; [32]yet when it is sown it grows up and becomes the greatest of all shrubs, and puts forth large branches, so that the birds of the air can make nests in its shade."

[33]With many such parables he spoke the word to them, as they were able to hear it; [34]he did not speak to them except in parables, but he explained everything in private to his disciples.

Primary Hymns and Songs for the Day

545 "The Church's One Foundation" (2 Cor.) (O)
383 "This Is a Day of New Beginnings" (2 Cor.)
H-3 Choir-196
2196 "We Walk by Faith" (2 Cor., Mark)
H-3 Choir-21
356 "Pues Si Vivimos" ("When We Are Living") (2 Cor., Mark) (C)
S-1 #320. Orff instrument arrangement
H-3 Choir-218; Organ-155

Hymn Suggestions

203 "Hail to the Lord's Anointed" (1 Sam.)
454 "Open My Eyes, That I May See" (1 Sam.)
497 "Send Me, Lord" (1 Sam.)
593 "Here I Am, Lord" (1 Sam.)
2123 "Loving Spirit" (1 Sam., Father's Day)
2236 "Gather Us In" (1 Sam., Mark)
2238 "In the Midst of New Dimensions" (1 Sam.)
2279 "The Trees of the Field" (Ps.)
160 "Rejoice, Ye Pure in Heart" (Ps.)
161 "Rejoice, Ye Pure in Heart" (Ps.)
292 "What Wondrous Love Is This" (2 Cor.)
294 "Alas! and Did My Savior Bleed" (2 Cor.)
359 "Alas! and Did My Savior Bleed" (2 Cor.)
384 "Love Divine, All Loves Excelling" (2 Cor.)
388 "O Come and Dwell in Me" (2 Cor.)
421 "Make Me a Captive, Lord" (2 Cor.)
508 "Faith, While Trees Are Still in Blossom" (2 Cor.)
524 "Beams of Heaven as I Go" (2 Cor.)
2046 "Womb of Life" (2 Cor.)
2083 "My Song Is Love Unknown" (2 Cor.)
2158 "Just a Closer Walk with Thee" (2 Cor.)
2282 "I'll Fly Away" (2 Cor.)
97 "For the Fruits of This Creation" (Mark)
118 "The Care the Eagle Gives Her Young" (Mark)
275 "The Kingdom of God" (Mark)
414 "Thou Hidden Love of God" (Mark)
565 "Father, We Thank You" (Mark)
583 "Sois la Semilla" ("You Are the Seed") (Mark)
694 "Come, Ye Thankful People, Come" (Mark)
707 "Hymn of Promise" (Mark)
2060 "God the Sculptor of the Mountains" (Mark)
2190 "Bring Forth the Kingdom" (Mark)
2211 "Faith Is Patience in the Night" (Mark)

Contemporary Suggestions

UM393 "Spirit of the Living God" (1 Sam.)
R90, SP131; S-1 #212 (vocal descant idea)
S2164 "Sanctuary" (1 Sam.)
R185, M52
M36 "Awesome in This Place" (1 Sam.)
WG14
M49 "Refresh My Heart" (1 Sam., 2 Cor.)
S2074 "Shout to the Lord" (Ps.)
M16, WY126; V-3 p. 56 (vocal solo)
S2159 "Jesus, Draw Me Close" (2 Cor.)
MM67 "We Want to See Jesus Lifted High" (2 Cor.)
WO149
MM82 "You Are My King" ("Amazing Love") (2 Cor.)
WY65
SP158 "The Battle Belongs to the Lord" (2 Cor.)
R244
WO78 "I Walk By Faith" (2 Cor.)
WO89 "I Will Not Forget You" (Mark)
M17 "This Kingdom" (Mark)

Vocal Solos

"Just a Closer Walk with Thee" (2 Cor.)
V-8 p. 323
"Father, We Thank You" (Mark)
UM563

Anthems

"Here I Am, Lord" (1 Sam.)
Schutte/Sherman; Hope Publishing C-5311
SAB with keyboard, opt. handbells (SATB C-5087)

"The Mustard Seed" (Mark)
Anna Laura Page; Choristers Guild CGA1011
Unison with piano (opt. flute)

Other Suggestions

Visuals:
O Several vials of oil, anointing
P Vials of oil, rejoicing, victory
E Cross wrapped with white cloth, resurrection, reconciliation
G Bag of seeds, several small plants, one larger plant, stalks of wheat

Call to Worship: S2124. "Come, O Holy Spirit, Come" (1 Sam.)
Greeting: BOW450 (Ps. 20) or BOW451 (Ps. 72)
Opening Prayer: BOW459 (1 Sam.)
Opening Prayer: BOW464 (Mark)
Prayer: BOW511. For God's Reign (1 Sam., Ps.)
Prayer: BOW544. For Leaders (1 Sam.)
Call to Prayer: UM388, st. 1. "O Come and Dwell in Me" (2 Cor.)
Prayer of Thanksgiving: BOW550 (2 Cor., Mark)
Blessing: BOW564 (1 Sam., 2 Cor.)
Benediction: S2241. "The Spirit Sends Us Forth to Serve" (1 Sam.)

1 Samuel 17:(1*a*, 4-11, 19-23) 32-49

1a Now the Philistines gathered their armies for battle.
4 And there came out from the camp of the Philistines a cham-
pion named Goliath, of Gath, whose height was six cubits and a span.
5 He had a helmet of bronze on his head, and he was armed with a
coat of mail; the weight of the coat was five thousand shekels of
bronze. 6 He had greaves of bronze on his legs and a javelin of bronze
slung between his shoulders. 7 The shaft of his spear was like a
weaver's beam, and his spear's head weighed six hundred shekels of
iron; and his shield-bearer went before him. 8 He stood and shouted
to the ranks of Israel, "Why have you come out to draw up for battle?
Am I not a Philistine, and are you not servants of Saul? Choose a man
for yourselves, and let him come down to me. 9 If he is able to fight
with me and kill me, then we will be your servants; but if I prevail
against him and kill him, then you shall be our servants and serve
us." 10 And the Philistine said, "Today I defy the ranks of Israel! Give
me a man, that we may fight together." 11 When Saul and all Israel
heard these words of the Philistine, they were dismayed and greatly
afraid.

19 Now Saul, and they, and all the men of Israel, were in the valley
of Elah, fighting with the Philistines. 20 David rose early in the morn-
ing, left the sheep with a keeper, took the provisions, and went as
Jesse had commanded him. He came to the encampment as the army
was going forth to the battle line, shouting the war cry. 21 Israel and
the Philistines drew up for battle, army against army. 22 David left the
things in charge of the keeper of the baggage, ran to the ranks, and
went and greeted his brothers. 23 As he talked with them, the cham-
pion, the Philistine of Gath, Goliath by name, came up out of the
ranks of the Philistines, and spoke the same words as before. And
David heard him.

32 David said to Saul, "Let no one's heart fail because of him; your
servant will go and fight with this Philistine." 33 Saul said to David,
"You are not able to go against this Philistine to fight with him; for
you are just a boy, and he has been a warrior from his youth." 34 But
David said to Saul, "Your servant used to keep sheep for his father;
and whenever a lion or a bear came, and took a lamb from the flock,
35 I went after it and struck it down, rescuing the lamb from its
mouth; and if it turned against me, I would catch it by the jaw, strike
it down, and kill it. 36 Your servant has killed both lions and bears;
and this uncircumcised Philistine shall be like one of them, since he
has defied the armies of the living God." 37 David said, "The LORD,
who saved me from the paw of the lion and from the paw of the bear,
will save me from the hand of this Philistine." So Saul said to David,
"Go, and may the LORD be with you!"

38 Saul clothed David with his armor; he put a bronze helmet on
his head and clothed him with a coat of mail. 39 David strapped Saul's
sword over the armor, and he tried in vain to walk, for he was not
used to them. Then David said to Saul, "I cannot walk with these; for
I am not used to them." So David removed them. 40 Then he took his
staff in his hand, and chose five smooth stones from the wadi, and
put them in his shepherd's bag, in the pouch; his sling was in his
hand, and he drew near to the Philistine.

41 The Philistine came on and drew near to David, with his shield-
bearer in front of him. 42 When the Philistine looked and saw David,
he disdained him, for he was only a youth, ruddy and handsome in
appearance. 43 The Philistine said to David, "Am I a dog, that you
come to me with sticks?" And the Philistine cursed David by his gods.
44 The Philistine said to David, "Come to me, and I will give your flesh
to the birds of the air and to the wild animals of the field." 45 But
David said to the Philistine, "You come to me with sword and spear
and javelin; but I come to you in the name of the LORD of hosts, the
God of the armies of Israel, whom you have defied. 46 This very day
the LORD will deliver you into my hand, and I will strike you down
and cut off your head; and I will give the dead bodies of the
Philistine army this very day to the birds of the air and to the wild ani-
mals of the earth, so that all the earth may know that there is a God
in Israel, 47 and that all this assembly may know that the LORD does
not save by sword and spear; for the battle is the LORD's and he will
give you into our hand."

48 When the Philistine drew nearer to meet David, David ran
quickly toward the battle line to meet the Philistine. 49 David put his
hand in his bag, took out a stone, slung it, and struck the Philistine
on his forehead; the stone sank into his forehead, and he fell face
down on the ground.

Psalm 9:9-20

9 The LORD is a stronghold for the oppressed, a stronghold in
times of trouble. 10 And those who know your name put their trust in
you, for you, O LORD, have not forsaken those who seek you. 11 Sing
praises to the LORD, who dwells in Zion. Declare his deeds among the
peoples. 12 For he who avenges blood is mindful of them; he does not
forget the cry of the afflicted. 13 Be gracious to me, O LORD. See what
I suffer from those who hate me; you are the one who lifts me up
from the gates of death, 14 so that I may recount all your praises, and,
in the gates of daughter Zion, rejoice in your deliverance. 15 The
nations have sunk in the pit that they made; in the net that they hid
has their own foot been caught. 16 The LORD has made himself
known, he has executed judgment; the wicked are snared in the work
of their own hands. 17 The wicked shall depart to Sheol, all the nations
that forget God. 18 For the needy shall not always be forgotten, nor
the hope of the poor perish forever. 19 Rise up, O LORD! Do not let
mortals prevail; let the nations be judged before you. 20 Put them in
fear, O LORD; let the nations know that they are only human.

2 Corinthians 6:1-13

1 As we work together with him, we urge you also not to accept
the grace of God in vain. 2 For he says, "At an acceptable time I have
listened to you, and on a day of salvation I have helped you." See,
now is the acceptable time; see, now is the day of salvation! 3 We are
putting no obstacle in anyone's way, so that no fault may be found
with our ministry, 4 but as servants of God we have commended our-
selves in every way: through great endurance, in afflictions, hard-
ships, calamities, 5 beatings, imprisonments, riots, labors, sleepless
nights, hunger; 6 by purity, knowledge, patience, kindness, holiness of
spirit, genuine love, 7 truthful speech, and the power of God; with the
weapons of righteousness for the right hand and for the left; 8 in
honor and dishonor, in ill repute and good repute. We are treated as
impostors, and yet are true; 9 as unknown, and yet are well known; as
dying, and see—we are alive; as punished, and yet not killed; 10 as sor-
rowful, yet always rejoicing; as poor, yet making many rich; as having
nothing, and yet possessing everything.

11 We have spoken frankly to you Corinthians; our heart is wide
open to you. 12 There is no restriction in our affections, but only in
yours. 13 In return—I speak as to children—open wide your hearts also.

Mark 4:35-41

35 On that day, when evening had come, he said to them, "Let us
go across to the other side." 36 And leaving the crowd behind, they
took him with them in the boat, just as he was. Other boats were with
him. 37 A great windstorm arose, and the waves beat into the boat, so
that the boat was already being swamped. 38 But he was in the stern,
asleep on the cushion; and they woke him up and said to him,
"Teacher, do you not care that we are perishing?" 39 He woke up and
rebuked the wind, and said to the sea, "Peace! Be still!" Then the
wind ceased, and there was a dead calm. 40 He said to them, "Why are
you afraid? Have you still no faith?" 41 And they were filled with great
awe and said to one another, "Who then is this, that even the wind
and the sea obey him?"

Primary Hymns and Songs for the Day

519 "Lift Every Voice and Sing" (1 Sam., 2 Cor.) (O)
H-3 Choir-128
377 "It Is Well with My Soul" (2 Cor., Mark)
H-3 Choir-113
2191 "Eternal Father, Strong to Save" (Mark)
H-3 Choir-63; Descant-74; Organ-89
512 "Stand By Me" (Mark) (C)
H-3 Choir-177

Hymn Suggestions

473 "Lead Me, Lord" (1 Sam.)
513 "Soldiers of Christ, Arise" (1 Sam.)
523 "Saranam, Saranam" ("Refuge") (1 Sam.)
110 "A Mighty Fortress Is Our God" (1 Sam., Ps., Mark)
517 "By Gracious Powers" (1 Sam., Ps.)
522 "Leave It There" (1 Sam., Ps.)
533 "We Shall Overcome" (1 Sam., Ps.)
577 "God of Grace and God of Glory" (1 Sam., Ps., Mark)
107 "La Palabra Del Señor Es Recta" ("Righteous and Just Is the Word of Our Lord") (Ps.)
2001 "We Sing to You, O God" (Ps.)
2030 "The First Song of Isaiah" (Ps.)
2216 "When We Are Called to Sing Your Praise" (Ps.)
2053 "If It Had Not Been for the Lord" (1 Sam., Ps.)
2218 "You Are Mine" (1 Sam., Mark)
450 "Creator of the Earth and Skies" (2 Cor.)
510 "Come, Ye Disconsolate" (2 Cor.)
511 "Am I Soldier of the Cross" (2 Cor.)
514 "Stand Up, Stand Up for Jesus" (2 Cor.)
730 "O Day of God, Draw Nigh" (2 Cor.)
2255 "In the Singing" (2 Cor., Communion)
2211 "Faith Is Patience in the Night" (2 Cor., Mark)
122 "God of the Sparrow, God of the Whale" (Mark)
129 "Give to the Winds Thy Fears" (Mark)
341 "I Sought the Lord" (Mark)
368 "My Hope Is Built" (Mark)
476 "Lonely the Boat" (Mark)
509 "Jesus, Savior, Pilot Me" (Mark)
525 "We'll Understand It Better By and By" (Mark)
529 "How Firm a Foundation" (Mark)
530 "Are Ye Able" (Mark)
532 "Jesus, Priceless Treasure" (Mark)
534 "Be Still, My Soul" (Mark)
479 "Jesus, Lover of My Soul" (Mark)
2142 "Blessed Quietness" (Mark)
2212 "My Life Flows On" ("How Can I Keep from Singing") (Mark)

Contemporary Suggestions

S2139 "Oh, I Know the Lord's Laid His Hands on Me" (1 Sam.)
S2054 "Nothing Can Trouble" (1 Sam., Ps.)
S2144 "Why We Sing" (Ps.)
SP2 "Ah, Lord God" (1 Sam., Ps.)
R254
SP3 "What a Mighty God" (1 Sam., Ps.)
S2021 "What Mighty God We Serve" (1 Sam., Ps.)
R159
SP4 "Great and Mighty Is He" (1 Sam., Ps.)
M11
SP158 "The Battle Belongs to the Lord" (1 Sam., 2 Cor.)
R244
WO78 "I Walk By Faith" (1 Sam., 2 Cor.)
MM67 "We Want to See Jesus Lifted High" (2 Cor.)
WO149
UM507 "Through It All" (2 Cor.)
S2040 "Awesome God" (1 Sam., Mark)
R245, SP11, WO9, WY3; V-10 (90) p. 21
S2057 "Be Still and Know That I Am God" (Mark)
R10, SP49
S2213 "Healer of Our Every Ill" (Mark)
WY145 "In Christ Alone" (Mark)

Vocal Solos

"What God Hath Promised" (2 Cor.)
V-8 p. 297
"Jesus, Lover of My Soul" (Mark)
V-1 p. 37

Anthems

"Pilot Me" (Mark)
Arr. Carol Barnett; Hal Leonard 08745078
SATB *divisi, a cappella*

"It Is Well with My Soul" (Mark)
Arr. John Helgen; Kjos 9051
SATB *divisi* with piano

Other Suggestions

Visuals:
O Armor, sword/spear, sling shot, stones, bag
P Globe, scales of justice, rejoicing
E Clock set for worship hour, all ages enduring hardship, poor smiling
G Boat, storm at sea, fear, peace, calm, sleeping, Jesus in command

Act of Congregational Centering: BOW472 (Mark)
Greeting: BOW327 (1 Sam., Mark)
Opening Prayer: BOW464 (Mark) or BOW466 (2 Cor.)
Opening Prayer: BOW466 (Father's Day)
Prayer of Confession and Assurance: BOW478 (1 Sam., Mark)
Prayer: BOW337, BOW506, or BOW522 (2 Cor.)
Prayer: BOW513 or BOW524 (1 Sam., Mark)
Prayer: BOW542. For Those in Military Service (1 Sam.)
Prayer: BOW437 or BOW441 (Father's Day)
Scripture Response: UM534, st. 2. "Be Still, My Soul" (Mark)
Dismissal: BOW559 (1 Sam., 2 Cor.)

2 Samuel 1:1, 17-27

1 After the death of Saul, when David had returned from defeating the Amalekites, David remained two days in Ziklag.

17 David intoned this lamentation over Saul and his son Jonathan. 18 (He ordered that The Song of the Bow be taught to the people of Judah; it is written in the Book of Jashar.) He said: 19 Your glory, O Israel, lies slain upon your high places! How the mighty have fallen! 20 Tell it not in Gath, proclaim it not in the streets of Ashkelon; or the daughters of the Philistines will rejoice, the daughters of the uncircumcised will exult. 21 You mountains of Gilboa, let there be no dew or rain upon you, nor bounteous fields! For there the shield of the mighty was defiled, the shield of Saul, anointed with oil no more. 22 From the blood of the slain, from the fat of the mighty, the bow of Jonathan did not turn back, nor the sword of Saul return empty. 23 Saul and Jonathan, beloved and lovely! In life and in death they were not divided; they were swifter than eagles, they were stronger than lions. 24 O daughters of Israel, weep over Saul, who clothed you with crimson, in luxury, who put ornaments of gold on your apparel.
25 How the mighty have fallen in the midst of the battle! Jonathan lies slain upon your high places. 26 I am distressed for you, my brother Jonathan; greatly beloved were you to me; your love to me was wonderful, passing the love of women. 27 How the mighty have fallen, and the weapons of war perished!

Psalm 130

1 Out of the depths I cry to you, O LORD. 2 Lord, hear my voice! Let your ears be attentive to the voice of my supplications! 3 If you, O LORD, should mark iniquities, Lord, who could stand? 4 But there is forgiveness with you, so that you may be revered. 5 I wait for the LORD, my soul waits, and in his word I hope; 6 my soul waits for the Lord more than those who watch for the morning, more than those who watch for the morning. 7 O Israel, hope in the LORD! For with the LORD there is steadfast love, and with him is great power to redeem. 8 It is he who will redeem Israel from all its iniquities.

---

2 Corinthians 8:7-15

7 Now as you excel in everything—in faith, in speech, in knowledge, in utmost eagerness, and in our love for you—so we want you to excel also in this generous undertaking.

8 I do not say this as a command, but I am testing the genuineness of your love against the earnestness of others. 9 For you know the generous act of our Lord Jesus Christ, that though he was rich, yet for your sakes he became poor, so that by his poverty you might become rich. 10 And in this matter I am giving my advice: it is appropriate for you who began last year not only to do something but even to desire to do something— 11 now finish doing it, so that your eagerness may be matched by completing it according to your means. 12 For if the eagerness is there, the gift is acceptable according to what one has—not according to what one does not have. 13 I do not mean that there should be relief for others and pressure on you, but it is a question of a fair balance between 14 your present abundance and their need, so that their abundance may be for your need, in order that there may be a fair balance. 15 As it is written, "The one who had much did not have too much, and the one who had little did not have too little."

Mark 5:21-43

21 When Jesus had crossed again in the boat to the other side, a great crowd gathered around him; and he was by the sea. 22 Then one of the leaders of the synagogue named Jairus came and, when he saw him, fell at his feet 23 and begged him repeatedly, "My little daughter is at the point of death. Come and lay your hands on her, so that she may be made well, and live." 24 So he went with him.

And a large crowd followed him and pressed in on him. 25 Now there was a woman who had been suffering from hemorrhages for twelve years. 26 She had endured much under many physicians, and had spent all that she had; and she was no better, but rather grew worse. 27 She had heard about Jesus, and came up behind him in the crowd and touched his cloak, 28 for she said, "If I but touch his clothes, I will be made well." 29 Immediately her hemorrhage stopped; and she felt in her body that she was healed of her disease. 30 Immediately aware that power had gone forth from him, Jesus turned about in the crowd and said, "Who touched my clothes?" 31 And his disciples said to him, "You see the crowd pressing in on you; how can you say, 'Who touched me?' " 32 He looked all around to see who had done it. 33 But the woman, knowing what had happened to her, came in fear and trembling, fell down before him, and told him the whole truth. 34 He said to her, "Daughter, your faith has made you well; go in peace, and be healed of your disease."

35 While he was still speaking, some people came from the leader's house to say, "Your daughter is dead. Why trouble the teacher any further?" 36 But overhearing what they said, Jesus said to the leader of the synagogue, "Do not fear, only believe." 37 He allowed no one to follow him except Peter, James, and John, the brother of James.
38 When they came to the house of the leader of the synagogue, he saw a commotion, people weeping and wailing loudly. 39 When he had entered, he said to them, "Why do you make a commotion and weep? The child is not dead but sleeping." 40 And they laughed at him. Then he put them all outside, and took the child's father and mother and those who were with him, and went in where the child was. 41 He took her by the hand and said to her, "Talitha cum," which means, "Little girl, get up!" 42 And immediately the girl got up and began to walk about (she was twelve years of age). At this they were overcome with amazement.
43 He strictly ordered them that no one should know this, and told them to give her something to eat.

Primary Hymns and Songs for the Day

117 "O God, Our Help in Ages Past" (2 Sam.) (O)
  H-3 Handbell-87; Choir-60, 143; Descant-93; Organ-132
  S-1 #293-96. Various treatments
427 "Where Cross the Crowded Ways of Life" (2 Cor., Mark)
  H-3 Choir-178, 180; Organ-44
  S-1 #141-43. Various treatments
434 "Cuando El Pobre" ("When the Poor Ones") (2 Cor., Mark)
474 "Precious Lord, Take My Hand" (2 Sam., Ps., Mark)
534 "Be Still, My Soul" (2 Sam., Ps., Mark) (C)
  H-3 Choir-36
2153 "I'm Gonna Live So God Can Use Me" (2 Cor.)

Hymn Suggestions

708 "Rejoice in God's Saints" (2 Sam.) (O)
510 "Come, Ye Disconsolate" (2 Sam., Ps., Comm.)
515 "Out of the Depths I Cry to You" (2 Sam., Ps.)
518 "O Thou, in Whose Presence" (2 Sam., Ps.)
700 "Abide with Me" (2 Sam., Ps.)
2110 "Why Has God Forsaken Me?" (2 Sam., Ps.)
2136 "Out of the Depths" (2 Sam., Ps.)
2213 "Healer of Our Every Ill" (2 Sam., Ps.)
2216 "When We Are Called to Sing Your Praise" (2 Sam., Ps.)
458 "Dear Lord, For All in Pain" (2 Sam., Ps., Mark)
250 "Once in Royal David's City" (2 Cor.)
372 "How Can We Sinners Know" (2 Cor.)
554 "All Praise to Our Redeeming Lord" (2 Cor.)
262 "Heal Me, Hands of Jesus" (Mark)
263 "When Jesus the Healer Passed Through Galilee" (Mark)
265 "O Christ, the Healer" (Mark)
266 "Heal Us, Emmanuel, Hear Our Prayer" (Mark)
274 "Woman in the Night" (Mark)
337 "Only Trust Him" (Mark)
340 "Come, Ye Sinners, Poor and Needy" (Mark)
341 "I Sought the Lord" (Mark)
351 "Pass Me Not, O Gentle Savior" (Mark)
357 "Just As I Am, Without One Plea" (Mark)
367 "He Touched Me" (Mark)
370 "Victory in Jesus" (Mark)
632 "Draw Us in the Spirit's Tether" (Mark, Comm.)
2104 "An Outcast among Outcasts" (Mark)
2266 "Here Is Bread, Here Is Wine" (Mark, Communion)

Contemporary Suggestions

S2215 "Cares Chorus" (Ps.., 2 Sam.)
S2244 "People Need the Lord" (Ps., Mark)
S2036 "Give Thanks" (2 Cor.)
S2163 "He Who Began a Good Work in You" (2 Cor.)
S2176 "Make Me a Servant" (2 Cor.)
MM98 "Take This Life" (2 Cor.)
MM101 "These Hands" (2 Cor.)
S2064 "Oh Lord, You're Beautiful" (Mark)
UM123 "El Shaddai" (Mark)
  S-2 #54 (stanzas for soloist)
UM328 "Surely the Presence of the Lord" (Mark)
  R167, SP243; S-2, #200 (stanzas for soloist)
UM347 "Spirit Song" (Mark)
UM349 "Turn Your Eyes upon Jesus" (Mark)
UM394 "Something Beautiful" (Mark)
S2040 "Awesome God" (Mark)
  R245, SP11, WO9, WY3; V-10 (90) p. 21
S2139 "Oh, I Know the Lord's Laid His Hands on Me" (Mark)
S2151 "I'm So Glad Jesus Lifted Me" (Mark)

Vocal Solos

"Like a Child" (2 Sam., Ps.)
V-8 p. 356
"Reason" (Ps.)
V-3 p. 102
"Jesus, Thou Art Watching Ever" (Ps.)
V-4 p. 6

Anthems

"Be Still, and Know That I Am God" (2 Sam., Ps., Mark)
Ralph M. Johnson; Kjos 8961
SATB with organ and English horn or clarinet

"Benediction" (Mark)
Bradley Ellingboe; Kjos 9025
SATB with organ

Other Suggestions

Visuals:
  O Bow/sword, mourning, dead soldiers
  P Darkness, prayer, patient waiting, early dawn, Ps. 130:5, 6*a*
  E Kindness, Jesus, poverty/wealth, full offering plate
  G Boat, child dead/woman reaching, child well/woman rejoicing, Jesus healing
If you address grief in today's message, related to the reading from Samuel, consider these resources:
  Services of Death and Resurrection: BOW, pp. 139-171
  Prayer: BOW548. On the Anniversary of a Death
  Response: BOW183. "God Hears Our Every Need"
Greeting: BOW327 (2 Sam., Ps.) or 455 (Mark)
Opening Prayer: BOW464 (Mark)
Prayer of Confession: BOW487 or BOW491 (Ps., Mark)
Canticle: UM516. "Canticle of Redemption" (Ps.) See S-1, p. 386.
Prayer: UM461. For Those Who Mourn (2 Sam.)
Prayer: BOW500. For Blessing, Mercy, and Courage (Mark)
Prayers: BOW545 and BOW546. For Those Who Suffer (2 Sam., Mark)
Prayers for Healing: BOW627, BOW628, BOW629 (Mark)
Benediction: UM665. "Go Now in Peace" (Mark)

2 Samuel 5:1-5, 9-10
1 Then all the tribes of Israel came to David at Hebron,
and said, "Look, we are your bone and flesh. 2 For some
time, while Saul was king over us, it was you who led out
Israel and brought it in. The LORD said to you: It is you who
shall be shepherd of my people Israel, you who shall be
ruler over Israel." 3 So all the elders of Israel came to the
king at Hebron; and King David made a covenant with
them at Hebron before the LORD, and they anointed David
king over Israel. 4 David was thirty years old when he began
to reign, and he reigned forty years. 5 At Hebron he reigned
over Judah seven years and six months; and at Jerusalem he
reigned over all Israel and Judah thirty-three years.
9 David occupied the stronghold, and named it the city
of David. David built the city all around from the Millo
inward. 10 And David became greater and greater, for the
LORD, the God of hosts, was with him.

Psalm 48
1 Great is the LORD and greatly to be praised in the city of
our God. His holy mountain, 2 beautiful in elevation, is the
joy of all the earth, Mount Zion, in the far north, the city of
the great King. 3 Within its citadels God has shown himself a
sure defense. 4 Then the kings assembled, they came on
together. 5 As soon as they saw it, they were astounded; they
were in panic, they took to flight; 6 trembling took hold of
them there, pains as of a woman in labor, 7 as when an east
wind shatters the ships of Tarshish. 8 As we have heard, so
have we seen in the city of the LORD of hosts, in the city of
our God, which God establishes forever. 9 We ponder your
steadfast love, O God, in the midst of your temple. 10 Your
name, O God, like your praise, reaches to the ends of the
earth. Your right hand is filled with victory. 11 Let Mount
Zion be glad, let the towns of Judah rejoice because of your
judgments. 12 Walk about Zion, go all around it, count its
towers,
13 consider well its ramparts; go through its citadels, that
you may tell the next generation 14 that this is God, our God
forever and ever. He will be our guide forever.

---

2 Corinthians 12:2-10
2 I know a person in Christ who fourteen years ago was
caught up to the third heaven—whether in the body or out
of the body I do not know; God knows. 3 And I know that
such a person—whether in the body or out of the body I do
not know; God knows— 4 was caught up into Paradise and
heard things that are not to be told, that no mortal is per-
mitted to repeat. 5 On behalf of such a one I will boast, but
on my own behalf I will not boast, except of my weaknesses.
6 But if I wish to boast, I will not be a fool, for I will be
speaking the truth. But I refrain from it, so that no one may
think better of me than what is seen in me or heard from
me, 7 even considering the exceptional character of the rev-
elations. Therefore, to keep me from being too elated, a
thorn was given me in the flesh, a messenger of Satan to
torment me, to keep me from being too elated. 8 Three
times I appealed to the Lord about this, that it would leave
me, 9 but he said to me, "My grace is sufficient for you, for
power is made perfect in weakness." So, I will boast all the
more gladly of my weaknesses, so that the power of Christ
may dwell in me. 10 Therefore I am content with weakness-
es, insults, hardships, persecutions, and calamities for the
sake of Christ; for whenever I am weak, then I am strong.

Mark 6:1-13
1 He left that place and came to his hometown, and his
disciples followed him. 2 On the sabbath he began to teach
in the synagogue, and many who heard him were astounded.
They said, "Where did this man get all this? What is this wis-
dom that has been given to him? What deeds of power are
being done by his hands! 3 Is not this the carpenter, the son
of Mary and brother of James and Joses and Judas and
Simon, and are not his sisters here with us?" And they took
offense at him. 4 Then Jesus said to them, "Prophets are not
without honor, except in their hometown, and among their
own kin, and in their own house." 5 And he could do no
deed of power there, except that he laid his hands on a few
sick people and cured them. 6 And he was amazed at their
unbelief.
Then he went about among the villages teaching. 7 He
called the twelve and began to send them out two by two,
and gave them authority over the unclean spirits. 8 He
ordered them to take nothing for their journey except a
staff; no bread, no bag, no money in their belts; 9 but to
wear sandals and not to put on two tunics. 10 He said to
them, "Wherever you enter a house, stay there until you
leave the place. 11 If any place will not welcome you and
they refuse to hear you, as you leave, shake off the dust that
is on your feet as a testimony against them." 12 So they went
out and proclaimed that all should repent. 13 They cast out
many demons, and anointed with oil many who were sick
and cured them.

Notes:

Primary Hymns and Songs for the Day

400 "Come, Thou Fount of Every Blessing" (2 Cor.) (O)
H-3 Choir-57; Descant-79; Organ-96
S-1 #244. Descant
2037 "I Sing Praises to Your Name" (Ps.)
R79, SP27
2130 "The Summons" (Mark)
2239 "Go Ye, Go Ye into the World" (Mark) (C)
584 "Lord, You Give the Great Commission" (Mark) (C)

Hymn Suggestions

206 "I Want to Walk as a Child of the Light" (2 Sam.)
518 "O Thou, in Whose Presence" (2 Sam., 2 Cor.)
732 "Come, We That Love the Lord" (2 Sam., Ps.)
733 "Marching to Zion" (2 Sam., Ps.)
77 "How Great Thou Art" (Ps.)
139 "Praise to the Lord, the Almighty" (Ps.)
726 "O Holy City, Seen of John" (Ps.)
727 "O What Their Joy and Their Glory Must Be" (Ps.)
731 "Glorious Things of Thee Are Spoken" (Ps.)
2208 "Guide My Feet" (Ps., 2 Cor., Mark)
88 "Maker, in Whom We Live" (Ps., 2 Cor.)
340 "Come, Ye Sinners, Poor and Needy" (2 Cor.)
365 "Grace Greater Than Our Sin" (2 Cor.)
378 "Amazing Grace" (2 Cor.)
386 "Come, O Thou Traveler Unknown" (2 Cor.)
480 "O Love That Wilt Not Let Me Go" (2 Cor.)
505 "When Our Confidence Is Shaken" (2 Cor.)
507 "Through It All" (2 Cor.)
581 "Lord, Whose Love Through Humble Service" (2 Cor., Mark)
582 "Whom Shall I Send?" (2 Cor., Mark)
2149 "Living for Jesus" (2 Cor., Mark)
257 "We Meet You, O Christ" (Mark)
263 "When Jesus the Healer Passed Through Galilee" (Mark)
358 "Dear Lord and Father of Mankind" (Mark) (Alternate Text: "Parent of Us All")
497 "Send Me, Lord" (Mark)
568 "Christ for the World We Sing" (Mark)
649 "How Shall They Hear the Word of God" (Mark)
2197 "Lord of All Hopefulness" (Mark)
2243 "We All Are One in Mission" (Mark)
2260 "Let Us Be Bread" (Mark, Communion)
2241 "The Spirit Sends Us Forth to Serve" (Mark) (C)
664 "Sent Forth by God's Blessing" (Mark) (C)
437 "This Is My Song" (Independence Day)

Contemporary Suggestions

MM103 "How Great Are You, Lord" (Ps.)
SP58 "Great Is the Lord Almighty!" (Ps.)
WO43 "God Will Make a Way" (Ps.)
SP40
S2022 "Great Is the Lord" (Ps.)
S2036 "Give Thanks" (2 Cor.)
S2162 "Grace Alone" (2 Cor.)
S2055 "You Are My Hiding Place" (2 Cor.)
M26 "The Power of Your Love" (2 Cor.)
WG133
SP220 "You Are My All in All" (2 Cor.)
WY39
MM92 "All Things Are Possible" (2 Cor.)
WG8
MM99 "Shout to the North" (2 Cor.)
WG114
WG54 "Good To Me" (2 Cor.)
MM55 "Jehovah Reigns" (Mark)
SP143 "Carry the Light" (Mark)
S2040 "Awesome God" (Mark)
R245, SP11, WO9, WY3; V-10 (90) p. 21
S2184 "Sent Out in Jesus' Name" (Mark)
S2186 "Song of Hope" (Mark)

Vocal Solos

"O Thou That Tellest Good Tidings to Zion" (2 Sam., Ps.)
"Rejoice Greatly, O Daughter of"Zion" (2 Sam., Ps.)
V-2
"What God Hath Promised" (2 Cor.)
V-8 p. 297
"Gospel Train" (Mark)
V-7 p. 74

Anthems

"Amazing Grace" (2 Cor.)
Mark A. Miller; Abingdon Press 0687493870
Unison/two-part with keyboard (opt. solo)

"Come, Thou Fount of Every Blessing" (2 Cor.)
Arr. Michael Braz; Hinshaw HMC1955
SATB with keyboard, opt. brass, handbells, congregation

Other Suggestions

Visuals:
O Shepherd, crown, oil
P People at worship, fear, globe, right hand
E Clay vessels of varying sizes, conditions, handicap sign
G Teams of two, staff, sandals, tunic, oil
Greeting: BOW452 (Ps.)
Prayer: BOW502. For the Church (Mark)
Prayer: BOW442 Independence Day
Prayer: BOW515 or BOW516 or BOW526. For the Nation and World (Independence Day)
Response to Scripture: UM206, refrain. "I Want to Walk as a Child of the Light" (2 Sam.)
Choral Response: UM77, st. 1. "How Great Thou Art" (Ps.)
Prayer of Thanksgiving: BOW550 (2 Cor.)
Hymn of Commitment: BOW223. "O Holy Spirit" (2 Cor, Mark)
Benediction: BOW177. "Amen Siakudumisa" (Ps.)
Benediction: S2241. "The Spirit Sends Us Forth" (Mark)

2 Samuel 6:1-5, 12*b*-19

1 David again gathered all the chosen men of Israel, thirty
thousand. 2 David and all the people with him set out and
went from Baale-judah, to bring up from there the ark of
God, which is called by the name of the LORD of hosts who is
enthroned on the cherubim. 3 They carried the ark of God
on a new cart, and brought it out of the house of Abinadab,
which was on the hill. Uzzah and Ahio, the sons of
Abinadab, were driving the new cart 4 with the ark of God;
and Ahio went in front of the ark. 5 David and all the house
of Israel were dancing before the LORD with all their might,
with songs and lyres and harps and tambourines and cas-
tanets and cymbals.

12b So David went and brought up the ark of God from
the house of Obed-edom to the city of David with rejoicing;
13 and when those who bore the ark of the LORD had gone
six paces, he sacrificed an ox and a fatling. 14 David danced
before the LORD with all his might; David was girded with a
linen ephod. 15 So David and all the house of Israel brought
up the ark of the LORD with shouting, and with the sound of
the trumpet.

16 As the ark of the LORD came into the city of David,
Michal daughter of Saul looked out of the window, and saw
King David leaping and dancing before the LORD; and she
despised him in her heart.

17 They brought in the ark of the LORD, and set it in its
place, inside the tent that David had pitched for it; and David
offered burnt offerings and offerings of well-being before the
LORD. 18 When David had finished offering the burnt offerings
and the offerings of well-being, he blessed the people in the
name of the LORD of hosts, 19 and distributed food among all
the people, the whole multitude of Israel, both men and
women, to each a cake of bread, a portion of meat, and a cake
of raisins. Then all the people went back to their homes.

Psalm 24

1 The earth is the LORD's and all that is in it, the world, and
those who live in it; 2 for he has founded it on the seas, and
established it on the rivers. 3 Who shall ascend the hill of the
LORD? And who shall stand in his holy place? 4 Those who
have clean hands and pure hearts, who do not lift up their
souls to what is false, and do not swear deceitfully.
5 They will receive blessing from the LORD, and vindication
from the God of their salvation. 6 Such is the company of
those who seek him, who seek the face of the God of Jacob.
7 Lift up your heads, O gates! and be lifted up, O ancient
doors! that the King of glory may come in. 8 Who is the King
of glory? The LORD, strong and mighty, the LORD, mighty in
battle. 9 Lift up your heads, O gates! and be lifted up, O
ancient doors! that the King of glory may come in. 10 Who is
this King of glory? The LORD of hosts, he is the King of glory.

Ephesians 1:3-14

3 Blessed be the God and Father of our Lord Jesus Christ,
who has blessed us in Christ with every spiritual blessing in
the heavenly places, 4 just as he chose us in Christ before the
foundation of the world to be holy and blameless before him
in love. 5 He destined us for adoption as his children through
Jesus Christ, according to the good pleasure of his will, 6 to
the praise of his glorious grace that he freely bestowed on us
in the Beloved. 7 In him we have redemption through his
blood, the forgiveness of our trespasses, according to the
riches of his grace 8 that he lavished on us. With all wisdom
and insight 9 he has made known to us the mystery of his will,
according to his good pleasure that he set forth in Christ, 10 as
a plan for the fullness of time, to gather up all things in him,
things in heaven and things on earth. 11 In Christ we have also
obtained an inheritance, having been destined according to
the purpose of him who accomplishes all things according to
his counsel and will, 12 so that we, who were the first to set our
hope on Christ, might live for the praise of his glory. 13 In him
you also, when you had heard the word of truth, the gospel
of your salvation, and had believed in him, were marked with
the seal of the promised Holy Spirit; 14 this is the pledge of
our inheritance toward redemption as God's own people, to
the praise of his glory.

Mark 6:14-29

14 King Herod heard of it, for Jesus' name had become
known. Some were saying, "John the baptizer has been
raised from the dead; and for this reason these powers are at
work in him." 15 But others said, "It is Elijah." And others
said, "It is a prophet, like one of the prophets of old." 16 But
when Herod heard of it, he said, "John, whom I beheaded,
has been raised."

17 For Herod himself had sent men who arrested John,
bound him, and put him in prison on account of Herodias,
his brother Philip's wife, because Herod had married her.
18 For John had been telling Herod, "It is not lawful for you
to have your brother's wife." 19 And Herodias had a grudge
against him, and wanted to kill him. But she could not,
20 for Herod feared John, knowing that he was a righteous
and holy man, and he protected him. When he heard him,
he was greatly perplexed; and yet he liked to listen to him.
21 But an opportunity came when Herod on his birthday gave
a banquet for his courtiers and officers and for the leaders
of Galilee. 22 When his daughter Herodias came in and
danced, she pleased Herod and his guests; and the king said
to the girl, "Ask me for whatever you wish, and I will give it."
23 And he solemnly swore to her, "Whatever you ask me, I will
give you, even half of my kingdom." 24 She went out and said
to her mother, "What should I ask for?" She replied, "The
head of John the baptizer."
25 Immediately she rushed back to the king and requested, "I
want you to give me at once the head of John the Baptist on
a platter." 26 The king was deeply grieved; yet out of regard
for his oaths and for the guests, he did not want to refuse
her. 27 Immediately the king sent a soldier of the guard with
orders to bring John's head. He went and beheaded him in
the prison, 28 brought his head on a platter, and gave it to
the girl. Then the girl gave it to her mother. 29 When his dis-
ciples heard about it, they came and took his body, and laid
it in a tomb.

Primary Hymns and Songs for the Day

213 "Lift Up Your Heads, Ye Mighty Gates" (Ps.) (O)
H-3 Handbell-50; Choir-129; Descant-101; Organ-167
S-1 #334-35. Descant/harmonization
2091 "The King of Glory Comes" (Ps.)
R267
99 "My Tribute" ("To God Be the Glory") (Eph.)
R68; V-8 p. 5 (vocal solo)
S-2 #130. Stanza for soloist
377 "It Is Well with My Soul" (Eph.) (C)
H-3 Choir-113

Hymn Suggestions

68 "When in Our Music God Is Glorified" (2 Sam.)
87 "What Gift Can We Bring" (2 Sam., Ps.)
93 "Let All the World in Every Corner Sing" (2 Sam., Ps.)
149 "Cantemos al Señor" ("Let's Sing Unto the Lord") (2 Sam., Ps.)
312 "Hail the Day That Sees Him Rise" (Ps.)
2044 "My Gratitude Now Accept, O God" (Ps.)
121 "There's a Wideness in God's Mercy" (Eph.)
141 "Children of the Heavenly Father" (Eph.)
182 "Word of God, Come Down on Earth" (Eph.)
194 "Morning Glory, Starlit Sky" (Eph.)
362 "Nothing But the Blood" (Eph.)
369 "Blessed Assurance" (Eph.)
370 "Victory in Jesus" (Eph.)
378 "Amazing Grace" (Eph.)
365 "Grace Greater Than Our Sin" (Eph.)
2248 "Baptized in Water" (Eph., Baptism)
2276 "Glory to God in the Highest" (Eph.)
108 "God Hath Spoken by the Prophets" (Mark)
525 "We'll Understand It Better By and By" (Mark)
529 "How Firm a Foundation" (Mark)
530 "Are Ye Able" (Mark)
534 "Be Still, My Soul" (Mark)
708 "Rejoice in God's Saints" (Mark)
711 "For All the Saints" (Mark)
2089 "Wild and Lone the Prophet's Voice" (Mark)
2155 "Blest Are They" (Mark)
2283 "For All the Saints" (Mark)

Contemporary Suggestions

S2028 "Clap Your Hands" (2 Sam.)
MM63 "I Could Sing of Your Love Forever" (2 Sam.)
WY44; V-3 p. 22 (vocal solo)
WO155 "We Will Dance" (2 Sam.)
M36 "Awesome in This Place" (2 Sam., Ps.)
WG14
S2272 "Holy Ground" (2 Sam., Ps.)
S2091 "The King of Glory Comes" (Ps.)
MM70 "No Higher Calling" (Ps.)
MM83 "Just Let Me Say" (Ps.)
WY108 "Audience of One" (Ps.)
S2039 "Holy, Holy" (Eph.)
S2162 "Grace Alone" (Eph.)
MM66 "We Fall Down" (Eph.)
WG169
MM82 "You Are My King" ("Amazing Love") (Eph.)
WY65
WG63 "Hallelujah" ("Your Love Is Amazing") (Eph.)
M7 "I Believe in Jesus" (Mark)
WO68
S2213 "Healer of Our Every Ill" (Mark)
UM507 "Through It All" (Mark)
UM527 "Do, Lord, Remember Me" (Mark)
UM533 "We Shall Overcome" (Mark)

Vocal Solos

"I Will Sing of Thy Great Mercies" (2 Sam., Eph.)
V-4 p. 43
"Lover of My Soul" (Ps.)
V-10 (90) p. 245
"And Can It Be That I Should Gain" (Eph.)
V-1 p. 29
"Amazing Grace" (Eph.)
V-5 p. 8
V-8 p. 56

Anthems

"The Earth Is the Lord's" (Ps.)
Glenn Wonacott; Abingdon Press 9780687645602
SATB with keyboard (opt. brass)

"Let All the World in Every Corner Sing" (2 Sam., Ps.)
David T. Childs; Kjos 6321
Two-part with organ

Other Suggestions

Visuals:
O Ark of Covenant, man dancing (video: David)
P Earth/sea/river, bowl/water/towel, hand with heart, gates
E Adoption papers, Christus Rex, last will and testament, rejoicing
G Feasting, dancing, dinner platter

This would be a good day to recognize musicians or dedicate a new instrument. See BOW604 and BOW606 for suggestions.

Call to Worship: BOW199 (2 Sam.)
Greeting: BOW450 (2 Sam.)
Prayer of Confession: BOW494 (Ps.)
Psalter: UM212. Psalm 24
Prayer: UM69 (2 Sam., Eph.) or UM713 (Mark)
Scripture Response: UM261, refrain. "Lord of the Dance" (2 Sam.)
Scripture Response: UM712, st. 1. "I Sing a Song of the Saints of God" (Mark)
Prayer of Thanksgiving: BOW557 (Ps.)
Dismissal: BOW559 (2 Sam., Mark)
Benediction: MM87. "Let the Peace of God Reign" (Eph.)

2 Samuel 7:1-14*a*

[1] Now when the king was settled in his house, and the
LORD had given him rest from all his enemies around him,
[2] the king said to the prophet Nathan, "See now, I am living
in a house of cedar, but the ark of God stays in a tent." [3]
Nathan said to the king, "Go, do all that you have in mind;
for the LORD is with you."

[4] But that same night the word of the LORD came to
Nathan: [5] Go and tell my servant David: Thus says the LORD:
Are you the one to build me a house to live in? [6] I have not
lived in a house since the day I brought up the people of
Israel from Egypt to this day, but I have been moving about
in a tent and a tabernacle. [7] Wherever I have moved about
among all the people of Israel, did I ever speak a word with
any of the tribal leaders of Israel, whom I commanded to
shepherd my people Israel, saying, "Why have you not built
me a house of cedar?" [8] Now therefore thus you shall say to
my servant David: Thus says the LORD of hosts: I took you
from the pasture, from following the sheep to be prince
over my people Israel; [9] and I have been with you wherever
you went, and have cut off all your enemies from before
you; and I will make for you a great name, like the name of
the great ones of the earth. [10] And I will appoint a place for
my people Israel and will plant them, so that they may live
in their own place, and be disturbed no more; and evildo-
ers shall afflict them no more, as formerly, [11] from the time
that I appointed judges over my people Israel; and I will
give you rest from all your enemies. Moreover the LORD
declares to you that the LORD will make you a house.
[12] When your days are fulfilled and you lie down with your
ancestors, I will raise up your offspring after you, who shall
come forth from your body, and I will establish his king-
dom. [13] He shall build a house for my name, and I will
establish the throne of his kingdom forever. [14] I will be a
father to him, and he shall be a son to me.

Psalm 89:20-37

[20] "I have found my servant David; with my holy oil I
have anointed him; [21] my hand shall always remain with
him; my arm also shall strengthen him. [22] The enemy shall
not outwit him, the wicked shall not humble him. [23] I will
crush his foes before him and strike down those who hate
him. [24] My faithfulness and steadfast love shall be with him;
and in my name his horn shall be exalted. [25] I will set his
hand on the sea and his right hand on the rivers. [26] He shall
cry to me, 'You are my Father, my God, and the Rock of my
salvation!' [27] I will make him the firstborn, the highest of
the kings of the earth. [28] Forever I will keep my steadfast
love for him, and my covenant with him will stand firm. [29] I
will establish his line forever, and his throne as long as the
heavens endure. [30] If his children forsake my law and do
not walk according to my ordinances, [31] if they violate my
statutes and do not keep my commandments, [32] then I will
punish their transgression with the rod and their iniquity
with scourges; [33] but I will not remove from him my stead-
fast love, or be false to my faithfulness. [34] I will not violate
my covenant, or alter the word that went forth from my
lips. [35] Once and for all I have sworn by my holiness; I will
not lie to David. [36] His line shall continue forever, and his
throne endure before me like the sun. [37] It shall be estab-
lished forever like the moon, an enduring witness in the
skies."

Ephesians 2:11-22

[11] So then, remember that at one time you Gentiles by
birth, called "the uncircumcision" by those who are called
"the circumcision"—a physical circumcision made in the
flesh by human hands— [12] remember that you were at that
time without Christ, being aliens from the commonwealth
of Israel, and strangers to the covenants of promise, having
no hope and without God in the world. [13] But now in Christ
Jesus you who once were far off have been brought near by
the blood of Christ. [14] For he is our peace; in his flesh he has
made both groups into one and has broken down the divid-
ing wall, that is, the hostility between us.
[15] He has abolished the law with its commandments and
ordinances, that he might create in himself one new
humanity in place of the two, thus making peace, [16] and
might reconcile both groups to God in one body through
the cross, thus putting to death that hostility through it.
[17] So he came and proclaimed peace to you who were far off
and peace to those who were near; [18] for through him both
of us have access in one Spirit to the Father. [19] So then you
are no longer strangers and aliens, but you are citizens with
the saints and also members of the household of God, [20]
built upon the foundation of the apostles and prophets,
with Christ Jesus himself as the cornerstone. [21] In him the
whole structure is joined together and grows into a holy
temple in the Lord; [22] in whom you also are built together
spiritually into a dwelling place for God.

Mark 6:30-34, 53-56

[30] The apostles gathered around Jesus, and told him all
that they had done and taught. [31] He said to them, "Come
away to a deserted place all by yourselves and rest a while."
For many were coming and going, and they had no leisure
even to eat. [32] And they went away in the boat to a deserted
place by themselves. [33] Now many saw them going and recog-
nized them, and they hurried there on foot from all the
towns and arrived ahead of them. [34] As he went ashore, he
saw a great crowd; and he had compassion for them, because
they were like sheep without a shepherd; and he began to
teach them many things.

[53] When they had crossed over, they came to land at
Gennesaret and moored the boat. [54] When they got out of
the boat, people at once recognized him, [55] and rushed
about that whole region and began to bring the sick on mats
to wherever they heard he was. [56] And wherever he went, into
villages or cities or farms, they laid the sick in the market-
places, and begged him that they might touch even the
fringe of his cloak; and all who touched it were healed.

Primary Hymns and Songs for the Day

116 "The God of Abraham Praise" (2 Sam.) (O)
H-3 Handbell-62, 95; Choir-59; Organ-77
S-1 #211. Harmonization

540 "I Love Thy Kingdom, Lord" (2 Sam., Eph.)
H-3 Handbell-16; Choir-106, 167; Descant-97; Organ-147
S-1 #311. Descant/harmonization

546 "The Church's One Foundation" (Eph.)
H-3 Handbell-94; Choir-180; Descant-16; Organ-9
S-1 #25-26. Descant/harmonization

358 "Dear Lord and Father of Mankind" (Mark)
(Alternate Text: "Parent of Us All")
H-3 Handbell-56; Choir-61; Organ-124
S-2 #151. Introduction
#152. Violin descant

559 "Christ Is Made the Sure Foundation" (Eph.) (C)
H-3 Choir-49; Descant-103; Organ-180
S-1 #346. Descant

Hymn Suggestions

580 "Lead On, O King Eternal" (2 Sam.)
115 "How Like a Gentle Spirit" (2 Sam., Eph.)
541 "See How Great a Flame Aspires" (2 Sam., Eph.)
463 "Lord, Speak to Me" (2 Sam., Ps.)
529 "How Firm a Foundation" (Ps., Eph.)
188 "Christ Is the World's Light" (Eph.)
377 "It Is Well with My Soul" (Eph.)
550 "Christ, from Whom All Blessings Flow" (Eph.)
552 "Here, O Lord, Your Servants Gather"
2128 "Come and Find the Quiet Center" (Eph.)
2135 "When Cain Killed Abel" (Eph.)
2158 "Just a Closer Walk with Thee" (Eph.)
2175 "Together We Serve" (Eph.)
2185 "For One Great Peace" (Eph.)
2218 "You Are Mine" (Eph.)
2220 "We Are God's People" (Eph.)
2228 "Sacred the Body" (Eph.)
178 "Hope of the World" (Eph., Mark)
187 "Rise, Shine, You People" (Mark)
261 "Lord of the Dance" (Mark)
263 "When Jesus the Healer Passed Through Galilee" (Mark)
266 "Heal Us, Emmanuel, Hear Our Prayer" (Mark)
472 "Near to the Heart of God" (Mark)
492 "Prayer Is the Soul's Sincere Desire" (Mark)
2202 "Come Away with Me" (Mark)

Contemporary Suggestions

S2139 "Oh, I Know the Lord's Laid His Hands on Me" (2 Sam.)
S2002 "I Will Call Upon the Lord" (Ps.)
S2066 "Praise the Name of Jesus" (Ps.)
UM143 "On Eagle's Wings" (Ps.)
R112; S-2 #143 (verses for soloist)
MM68 "Forever" (Ps.)
WY57
MM93 "Rock of Ages" (Ps.)
WO125
S2043 "Alleluia" (Eph.)
S2159 "Jesus, Draw Me Close" (Eph.)
S2226 "Bind Us Together" (Eph.)
S2164 "Sanctuary" (Eph.)
SP177 "Cornerstone" (Eph.)
M9 "Firm Foundation" (Eph.)
S2064 "Oh Lord, You're Beautiful" (Mark)
S2244 "People Need the Lord" (Mark)
S2266 "Here Is Bread, Here Is Wine" (Mark, Communion)
MM104 "There Is None Like You" (Mark)
WO137

Vocal Solos

"How Firm a Foundation" (Eph.)
V-6 p. 31
"Just a Closer Walk with Thee" (Eph.)
V-8 p. 323
"Serenity" (Mark)
UM499

Anthems

"The Church's One Foundation" (Eph.)
Arr. Craig Courtney; Beckenhorst BP1353
SATB with keyboard

"Loving Shepherd of Thy Sheep" (Mark)
John Rutter; Hinshaw HMC1192
SATB *a cappella*

Other Suggestions

Visuals:
O Cedar, churches under construction
P Rock, star of David, oil, genealogical chart, father/son
E Walls crumbling, family, Christian unity, cornerstone
G Resting, boat, sheep, healing, cloak with fringe

Call to Worship: S2057. "Be Still and Know That I Am God" (Eph.)
Greeting: BOW307, BOW455, or BOW456 (Eph., Mark)
Opening Prayer: BOW460 (Mark)
Prayer of Confession: BOW492 or BOW493 (Eph.)
Litany: BOW495. For the Church and For the World (Eph., Mark)
Prayer: BOW503 or BOW506. For the Church (Eph.)
Prayer: BOW514. For the Mind of Christ (Mark)
Response: BOW191. "May This Mind Be in Us" (Mark)
Prayer: BOW546. For Those Who Suffer (Mark)
Scripture Response: UM541, st. 1. "See How Great a Flame Aspires" (2 Sam., Eph.)
Prayer of Thanksgiving: BOW551 (Mark)
Dismissal: BOW559 (Eph.)
Benediction: S2156. "Give Peace" (Eph.)

2 Samuel 11:1-15

1 In the spring of the year, the time when kings go out to
battle, David sent Joab with his officers and all Israel with
him; they ravaged the Ammonites, and besieged Rabbah. But
David remained at Jerusalem.

2 It happened, late one afternoon, when David rose from
his couch and was walking about on the roof of the king's
house, that he saw from the roof a woman bathing; the
woman was very beautiful. 3 David sent someone to inquire
about the woman. It was reported, "This is Bathsheba daugh-
ter of Eliam, the wife of Uriah the Hittite." 4 So David sent
messengers to get her, and she came to him, and he lay with
her. (Now she was purifying herself after her period.) Then
she returned to her house. 5 The woman conceived; and she
sent and told David, "I am pregnant."

6 So David sent word to Joab, "Send me Uriah the Hittite."
And Joab sent Uriah to David. 7 When Uriah came to him,
David asked how Joab and the people fared, and how the war
was going. 8 Then David said to Uriah, "Go down to your
house, and wash your feet." Uriah went out of the king's
house, and there followed him a present from the king. 9 But
Uriah slept at the entrance of the king's house with all the
servants of his lord, and did not go down to his house. 10
When they told David, "Uriah did not go down to his house,"
David said to Uriah, "You have just come from a journey.
Why did you not go down to your house?" 11 Uriah said to
David, "The ark and Israel and Judah remain in booths; and
my lord Joab and the servants of my lord are camping in the
open field; shall I then go to my house, to eat and to drink,
and to lie with my wife? As you live, and as your soul lives, I
will not do such a thing."
12 Then David said to Uriah, "Remain here today also, and
tomorrow I will send you back." So Uriah remained in
Jerusalem that day. On the next day, 13 David invited him to
eat and drink in his presence and made him drunk; and in
the evening he went out to lie on his couch with the servants
of his lord, but he did not go down to his house.

14 In the morning David wrote a letter to Joab, and sent it
by the hand of Uriah. 15 In the letter he wrote, "Set Uriah in
the forefront of the hardest fighting, and then draw back
from him, so that he may be struck down and die."

Psalm 14

1 Fools say in their hearts, "There is no God." They are
corrupt, they do abominable deeds; there is no one who does
good. 2 The LORD looks down from heaven on humankind to
see if there are any who are wise, who seek after God. 3 They
have all gone astray, they are all alike perverse; there is no
one who does good, no, not one. 4 Have they no knowledge,
all the evildoers who eat up my people as they eat bread, and
do not call upon the LORD? 5 There they shall be in great ter-
ror, for God is with the company of the righteous. 6 You
would confound the plans of the poor, but the LORD is their
refuge. 7 O that deliverance for Israel would come from Zion!
When the LORD restores the fortunes of his people, Jacob will
rejoice; Israel will be glad.

Ephesians 3:14-21

14 For this reason I bow my knees before the Father,
15 from whom every family in heaven and on earth takes its
name. 16 I pray that, according to the riches of his glory, he
may grant that you may be strengthened in your inner being
with power through his Spirit, 17 and that Christ may dwell in
your hearts through faith, as you are being rooted and
grounded in love. 18 I pray that you may have the power to
comprehend, with all the saints, what is the breadth and
length and height and depth, 19 and to know the love of
Christ that surpasses knowledge, so that you may be filled
with all the fullness of God.

20 Now to him who by the power at work within us is able
to accomplish abundantly far more than all we can ask or
imagine, 21 to him be glory in the church and in Christ Jesus
to all generations, forever and ever. Amen.

John 6:1-21

1 After this Jesus went to the other side of the Sea of
Galilee, also called the Sea of Tiberias. 2 A large crowd kept
following him, because they saw the signs that he was doing
for the sick. 3 Jesus went up the mountain and sat down there
with his disciples. 4 Now the Passover, the festival of the Jews,
was near. 5 When he looked up and saw a large crowd coming
toward him, Jesus said to Philip, "Where are we to buy bread
for these people to eat?" 6 He said this to test him, for he him-
self knew what he was going to do.
7 Philip answered him, "Six months' wages would not buy
enough bread for each of them to get a little." 8 One of his
disciples, Andrew, Simon Peter's brother, said to him,
9 "There is a boy here who has five barley loaves and two fish.
But what are they among so many people?" 10 Jesus said,
"Make the people sit down." Now there was a great deal of
grass in the place; so they sat down, about five thousand in
all. 11 Then Jesus took the loaves, and when he had given
thanks, he distributed them to those who were seated; so also
the fish, as much as they wanted. 12 When they were satisfied,
he told his disciples, "Gather up the fragments left over, so
that nothing may be lost." 13 So they gathered them up, and
from the fragments of the five barley loaves, left by those who
had eaten, they filled twelve baskets. 14 When the people saw
the sign that he had done, they began to say, "This is indeed
the prophet who is to come into the world."

15 When Jesus realized that they were about to come and
take him by force to make him king, he withdrew again to the
mountain by himself.

16 When evening came, his disciples went down to the sea,
17 got into a boat, and started across the sea to Capernaum. It
was now dark, and Jesus had not yet come to them. 18 The sea
became rough because a strong wind was blowing. 19 When
they had rowed about three or four miles, they saw Jesus
walking on the sea and coming near the boat, and they were
terrified. 20 But he said to them, "It is I; do not be afraid."
21 Then they wanted to take him into the boat, and immedi-
ately the boat reached the land toward which they were
going.

Primary Hymns and Songs for the Day

111 "How Can We Name a Love" (Eph.) (O)
H-3 Handbell-99; Choir-102, 197; Organ-159
S-1 #326. Transposition in D major

175 "Jesus, the Very Thought of Thee" (Eph.)
H-3 Handbell-52; Choir-90; Descant-92; Organ-131
S-1 #291-92. Descant/harmonization

191 "Jesus Loves Me" (Eph.)
H-3 Choir-117

599 "Break Thou the Bread of Life" (John, Communion) (C)
H-3 Choir-44; Organ-15

Hymn Suggestions

425 "O Crucified Redeemer" (2 Sam.)
439 "We Utter Our Cry" (2 Sam.)
441 "What Does the Lord Require" (2 Sam.)
2048 "God Weeps" (2 Sam., Ps.)
120 "Your Love, O God" (2 Sam., Eph.)
523 "Saranam, Saranam" ("Refuge") (Ps.)
2004 "Praise the Source of Faith and Learning" (Ps.)
2027 "Now Praise the Hidden God of Love" (Ps., Eph.)
98 "To God Be the Glory" (Eph.)
267 "O Love, How Deep" (Eph.)
356 "Pues Si Vivimos" ("When We Are Living") (Eph.)
372 "How Can We Sinners Know" (Eph.)
388 "O Come and Dwell in Me" (Eph.)
414 "Thou Hidden Love of God" (Eph.)
551 "Awake, O Sleeper" (Eph.)
627 "O the Depth of Love Divine" (Eph.)
102 "Now Thank We All Our God" (John)
350 "Come, All of You" (John)
427 "Where Cross the Crowded Ways of Life" (John)
444 "O Young and Fearless Prophet" (John)
507 "Through It All" (John)
368 "My Hope Is Built" (John)
476 "Lonely the Boat" (John)
479 "Jesus, Lover of My Soul" (John)
509 "Jesus, Savior, Pilot Me" (John)
525 "We'll Understand It Better By and By" (John)
529 "How Firm a Foundation" (John)
532 "Jesus, Priceless Treasure" (John)
534 "Be Still, My Soul" (John)
612 "Deck Thyself, My Soul, with Gladness" (John, Communion)
617 "I Come with Joy" (John, Communion)
629 "You Satisfy the Hungry Heart" (John, Communion)
631 "O Food to Pilgrims Given" (John, Communion)
2142 "Blessed Quietness" (John)
2202 "Come Away with Me" (John)
2218 "You Are Mine" (John)
539 "O Spirit of the Living God" (Eph.) (C)

Contemporary Suggestions

S2053 "If It Had Not Been for the Lord" (Ps.)
UM347 "Spirit Song" (Eph.)
S2073 "Celebrate Love" (Eph.)
S2141 "There's a Song" (Eph.)
S2143 "O Lord, Your Tenderness" (Eph.)
S2150 "Lord, Be Glorified" (Eph.)
M13 "Be Glorified" (Eph.)
M25 "No Greater Love" (Eph.)
M37 "He Is Able" (Eph.)
WO49
MM63 "I Could Sing of Your Love Forever" (Eph.)
WY44; V-3 p. 22 (vocal solo)
SP50 "Think about His Love" (Eph.)
WG138
WY145 "In Christ Alone" (John)
S2072 "Amen, Amen" (John)
UM628 "Eat This Bread" (John)

Vocal Solos

"Wondrous Love" (Eph.)
V-6 p. 47
"May the Mind of Christ" (Eph.)
V-8 p. 114
"Give Me Jesus" (Eph.)
V-8 p. 256

Anthems

"Lonely the Boat" (John)
Arr. William Rose; Abingdon Press 06874995199
SATB with piano

"Be Still, My Soul" (John)
Arr. Benjamin Harlan; Brookfield Press 08745057
SATB with keyboard

Other Suggestions

Visuals:
O Bath towel, sword
P Broken bread, fear, rescue, rejoicing
E Kneeling in prayer, globe, flags of nations, missions, love
G Dried fish, five loaves, twelve baskets, boat, storm, Jesus walking

Call to Worship: S2118. "Holy Spirit, Come to Us" (Ps.)
Greeting: BOW449 (2 Sam.)
Opening Prayer: BOW460 (2 Sam., Ps., Eph.)
Call to Prayer: S2207. "Lord, Listen to Your Children"
Prayer of Confession and Assurance: BOW478 (2 Sam., John)
Prayer: BOW510 (2 Sam., Eph.)
Prayer: BOW431 or UM446 (John, Communion)
Prayer: BOW522 or BOW525 (Ps.)
Response: BOW193. "Prayer for Wisdom" (Ps.)
Scripture Response: UM441, st. 2. "What Does the Lord Require?" (2 Sam.)
Scripture Response: UM292, st. 2. "What Wondrous Love Is This" (Eph.)
Blessing: BOW529. A Prayer of Saint Patrick (Eph.)

2 Samuel 11:26–12:13*a*

26 When the wife of Uriah heard that her husband was dead,
she made lamentation for him. 27 When the mourning was over,
David sent and brought her to his house, and she became his
wife, and bore him a son.
But the thing that David had done displeased the LORD,
1 and the LORD sent Nathan to David. He came to him, and
said to him, "There were two men in a certain city, the one rich
and the other poor. 2 The rich man had very many flocks and
herds; 3 but the poor man had nothing but one little ewe lamb,
which he had bought. He brought it up, and it grew up with
him and with his children; it used to eat of his meager fare, and
drink from his cup, and lie in his bosom, and it was like a
daughter to him. 4 Now there came a traveler to the rich man,
and he was loath to take one of his own flock or herd to prepare
for the wayfarer who had come to him, but he took the poor
man's lamb, and prepared that for the guest who had come to
him." 5 Then David's anger was greatly kindled against the man.
He said to Nathan, "As the LORD lives, the man who has done
this deserves to die; 6 he shall restore the lamb fourfold, because
he did this thing, and because he had no pity."
7 Nathan said to David, "You are the man! Thus says the
LORD, the God of Israel: I anointed you king over Israel, and I
rescued you from the hand of Saul; 8 I gave you your master's
house, and your master's wives into your bosom, and gave you
the house of Israel and of Judah; and if that had been too little,
I would have added as much more. 9 Why have you despised the
word of the LORD, to do what is evil in his sight? You have struck
down Uriah the Hittite with the sword, and have taken his wife
to be your wife, and have killed him with the sword of the
Ammonites. 10 Now therefore the sword shall never depart from
your house, for you have despised me, and have taken the wife
of Uriah the Hittite to be your wife. 11 Thus says the LORD: I will
raise up trouble against you from within your own house; and I
will take your wives before your eyes, and give them to your
neighbor, and he shall lie with your wives in the sight of this
very sun. 12 For you did it secretly; but I will do this thing before
all Israel, and before the sun."
13a David said to Nathan, "I have sinned against the LORD."

Psalm 51:1-12

1 Have mercy on me, O God, according to your steadfast
love; according to your abundant mercy blot out my transgres-
sions. 2 Wash me thoroughly from my iniquity, and cleanse me
from my sin. 3 For I know my transgressions, and my sin is ever
before me. 4 Against you, you alone, have I sinned, and done
what is evil in your sight, so that you are justified in your sen-
tence and blameless when you pass judgment. 5 Indeed, I was
born guilty, a sinner when my mother conceived me. 6 You
desire truth in the inward being; therefore teach me wisdom in
my secret heart. 7 Purge me with hyssop, and I shall be clean;
wash me, and I shall be whiter than snow. 8 Let me hear joy and
gladness; let the bones that you have crushed rejoice.
9 Hide your face from my sins, and blot out all my iniquities.
10 Create in me a clean heart, O God, and put a new and right
spirit within me. 11 Do not cast me away from your presence,
and do not take your holy spirit from me. 12 Restore to me the
joy of your salvation, and sustain in me a willing spirit.

Ephesians 4:1-16

1 I therefore, the prisoner in the Lord, beg you to lead a life
worthy of the calling to which you have been called,
2 with all humility and gentleness, with patience, bearing with
one another in love, 3 making every effort to maintain the unity
of the Spirit in the bond of peace. 4 There is one body and one
Spirit, just as you were called to the one hope of your calling,
5 one Lord, one faith, one baptism, 6 one God and Father of all,
who is above all and through all and in all.
7 But each of us was given grace according to the measure of
Christ's gift. 8 Therefore it is said, "When he ascended on high
he made captivity itself a captive; he gave gifts to his people."
9 (When it says, "He ascended," what does it mean but that he
had also descended into the lower parts of the earth? 10 He who
descended is the same one who ascended far above all the heav-
ens, so that he might fill all things.) 11 The gifts he gave were
that some would be apostles, some prophets, some evangelists,
some pastors and teachers, 12 to equip the saints for the work of
ministry, for building up the body of Christ,
13 until all of us come to the unity of the faith and of the knowl-
edge of the Son of God, to maturity, to the measure of the full
stature of Christ. 14 We must no longer be children, tossed to
and fro and blown about by every wind of doctrine, by people's
trickery, by their craftiness in deceitful scheming. 15 But speak-
ing the truth in love, we must grow up in every way into him
who is the head, into Christ, 16 from whom the whole body,
joined and knit together by every ligament with which it is
equipped, as each part is working properly, promotes the
body's growth in building itself up in love.

John 6:24-35

24 So when the crowd saw that neither Jesus nor his disciples
were there, they themselves got into the boats and went to
Capernaum looking for Jesus.
25 When they found him on the other side of the sea, they
said to him, "Rabbi, when did you come here?" 26 Jesus
answered them, "Very truly, I tell you, you are looking for me,
not because you saw signs, but because you ate your fill of the
loaves. 27 Do not work for the food that perishes, but for the
food that endures for eternal life, which the Son of Man will
give you. For it is on him that God the Father has set his seal."
28 Then they said to him, "What must we do to perform the
works of God?" 29 Jesus answered them, "This is the work of
God, that you believe in him whom he has sent." 30 So they said
to him, "What sign are you going to give us then, so that we may
see it and believe you? What work are you performing? 31 Our
ancestors ate the manna in the wilderness; as it is written, 'He
gave them bread from heaven to eat.' "
32 Then Jesus said to them, "Very truly, I tell you, it was not
Moses who gave you the bread from heaven, but it is my Father
who gives you the true bread from heaven. 33 For the bread of
God is that which comes down from heaven and gives life to the
world." 34 They said to him, "Sir, give us this bread always."
35 Jesus said to them, "I am the bread of life. Whoever comes
to me will never be hungry, and whoever believes in me will
never be thirsty."

Primary Hymns and Songs for the Day

546 "The Church's One Foundation" (Eph.) (O)
H-3 Handbell-94; Choir-180; Descant-16; Organ-9
S-1 #25-26. Descant/harmonization
355 "Depth of Mercy" (2 Sam., Ps.)
H-3 Choir-63, 100
S-1 #53. Descant
628 "Eat This Bread" (John, Communion)
629 "You Satisfy the Hungry Heart" (John)
S-1 #144. Four-part setting of refrain
641 "Fill My Cup, Lord" (John, Communion) (C)
S-2 #62. Stanzas for soloist

Hymn Suggestions

421 "Make Me a Captive, Lord" (2 Sam.) (O)
439 "We Utter Our Cry" (2 Sam.)
441 "What Does the Lord Require" (2 Sam.)
357 "Just as I Am, Without One Plea" (2 Sam., Ps.)
417 "O For a Heart to Praise My God" (Ps.)
2134 "Forgive Us, Lord" ("Perdón, Señor") (Ps.)
108 "God Hath Spoken by the Prophets" (Eph.)
410 "I Want a Principle Within" (Eph.)
505 "When Our Confidence Is Shaken" (Eph.)
547 "O Church of God, United" (Eph.)
551 "Awake, O Sleeper" (Eph.)
554 "All Praise to Our Redeeming Lord" (Eph.)
555 "Forward Through the Ages" (Eph.)
604 "Praise and Thanksgiving Be to God" (Eph., Baptism
620 "One Bread, One Body" (Eph., Communion)
649 "How Shall They Hear the Word of God" (Eph.)
709 "Come, Let Us Join Our Friends Above" (Eph.)
712 "I Sing a Song of the Saints of God" (Eph.)
2175 "Together We Serve" (Eph.)
2220 "We Are God's People" (Eph.)
2221 "In Unity We Lift Our Song" (Eph., John)
2229 "We Are One in Christ Jesus" (Eph.)
2240 "One God and Father of Us All" (Eph.)
2269 "Come, Share the Lord" (Eph., Communion)
127 "Guide Me, O Thou Great Jehovah" (John)
350 "Come, All of You" (John)
565 "Father, We Thank You" (John)
624 "Bread of the World" (John, Communion)
631 "O Food to Pilgrims Given" (John, Communion)
2236 "Gather Us In" (John, Communion)
2261 "Life-giving Bread" (Eph., John, Communion)

Contemporary Suggestions

S2152 "Change My Heart, O God" (2 Sam., Ps.)
S2133 "Give Me a Clean Heart" (2 Sam., Ps.)
M50 "Refiner's Fire" (Ps.)
M26 "The Power of Your Love" (Ps.)
WG133
M35 "White as Snow" (Ps.)
MM90 "Purify My Heart" (Ps.)
R187
MM77 "Above All" (Eph.)
WO2; V-3 p. 17 or V-10(03) p. 18 (vocal solo)
MM68 "Forever" (Eph.)
WY57
S2224 "Make Us One" (Eph.)
S2227 "We Are the Body of Christ" (Eph.)
S2223 "They'll Know We Are Christians by Our Love" (Eph.)
S2226 "Bind Us Together" (Eph.)
S2026b "Halle, Halle, Halleluja" (John)
S2071 "Jesus, Name Above All Names" (John)
S2132 "You Who Are Thirsty" (John, Communion)
M32 "Holy and Anointed One" (John)
M32

Vocal Solos

"A Contrite Heart" (Ps.)
V-4 p. 10
"Clean Before My Lord" (Ps.)
V-8 p. 233
"Life Indeed" (John, Communion)
V-8 p. 271
"Father, We Thank You" (John)
UM563

Anthems

"Kyrie" (2 Sam.)
Mark Burrows; Abingdon Press 0687330394
SATB with piano

"Fill All That's Within Me" (John)
Ken Dosso; Abingdon 0687044286
SATB with keyboard

Other Suggestions

Visuals:
O Lamb, sword
P Water, hyssop, snow, rejoicing, heart, baptism
E Unity, no. 1, baptism, gifts, building, Christ, ministry, binding
G Boat, seal, bread, feeding, pitcher of water, flowing water

Greeting: BOW454 (2 Sam., Ps.)
Opening Prayer: BOW461 (2 Sam., Ps.)
Call to Prayer: S2157. "Come and Fill Our Hearts" (Ps.)
Prayer of Confession: BOW486 (Ps., Eph.)
Response: UM483, UM484 or S2275. "Kyrie" (Ps.)
Response: UM482 or S2277. "Lord, Have Mercy" (Ps.)
Prayer: UM353, UM366, UM456, or UM535 (2 Sam., Ps.)
Prayer: UM713. All Saints (Eph.)
Prayer: BOW399 Week 2 or BOW431 (John)
Prayers: BOW505 and BOW506. For the Church (Eph.)
Call to Communion: BOW431 by Andy Langford (John)
Prayer of Thanksgiving or Communion Prayer: BOW431 by Barbara Dunlap-Berg (John, Communion)
Prayer of Thanksgiving: BOW554 (Eph., John)
Blessing: BOW564 (John)

2 Samuel 18:5-9, 15, 31-33

5 The king ordered Joab and Abishai and Ittai, saying,
"Deal gently for my sake with the young man Absalom."
And all the people heard when the king gave orders to all
the commanders concerning Absalom.
6 So the army went out into the field against Israel; and
the battle was fought in the forest of Ephraim. 7 The men of
Israel were defeated there by the servants of David, and the
slaughter there was great on that day, twenty thousand
men. 8 The battle spread over the face of all the country;
and the forest claimed more victims that day than the
sword.
9 Absalom happened to meet the servants of David.
Absalom was riding on his mule, and the mule went under
the thick branches of a great oak. His head caught fast in
the oak, and he was left hanging between heaven and
earth, while the mule that was under him went on.
15 And ten young men, Joab's armor-bearers, surrounded
Absalom and struck him, and killed him.
31 Then the Cushite came; and the Cushite said, "Good
tidings for my lord the king! For the LORD has vindicated
you this day, delivering you from the power of all who rose
up against you." 32 The king said to the Cushite, "Is it well
with the young man Absalom?" The Cushite answered,
"May the enemies of my lord the king, and all who rise up
to do you harm, be like that young man."
33 The king was deeply moved, and went up to the cham-
ber over the gate, and wept; and as he went, he said, "O my
son Absalom, my son, my son Absalom! Would I had died
instead of you, O Absalom, my son, my son!"

Psalm 130

1 Out of the depths I cry to you, O LORD. 2 Lord, hear my
voice! Let your ears be attentive to the voice of my supplica-
tions! 3 If you, O LORD, should mark iniquities, Lord, who
could stand? 4 But there is forgiveness with you, so that you
may be revered. 5 I wait for the LORD, my soul waits, and in
his word I hope; 6 my soul waits for the Lord more than
those who watch for the morning, more than those who
watch for the morning. 7 O Israel, hope in the LORD! For
with the LORD there is steadfast love, and with him is great
power to redeem. 8 It is he who will redeem Israel from all
its iniquities.

Ephesians 4:25–5:2

25 So then, putting away falsehood, let all of us speak the
truth to our neighbors, for we are members of one anoth-
er. 26 Be angry but do not sin; do not let the sun go down
on your anger, 27 and do not make room for the devil. 28
Thieves must give up stealing; rather let them labor and
work honestly with their own hands, so as to have some-
thing to share with the needy. 29 Let no evil talk come out of
your mouths, but only what is useful for building up, as
there is need, so that your words may give grace to those
who hear. 30 And do not grieve the Holy Spirit of God, with
which you were marked with a seal for the day of redemp-
tion. 31 Put away from you all bitterness and wrath and
anger and wrangling and slander, together with all malice,
32 and be kind to one another, tenderhearted, forgiving one
another, as God in Christ has forgiven you.
1 Therefore be imitators of God, as beloved children,
2 and live in love, as Christ loved us and gave himself up for
us, a fragrant offering and sacrifice to God.

John 6:35, 41-51

35 Jesus said to them, "I am the bread of life. Whoever
comes to me will never be hungry, and whoever believes in
me will never be thirsty."
41 Then the Jews began to complain about him because
he said, "I am the bread that came down from heaven."
42 They were saying, "Is not this Jesus, the son of Joseph,
whose father and mother we know? How can he now say, 'I
have come down from heaven'?" 43 Jesus answered them,
"Do not complain among yourselves. 44 No one can come to
me unless drawn by the Father who sent me; and I will raise
that person up on the last day. 45 It is written in the
prophets, 'And they shall all be taught by God.' Everyone
who has heard and learned from the Father comes to me.
46 Not that anyone has seen the Father except the one who
is from God; he has seen the Father. 47 Very truly, I tell you,
whoever believes has eternal life. 48 I am the bread of life.
49 Your ancestors ate the manna in the wilderness, and they
died. 50 This is the bread that comes down from heaven, so
that one may eat of it and not die. 51 I am the living bread
that came down from heaven. Whoever eats of this bread
will live forever; and the bread that I will give for the life of
the world is my flesh."

Notes:

Primary Hymns and Songs for the Day

178 "Hope of the World" (Eph., John) (O)
H-3 Choir-100
S-1 #343. Descant
S-2 #189. Introduction
136 "The Lord's My Shepherd, I'll Not Want" (2 Sam.)
H-3 Choir-75, 188
2261 "Life-giving Bread" (John, Communion)
474 "Precious Lord, Take My Hand" (2 Sam., Ps.) (C)
H-3 Choir-164; Organ-116

Hymn Suggestions

443 "O God Who Shaped Creation" (2 Sam.) (O)
458 "Dear Lord, For All in Pain" (2 Sam., Ps.)
515 "Out of the Depths I Cry to You" (2 Sam., Ps.)
534 "Be Still, My Soul" (2 Sam., Ps.)
700 "Abide with Me" (2 Sam., Ps.)
2110 "Why Has God Forsaken Me?" (2 Sam., Ps.)
2136 "Out of the Depths" (2 Sam., Ps.)
510 "Come, Ye Disconsolate" (2 Sam., John)
399 "Take My Life, and Let It Be" (Eph.)
430 "O Master, Let Me Walk with Thee" (Eph.)
431 "Let There Be Peace on Earth" (Eph.)
608 "This Is the Spirit's Entry Now" (Eph.)
2082 "Woke Up This Morning" (Eph.)
2167 "More Like You" (Eph.)
2205 "The Fragrance of Christ" (Eph.)
2213 "Healer of Our Every Ill" (Eph.)
350 "Come, All of You" (John)
127 "Guide Me, O Thou Great Jehovah" (John)
612 "Deck Thyself, My Soul, with Gladness" (John, Communion)
616 "Come, Sinners, to the Gospel Feast" (John, Communion)
624 "Bread of the World" (John, Communion)
627 "O the Depth of Love Divine" (John, Communion)
629 "You Satisfy the Hungry Heart" (John, Communion)
630 "Become to Us the Living Bread" (John, Communion)
631 "O Food to Pilgrims Given" (John)
633 "The Bread of Life for All Is Broken" (John, Communion)
2060 "God the Sculptor of the Mountains" (John)
2062 "The Lily of the Valley" (John)
2132 "You Who Are Thirsty" (John)
2236 "Gather Us In" (John)
672 "God Be with You Till We Meet Again" (2 Sam., John) (C)
673 "God Be with You Till We Meet Again" (2 Sam., John) (C)

Contemporary Suggestions

WO63 "Hungry" ("Falling On My Knees") (Ps., John)
WY52
S2039 "Holy, Holy" (Eph.)
S2073 "Celebrate Love" (Eph.)
S2108 "O How He Loves You and Me!" (Eph.)
S2145 "I've Got Peace Like a River" (Eph.)
S2161 "To Know You More" (Eph.)
M38 "In the Secret" ("I Want to Know You") (Eph.)
WO103; V-3 p. 36 (vocal solo)
S2026b "Halle, Halle, Halleluja" (John)
S2038 "Father, I Adore You" (John)
S2071 "Jesus, Name Above All Names" (John)
S2204 "Light of the World" (John)
UM628 "Eat This Bread" (John, Communion)
UM640 "Take Our Bread" (John, Communion)
UM641 "Fill My Cup, Lord" (John, Communion)

Vocal Solos

"Reason" (Ps.)
V-3 p. 102
"Like a Child" (Ps., Eph.)
V-8 p. 356
"Mirror" (Eph.)
V-8 p. 21
"Christ Living Within You" (Eph.)
V-8 p. 177
"My Father's Heart" (Eph.)
V-3 p. 134

Anthems

"Let the Peace of Christ Rule in Your Hearts" (Eph.)
Craig Courtney; Brookfield Press 08744177
SATB with keyboard

"I Am the Bread of Life" (John)
Simon Lole; GIA G- 4473
Unison with keyboard

Other Suggestions

Visuals:
O Tree limb, man weeping
P Waiting for dawn, forgiveness, praying hands, weeping
E Setting sun, children, sacrificial offering, portrait of Christ
G Bread, love feast, communion, anointing with oil, baptism

Greeting: BOW453 (2 Sam., John)
Opening Prayer: BOW469 (John)
Canticle: UM516. "Canticle of Redemption" (Ps.)
Prayer: UM461. For Those Who Mourn (2 Sam.)
Prayer: UM481. The Prayer of Saint Francis (Eph.)
Prayer: BOW514. "For the Mind of Christ" (Eph.)
Call to Communion: BOW431 by Andy Langford (John)
Prayer of Thanksgiving or Communion Prayer: BOW431 by Barbara Dunlap-Berg (John, Communion)
Benediction: S2161. "To Know You More" (Eph.)

1 Kings 2:10-12; 3:3-14

[10] Then David slept with his ancestors, and was buried in
the city of David. [11] The time that David reigned over Israel
was forty years; he reigned seven years in Hebron, and thir-
ty-three years in Jerusalem. [12] So Solomon sat on the throne
of his father David; and his kingdom was firmly established.

[3] Solomon loved the LORD, walking in the statutes of his
father David; only, he sacrificed and offered incense at the
high places. [4] The king went to Gibeon to sacrifice there,
for that was the principal high place; Solomon used to offer
a thousand burnt offerings on that altar. [5] At Gibeon the
LORD appeared to Solomon in a dream by night; and God
said, "Ask what I should give you." [6] And Solomon said,
"You have shown great and steadfast love to your servant my
father David, because he walked before you in faithfulness,
in righteousness, and in uprightness of heart toward you;
and you have kept for him this great and steadfast love, and
have given him a son to sit on his throne today. [7] And now,
O LORD my God, you have made your servant king in place
of my father David, although I am only a little child; I do
not know how to go out or come in. [8] And your servant is in
the midst of the people whom you have chosen, a great
people, so numerous they cannot be numbered or count-
ed. [9] Give your servant therefore an understanding mind to
govern your people, able to discern between good and evil;
for who can govern this your great people?"

[10] It pleased the Lord that Solomon had asked this.
[11] God said to him, "Because you have asked this, and have
not asked for yourself long life or riches, or for the life of
your enemies, but have asked for yourself understanding to
discern what is right, [12] I now do according to your word.
Indeed I give you a wise and discerning mind; no one like
you has been before you and no one like you shall arise
after you. [13] I give you also what you have not asked, both
riches and honor all your life; no other king shall compare
with you. [14] If you will walk in my ways, keeping my statutes
and my commandments, as your father David walked, then
I will lengthen your life."

Psalm 111

[1] Praise the LORD! I will give thanks to the LORD with my
whole heart, in the company of the upright, in the congre-
gation. [2] Great are the works of the LORD, studied by all who
delight in them. [3] Full of honor and majesty is his work, and
his righteousness endures forever. [4] He has gained renown
by his wonderful deeds; the LORD is gracious and merciful. [5]
He provides food for those who fear him; he is ever mind-
ful of his covenant. [6] He has shown his people the power of
his works, in giving them the heritage of the nations. [7] The
works of his hands are faithful and just; all his precepts are
trustworthy. [8] They are established forever and ever, to be
performed with faithfulness and uprightness. [9] He sent
redemption to his people; he has commanded his covenant
forever. Holy and awesome is his name. [10] The fear of the
LORD is the beginning of wisdom; all those who practice it
have a good understanding. His praise endures forever.

Ephesians 5:15-20

[15] Be careful then how you live, not as unwise people but
as wise, [16] making the most of the time, because the days are
evil. [17] So do not be foolish, but understand what the will of
the Lord is. [18] Do not get drunk with wine, for that is
debauchery; but be filled with the Spirit, [19] as you sing
psalms and hymns and spiritual songs among yourselves,
singing and making melody to the Lord in your hearts,
[20] giving thanks to God the Father at all times and for every-
thing in the name of our Lord Jesus Christ.

John 6:51-58

[51] "I am the living bread that came down from heaven.
Whoever eats of this bread will live forever; and the bread
that I will give for the life of the world is my flesh."

[52] The Jews then disputed among themselves, saying,
"How can this man give us his flesh to eat?" [53] So Jesus said
to them, "Very truly, I tell you, unless you eat the flesh of
the Son of Man and drink his blood, you have no life in
you. [54] Those who eat my flesh and drink my blood have
eternal life, and I will raise them up on the last day; [55] for
my flesh is true food and my blood is true drink. [56] Those
who eat my flesh and drink my blood abide in me, and I in
them. [57] Just as the living Father sent me, and I live because
of the Father, so whoever eats me will live because of me.
[58] This is the bread that came down from heaven, not like
that which your ancestors ate, and they died. But the one
who eats this bread will live forever."

Notes:

Primary Hymns and Songs for the Day

60 "I'll Praise My Maker While I've Breath" (Ps., Eph.) (O)
 H-3 Choir-109; Organ-105
 S-2 #141. Harmonization
500 "Spirit of God, Descend Upon My Heart" (Eph.)
 H-3 Choir-175; Descant-77; Organ-94
 S-2 #125-28. Various treatments
624 "Bread of the World" (John, Communion)
2254 "In Remembrance of Me" (John, Communion)

Hymn Suggestions

140 "Great Is Thy Faithfulness" (1 Kings, Ps.) (O)
407 "Close to Thee" (1 Kings)
410 "I Want a Principle Within" (1 Kings)
411 "Dear Lord, Lead Me Day by Day" (1 Kings)
430 "O Master, Let Me Walk with Thee" (1 Kings, Ps.)
441 "What Does the Lord Require" (1 Kings)
451 "Be Thou My Vision" (1 Kings)
73 "O Worship the King" (Ps., Eph.)
2004 "Praise the Source of Faith and Learning" (Ps., Eph.)
2121 "O Holy Spirit, Root of Life" (Ps., Eph.)
2195 "In the Lord I'll Be Ever Thankful" (Ps., Eph.)
2216 "When We Are Called to Sing Your Praise" (Eph.)
2255 "In the Singing" (Eph, Communion)
68 "When in Our Music God Is Glorified" (Eph.)
395 "Take Time to Be Holy" (Eph.)
537 "Filled with the Spirit's Power" (Eph.)
539 "O Spirit of the Living God" (Eph.)
164 "Come, My Way, My Truth, My Life" (John)
339 "Come, Sinners, to the Gospel Feast" (John)
616 "Come, Sinners, to the Gospel Feast" (John, Comm.)
630 "Become to Us the Living Bread" (John)
631 "O Food to Pilgrims Given" (John, Communion)
2060 "God the Sculptor of the Mountains" (John)
2062 "The Lily of the Valley" (John)
2263 "Broken for Me" (John, Communion)

Contemporary Suggestions

WY202 "Be Thou My Vision" (1 Kings)
MM72 "Jesus, Lover of My Soul" ("It's All about You") (1 Kings)
MM104 "There Is None Like You" (1 Kings)
 WO137
MM103 "How Great Are You, Lord" (Ps.)
UM84 "Thank You, Lord" (Ps.)
SP2 "Ah, Lord God" (Ps.)
 R254
SP58 "Great Is the Lord Almighty!" (Ps.)
SP102 "Great Are You, Lord" (Ps.)
 R69
S2040 "Awesome God" (Ps.)
 R245, SP11, WO9, WY3; V-10 (90) p. 21
S2022 "Great Is the Lord" (Ps.)
 R22, SP30, WG59
S2036 "Give Thanks" (Eph.)
 R266, SP170
S2144 "Why We Sing" (Eph.)
S2173 "Shine, Jesus, Shine" (Eph.)
 R247, SP142, WO133
S2038 "Father, I Adore You" (John)
 SP194
S2266 "Here Is Bread, Here Is Wine" (John, Communion)

Vocal Solos

"Be Thou My Vision" (1 Kings)
V-6 p. 13
"Now Thank We All Our God" (Ps.)
V-6 p. 8
"Thanks to God" (Ps.)
V-8 p. 296
"Author of Life Divine" (Eph., John)
V-1 p. 39

Anthems

"Be Thou My Vision" (1 Kings)
Claren D. Wilson; Kjos 9045
SATB with piano

"Sing for Joy" (Eph.)
Allen Pote; Choristers Guild CGA161
SATB with piano, opt. instruments

Other Suggestions

Visuals:
 O Crown, scepter, royal robe, people exhibiting wisdom
 P Images of creation, feasting, heart, humble praise
 E Singing, musical instruments, hymnal, worship/revelry
 G Communion broken bread, chalice, crucifix
Call to Worship: S2271, BOW199. "Come! Come! Everybody Worship" (Eph.)
Call to Worship: S2265. "Time Now to Gather" (John, Communion)
Greeting: BOW451 (1 Kings, Ps.)
Opening Prayer: BOW468 (1 Kings)
Canticle: UM112. "Canticle of Wisdom" (1 Kings, Wisdom of Solomon) (see S-1, p. 377)
Prayer of Confession: UM586 or BOW487 (1 Kings, Eph.)
Intercessory Prayer: UM429. For Our Country (1 Kings)
Prayer: BOW399 Week 2 or BOW431 (John)
Prayer: BOW510, BOW525, or BOW530 (1 Kings, Ps., Eph.)
Response: BOW193. "Prayer for Wisdom" (1 Kings, Ps.)
Prayer of Thanksgiving: BOW555 (1 Kings, Eph.)
Response: UM84. "Thank You, Lord" (Ps.)
Blessing: BOW564 (1 Kings, Ps., John)
Benediction: 2067, BOW177. "Amen, We Praise Your Name, O God" ("Amen Siakudumisa") (Ps., Eph.)

1 Kings 8:(1, 6, 10-11) 22-30, 41-43

1 Then Solomon assembled the elders of Israel and all the
heads of the tribes, the leaders of the ancestral houses of the
Israelites, before King Solomon in Jerusalem, to bring up the ark
of the covenant of the LORD out of the city of David, which is
Zion.

6 Then the priests brought the ark of the covenant of the
LORD to its place, in the inner sanctuary of the house, in the
most holy place, underneath the wings of the cherubim.

10 And when the priests came out of the holy place, a cloud
filled the house of the LORD, 11 so that the priests could not stand
to minister because of the cloud; for the glory of the LORD filled
the house of the LORD.

22 Then Solomon stood before the altar of the LORD in the
presence of all the assembly of Israel, and spread out his hands
to heaven. 23 He said, "O LORD, God of Israel, there is no God
like you in heaven above or on earth beneath, keeping covenant
and steadfast love for your servants who walk before you with all
their heart, 24 the covenant that you kept for your servant my
father David as you declared to him; you promised with your
mouth and have this day fulfilled with your hand.
25 Therefore, O LORD, God of Israel, keep for your servant my
father David that which you promised him, saying, 'There shall
never fail you a successor before me to sit on the throne of Israel,
if only your children look to their way, to walk before me as you
have walked before me.' 26 Therefore, O God of Israel, let your
word be confirmed, which you promised to your servant my
father David.

27 "But will God indeed dwell on the earth? Even heaven and
the highest heaven cannot contain you, much less this house
that I have built! 28 Regard your servant's prayer and his plea, O
LORD my God, heeding the cry and the prayer that your servant
prays to you today; 29 that your eyes may be open night and day
toward this house, the place of which you said, 'My name shall
be there,' that you may heed the prayer that your servant prays
toward this place. 30 Hear the plea of your servant and of your
people Israel when they pray toward this place; O hear in heaven
your dwelling place; heed and forgive.

41 "Likewise when a foreigner, who is not of your people
Israel, comes from a distant land because of your name
42—for they shall hear of your great name, your mighty hand,
and your outstretched arm—when a foreigner comes and prays
toward this house, 43 then hear in heaven your dwelling place,
and do according to all that the foreigner calls to you, so that all
the peoples of the earth may know your name and fear you, as
do your people Israel, and so that they may know that your name
has been invoked on this house that I have built."

Psalm 84

1 How lovely is your dwelling place, O LORD of hosts!
2 My soul longs, indeed it faints for the courts of the LORD; my
heart and my flesh sing for joy to the living God. 3 Even the spar-
row finds a home, and the swallow a nest for herself, where she
may lay her young, at your altars, O LORD of hosts, my King and
my God. 4 Happy are those who live in your house, ever singing
your praise. 5 Happy are those whose strength is in you, in whose
heart are the highways to Zion. 6 As they go through the valley of
Baca they make it a place of springs; the early rain also covers it
with pools. 7 They go from strength to strength; the God of gods
will be seen in Zion. 8 O LORD God of hosts, hear my prayer; give
ear, O God of Jacob! 9 Behold our shield, O God; look on the face
of your anointed. 10 For a day in your courts is better than a thou-
sand elsewhere. I would rather be a doorkeeper in the house of
my God than live in the tents of wickedness. 11 For the LORD God
is a sun and shield; he bestows favor and honor. No good thing
does the LORD withhold from those who walk uprightly. 12 O LORD
of hosts, happy is everyone who trusts in you.

Ephesians 6:10-20

10 Finally, be strong in the Lord and in the strength of his
power. 11 Put on the whole armor of God, so that you may be
able to stand against the wiles of the devil. 12 For our struggle is
not against enemies of blood and flesh, but against the rulers,
against the authorities, against the cosmic powers of this pres-ent
darkness, against the spiritual forces of evil in the heavenly
places. 13 Therefore take up the whole armor of God, so that you
may be able to withstand on that evil day, and having done every-
thing, to stand firm. 14 Stand therefore, and fasten the belt of
truth around your waist, and put on the breastplate of righ-teous-
ness. 15 As shoes for your feet put on whatever will make you
ready to proclaim the gospel of peace. 16 With all of these, take
the shield of faith, with which you will be able to quench all the
flaming arrows of the evil one. 17 Take the helmet of salvation,
and the sword of the Spirit, which is the word of God.

18 Pray in the Spirit at all times in every prayer and supplica-
tion. To that end keep alert and always persevere in supplication
for all the saints. 19 Pray also for me, so that when I speak, a mes-
sage may be given to me to make known with boldness the mys-
tery of the gospel, 20 for which I am an ambassador in chains.
Pray that I may declare it boldly, as I must speak.

John 6:56-69

56 "Those who eat my flesh and drink my blood abide in me,
and I in them. 57 Just as the living Father sent me, and I live
because of the Father, so whoever eats me will live because of
me. 58 This is the bread that came down from heaven, not like
that which your ancestors ate, and they died. But the one who
eats this bread will live forever." 59 He said these things while he
was teaching in the synagogue at Capernaum.

60 When many of his disciples heard it, they said, "This teach-
ing is difficult; who can accept it?" 61 But Jesus, being aware that
his disciples were complaining about it, said to them, "Does this
offend you? 62 Then what if you were to see the Son of Man
ascending to where he was before? 63 It is the spirit that gives life;
the flesh is useless. The words that I have spoken to you are spirit
and life. 64 But among you there are some who do not believe."
For Jesus knew from the first who were the ones that did not
believe, and who was the one that would betray him. 65 And he
said, "For this reason I have told you that no one can come to
me unless it is granted by the Father."

66 Because of this many of his disciples turned back and no
longer went about with him. 67 So Jesus asked the twelve, "Do you
also wish to go away?" 68 Simon Peter answered him, "Lord, to
whom can we go? You have the words of eternal life. 69 We have
come to believe and know that you are the Holy One of God."

Primary Hymns and Songs for the Day

514 "Stand Up, Stand Up for Jesus" (Eph.) (O)
  H-3 Choir-177; Organ-177
  S-2 #192-94. Various treatments
2042 "How Lovely, Lord, How Lovely" (Ps.)
  H-3 Handbell-70; Choir-103, 174; Descant-76; Organ-90
513 "Soldiers of Christ, Arise" (Eph.)
  H-3 Handbell-55; Choir-60; Descant-30; Organ-27
  S-1 #86-88. Various treatments
600 "Wonderful Words of Life" (John)
  H-3 Choir-221; Organ-186
178 "Hope of the World" (Eph., John) (C)

Hymn Suggestions

88 "Maker, in Whom We Live" (1 Kings) (O)
93 "Let All the World in Every Corner Sing" (1 Kings)
119 "O God in Heaven" (1 Kings)
2142 "Blessed Quietness" (Ps.)
374 "Standing on the Promises" (Eph.)
435 "O God of Every Nation" (Eph.)
575 "Onward, Christian Soldiers" (Eph.)
580 "Lead On, O King Eternal" (Eph.)
2202 "Come Away with Me" (Eph.)
369 "Blessed Assurance" (John)
462 " 'Tis So Sweet to Trust in Jesus" (John)
596 "Blessed Jesus, at Thy Word" (John)
598 "O Word of God Incarnate" (John)
630 "Become to Us the Living Bread" (John, Communion)
2254 "In Remembrance of Me" (John, Communion)
2263 "Broken for Me" (John, Communion)
2265 "Time Now to Gather" (John, Communion)
670 "Go Forth for God" (Eph.) (C)

Contemporary Suggestions

S2272 "Holy Ground" (1 Kings)
M36 "Awesome in this Place" (1 Kings)
  WG14
MM61 "Breathe" (Ps., John)
  WG20, WY8; V-3 p. 42 (vocal solo)
S2080 "All I Need Is You" (Ps.)
S2025 "As the Deer" (Ps.)
M28 "Who Can Satisfy My Soul Like You?" (Ps.)
MM60 "Better Is One Day" (Ps.)
  WY170, WO13
MM110 "Love You So Much" (Ps.)
SP220 "You Are My All in All" (Ps., Eph.)
  WY39
SP158 "The Battle Belongs to the Lord" (Eph.)
  R244
S2055 "You Are My Hiding Place" (Eph.)
MM67 "We Want to See Jesus Lifted High" (Eph.)
  WO149
MM92 "All Things Are Possible" (Eph.)
  WG8
MM99 "Shout to the North" (Eph.)
  WG114
WG54 "Good to Me" (Eph.)
S2038 "Father, I Adore You" (John)
S2266 "Here Is Bread, Here Is Wine" (John, Communion)
UM628 "Eat This Bread" (John, Communion)
M7 "I Believe in Jesus" (John)
  WO68
MM72 "Jesus, Lover of My Soul" (John)

Vocal Solos

"Ivory Palaces" (Ps.)
V-8 p. 136
"Joy" (Ps.)
V-3 p. 94
"I Walk By Faith" (Eph.)
WO78

Anthems

"How Lovely" (Ps.)
Mark Burrows; Abingdon 068704427X
SATB with piano

"Psalm 84: Cantique de Jean Racine" (Ps.)
Fauré/Hopson; Carl Fischer N6169
SATB with keyboard

Other Suggestions

Visuals:
  O Praying hands, temple (church), hand, outstretched arm
  P Churches, sparrows and nest, rain, water pooling, door
  E Armor, praying hands, people in prayer
  G Bread/wine/communion, line drawn, question mark, Christ
Call to Worship: S2273, BOW187. "Jesus, We Are Here" (Eph.)
Opening Prayer: BOW467 (John)
Prayer of Confession: BOW486 (1 Kings, Eph.)
Sung Prayers: S2201. "Prayers of the People" (Ps., Eph.)
Prayer: UM423. Finding Rest in God (Ps.)
Prayer: BOW399 Week 2 or BOW431 (John)
Prayer: BOW504, BOW521, or BOW528 (Eph.)
Prayer: BOW516. For the Nation (1 Kings, Eph.)
Response: S2193. "Lord, Listen to Your Children Praying" (Ps., Eph.)
Scripture Response: UM600, st. 1. "Wonderful Words of Life" (John)
Prayer of Thanksgiving: BOW553 (Eph., John)
Response: S2262. "Let Us Offer to the Father" (Ps., Eph.)
Blessing: BOW564 (Eph., John)
Benediction: S2281. "May You Run and Not Be Weary" (Eph.)

Song of Solomon 2:8-13

8 The voice of my beloved! Look, he comes, leaping upon the mountains, bounding over the hills. 9 My beloved is like a gazelle or a young stag. Look, there he stands behind our wall, gazing in at the windows, looking through the lattice. 10 My beloved speaks and says to me: "Arise, my love, my fair one, and come away; 11 for now the winter is past, the rain is over and gone. 12 The flowers appear on the earth; the time of singing has come, and the voice of the turtledove is heard in our land. 13 The fig tree puts forth its figs, and the vines are in blossom; they give forth fragrance. Arise, my love, my fair one, and come away."

Psalm 45:1-2, 6-9 (or Psalm 72)

1 My heart overflows with a goodly theme; I address my verses to the king; my tongue is like the pen of a ready scribe. 2 You are the most handsome of men; grace is poured upon your lips; therefore God has blessed you forever.

6 Your throne, O God, endures forever and ever. Your royal scepter is a scepter of equity; 7 you love righteousness and hate wickedness. Therefore God, your God, has anointed you with the oil of gladness beyond your companions; 8 your robes are all fragrant with myrrh and aloes and cassia. From ivory palaces stringed instruments make you glad; 9 daughters of kings are among your ladies of honor; at your right hand stands the queen in gold of Ophir.

James 1:17-27

17 Every generous act of giving, with every perfect gift, is from above, coming down from the Father of lights, with whom there is no variation or shadow due to change. 18 In fulfillment of his own purpose he gave us birth by the word of truth, so that we would become a kind of first fruits of his creatures.

19 You must understand this, my beloved: let everyone be quick to listen, slow to speak, slow to anger; 20 for your anger does not produce God's righteousness. 21 Therefore rid yourselves of all sordidness and rank growth of wickedness, and welcome with meekness the implanted word that has the power to save your souls.

22 But be doers of the word, and not merely hearers who deceive themselves. 23 For if any are hearers of the word and not doers, they are like those who look at themselves in a mirror; 24 for they look at themselves and, on going away, immediately forget what they were like. 25 But those who look into the perfect law, the law of liberty, and persevere, being not hearers who forget but doers who act—they will be blessed in their doing.

26 If any think they are religious, and do not bridle their tongues but deceive their hearts, their religion is worthless. 27 Religion that is pure and undefiled before God, the Father, is this: to care for orphans and widows in their distress, and to keep oneself unstained by the world.

Mark 7:1-8, 14-15, 21-23

1 Now when the Pharisees and some of the scribes who had come from Jerusalem gathered around him, 2 they noticed that some of his disciples were eating with defiled hands, that is, without washing them. 3 (For the Pharisees, and all the Jews, do not eat unless they thoroughly wash their hands, thus observing the tradition of the elders; 4 and they do not eat anything from the market unless they wash it; and there are also many other traditions that they observe, the washing of cups, pots, and bronze kettles.) 5 So the Pharisees and the scribes asked him, "Why do your disciples not live according to the tradition of the elders, but eat with defiled hands?" 6 He said to them, "Isaiah prophesied rightly about you hypocrites, as it is written, 'This people honors me with their lips, but their hearts are far from me; 7 in vain do they worship me, teaching human precepts as doctrines.' 8 You abandon the commandment of God and hold to human tradition."

14 Then he called the crowd again and said to them, "Listen to me, all of you, and understand: 15 there is nothing outside a person that by going in can defile, but the things that come out are what defile.

21 "For it is from within, from the human heart, that evil intentions come: fornication, theft, murder, 22 adultery, avarice, wickedness, deceit, licentiousness, envy, slander, pride, folly. 23 All these evil things come from within, and they defile a person."

Notes:

Primary Hymns and Songs for the Day

549 "Where Charity and Love Prevail" (James) (O)
H-3 Handbell-71, 104; Choir-219; Descant-95; Organ-143
S-2 #162. Harmonization

408 "The Gift of Love" (Song of Sol., Ps.)
H-3 Choir-200; Organ-45

642 "As Man and Woman We Were Made" (Song of Sol., Ps.)
S-2 #168-69. Descants

402 "Lord, I Want to Be a Christian" (James, Mark) (C)
H-3 Choir-130

Hymn Suggestions

553 "And Are We Yet Alive" (James) (O)
675 "As the Sun Doth Daily Rise" (James) (O)
643 "When Love Is Found" (Song of Sol., Ps.)
644 "Jesus, Joy of Our Desiring" (Song of Sol., Ps.)
647 "Your Love, O God, Has Called Us Here" (Song of Sol., Ps.)
2062 "The Lily of the Valley" (Song of Sol.)
247 "O Morning Star, How Fair and Bright" (Ps.)
140 "Great Is Thy Faithfulness" (James)
554 "All Praise to Our Redeeming Lord" (James)
563 "Father, We Thank You" (James)
565 "Father, We Thank You" (James)
566 "Blest Be the Dear Uniting Love" (James)
588 "All Things Come of Thee" (James)
2061 "Praise Our God Above" ("Harvest Song") (James)
2175 "Together We Serve" (James)
2178 "Here Am I" (James)
410 "I Want a Principle Within" (James, Mark)
444 "O Young and Fearless Prophet" (James, Mark)
261 "Lord of the Dance" (Mark)
399 "Take My Life, and Let It Be" (James) (C)
557 "Blest Be the Tie That Binds" (James) (C)

Contemporary Suggestions

S2071 "Jesus, Name Above All Names" (Song of Sol.)
R26, SP76
S2068 "I Love You, Lord" (Ps.)
R36, SP72
S2195 "In the Lord I'll Be Ever Thankful" (James)
S2150 "Lord, Be Glorified" (James)
R172, SP196
S2176 "Make Me a Servant" (James)
SP193
S2270 "I Will Enter His Gates" (James, Mark)
SP168
S2152 "Change My Heart, O God" (James, Mark)
R143, SP195
S2036 "Give Thanks" (James, Mark)
R266, SP170
S2086 "Open Our Eyes, Lord" (Mark)
SP199, R91
MM57 "Open the Eyes of My Heart" (Mark)
V-3 p. 162 (vocal solo)

Vocal Solos

"The Call" (Song of Sol.)
V-4 p. 31
"Set Me As a Seal" (Song of Sol.)
V-4 p. 34
"Thank You for These Gifts" (Song of Sol., James)
V-8 p. 129
"Take My Life" (James, Mark)
V-8 p. 262

Anthems

"Take My Life, and Let It Be" (James)
Michael Larkin; Concordia 98-3627
SATB with keyboard

"Ubi caritas" (James)
James Biery; MorningStar MSM-50-3055
SATB *a cappella*

Other Suggestions

Visuals:
O Gazelle, stag, heart, flowers, birds, fruit, fig tree, lovers
P Scepter, robe, oil, instruments
E Images of giving, listening, ministry to children, widows, elderly
G Hands/ dishwashing (pots, pans, cups), heart

The Song of Solomon and Psalm lections make this an appropriate day to plan a reaffirmation of marital vows or a celebration of marriage anniversaries/ engagements. BOW resources related to marriage include:
Reaffirmation of the Marriage Covenant: BOW135
Marriage Anniversary Prayers: BOW138
Prayer for an Engaged Couple: BOW537
Ministry with Persons Going Through Divorce: BOW626

Greeting: BOW458 (Song of Sol., James)
Opening Prayer: BOW460 (James)
Canticle: UM646. "Canticle of Love" (Song of Sol.) (see S-1, p. 387)
Prayer of Confession: BOW488 (Song of Sol., James, John)
Prayer: UM69 or UM409 (James)
Prayer: BOW502 or BOW530 (James, Mark)
Prayer of Thanksgiving: BOW550 or BOW555 (James)
Doxology: S2044. "My Gratitude Now Accept, O God" (James)
Closing Words: BOW559 or BOW567 (James)
Blessing: BOW565 (Song of Sol.)

INDEX OF SCRIPTURES REFERENCED

WORSHIP PLANNING SHEET 1

Date: ____________________ Color: ____________________

Preacher: ____

Liturgist: ____

Selected Scripture: ____________________________________

Selected Hymns	No.	Placement

Psalter #____________________

Keyboard Selections

Title	Composer	Placement

Anthems

Title	Choir	Composer	Placement

Vocal Solos

Title	Singer	Composer	Placement

Other Ideas:

Acolytes: ____

Head Usher: ____

Altar Guild Contact: ___________________________________

Other Participants:

____

____

WORSHIP PLANNING SHEET 2

Date: ____________________ Sunday: ______________________________ Color: ____________________

Preacher: ____

Liturgist: ____

Opening Voluntary Composer

____

Hymn Tune Name No.

____

Opening Prayer: ____

Prayer for Illumination: ____

First Lesson: ____

Psalter: ____

Second Lesson: ____

Gospel Lesson: ____

Hymn Tune Name No.

____

Response to the Word: ____

Prayers of the People: ____

Offertory Composer

____

Communion Setting: ____

Communion Hymns Tune Name No.

____

____

____

Closing Hymn Tune Name No.

____

Benediction: ____

Closing Voluntary Composer

____

CONTEMPORARY WORSHIP PLANNING SHEET

Because of the diversity in orders of worship, you will want to adjust this planning sheet to meet the needs of your worship planning team. A common order used would consist of three to four opening praise choruses and lively hymns, a time of informal prayers of the congregation along with songs of prayer, reading of the primary scripture for the day, a drama or video to illustrate the day's theme, a message from the preacher, a testimony on the theme for the day (if a drama or video was not presented earlier), followed by closing songs appropriate to the mood of the service and the message. Any offering would usually be taken early in the service, and Holy Communion would normally take place following the message—with an invitation reminding people that all persons who claim Christ are welcome to partake of Holy Communion in The United Methodist Church. Special music (solos, duets, instrumental music) can be used wherever it best expresses the theme of the service.

Date: ______________________________ Sunday: ______________________________

Thematic Emphasis or Topic: ______________________________

Color: ______________________________ Visual Focus: ______________________________

Opening Songs: ______________________________

____

____

Prayer Songs: ______________________________

____

Scripture Selection(s): ______________________________

____

____

Drama or Video: ______________________________

Message Title: ______________________________

Testimony: ______________________________

Special Music: ______________________________

____

____

Closing Songs: ______________________________

____

Preacher: ______________________________ Music Leader: ______________________________

Worship Facilitator: ______________________________ Prayer Leader: ______________________________

Notes

Notes

Notes

Notes